4th Grade

GEORGIA MATH TEST PREP

Common Core State Standards

Send all inquiries to:

sales@teacherstreasures.com
http://www.teacherstreasures.com

INTRODUCTION

Our 4th Grade Math Test Prep for Common Core State Standards is an excellent resource to supplement your classroom's curriculum to assess and manage students' understanding of concepts outlined in the Common Core State Standards Initiative. This resource is divided into three sections: Diagnostic, Practice, and Assessment with multiple choice questions in each section. We recommend you use the Diagnostic section as a tool to determine the students' areas that need to be retaught. We also recommend you encourage your students to show their work to determine *how* and *why* the student arrived at an answer. The Practice section should be used to strengthen the students' knowledge by re-testing the standard to ensure comprehension of each standard. To ensure students' apply taught concepts in the classroom, we advise you use the Assessment section as a final test to verify the students' have mastered the standard.

This resource contains 600 practice problems aligned to the Common Core State Standards. To view the standards, refer to pages *i* through *vi*.

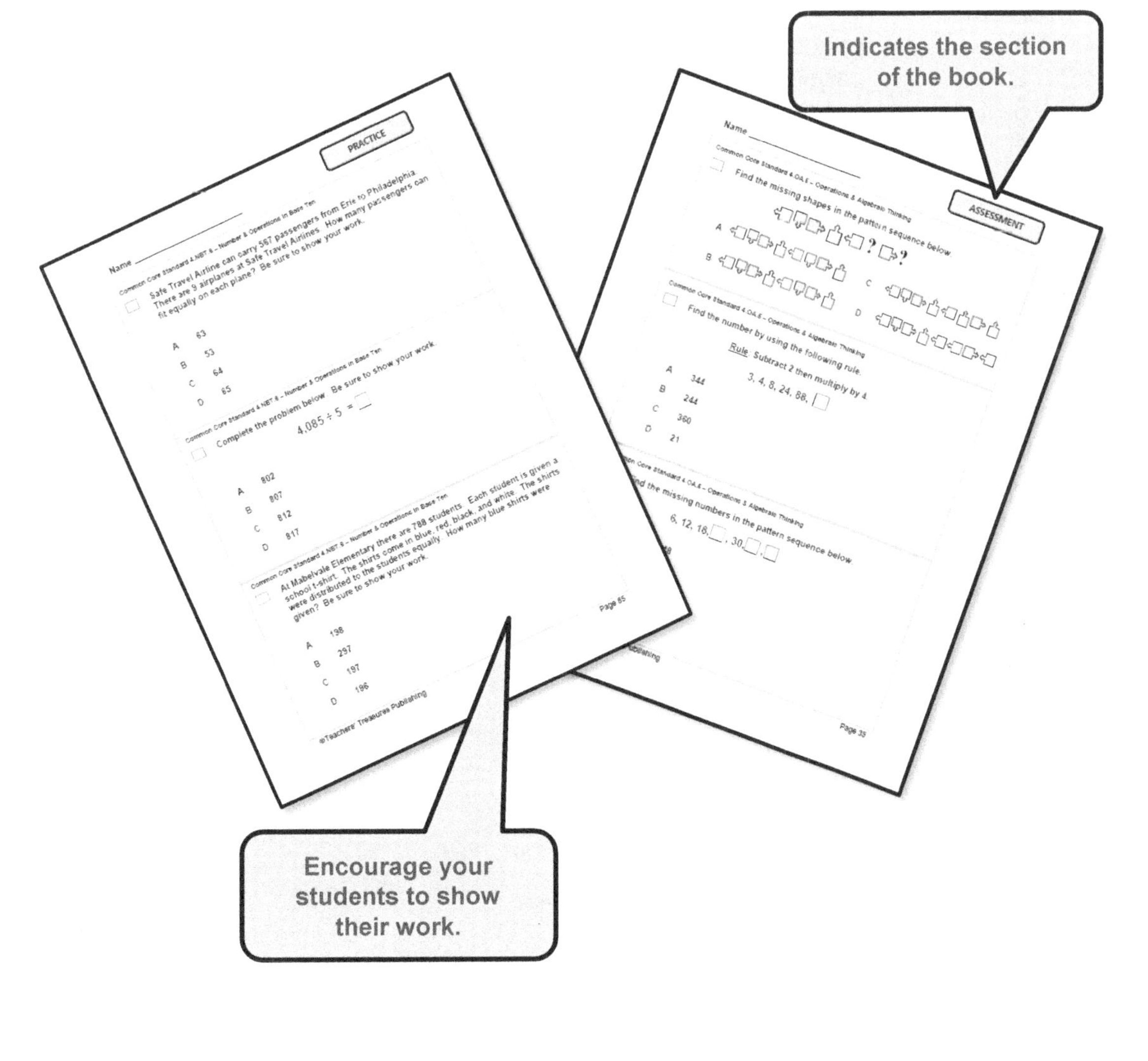

TABLE OF CONTENTS

4th Grade
Math Test Prep
FOR
Common Core Standards

COMMON CORE STATE STANDARDS

Operations & Algebraic Thinking **4.OA.1**

Interpret a multiplication equation as a comparison, e.g., interpret 35 = 5 × 7 as a statement that 35 is 5 times as many as 7 and 7 times as many as 5. Represent verbal statements of multiplicative comparisons as multiplication equations.

Operations & Algebraic Thinking **4.OA.2**

Multiply or divide to solve word problems involving multiplicative comparison, e.g., by using drawings and equations with a symbol for the unknown number to represent the problem, distinguishing multiplicative comparison from additive comparison.

Operations & Algebraic Thinking **4.OA.3**

Solve multistep word problems posed with whole numbers and having whole-number answers using the four operations, including problems in which remainders must be interpreted. Represent these problems using equations with a letter standing for the unknown quantity. Assess the reasonableness of answers using mental computation and estimation strategies including rounding.

Operations & Algebraic Thinking **4.OA.4**

Find all factor pairs for a whole number in the range 1–100. Recognize that a whole number is a multiple of each of its factors. Determine whether a given whole number in the range 1–100 is a multiple of a given one-digit number. Determine whether a given whole number in the range 1–100 is prime or composite.

Operations & Algebraic Thinking **4.OA.5**

Generate a number or shape pattern that follows a given rule. Identify apparent features of the pattern that were not explicit in the rule itself. *For example, given the rule “Add 3” and the starting number 1, generate terms in the resulting sequence and observe that the terms appear to alternate between odd and even numbers. Explain informally why the numbers will continue to alternate in this way.*

COMMON CORE STATE STANDARDS

Number & Operations in Base Ten **4.NBT.1**

Recognize that in a multi-digit whole number, a digit in one place represents ten times what it represents in the place to its right. *For example, recognize that 700 ÷ 70 = 10 by applying concepts of place value and division.*

Number & Operations in Base Ten **4.NBT.2**

Read and write multi-digit whole numbers using base-ten numerals, number names, and expanded form. Compare two multi-digit numbers based on meanings of the digits in each place, using >, =, and < symbols to record the results of comparisons.

Number & Operations in Base Ten **4.NBT.3**

Use place value understanding to round multi-digit whole numbers to any place.

Number & Operations in Base Ten **4.NBT.4**

Fluently add and subtract multi-digit whole numbers using the standard algorithm.

Number & Operations in Base Ten **4.NBT.5**

Multiply a whole number of up to four digits by a one-digit whole number, and multiply two two-digit numbers, using strategies based on place value and the properties of operations. Illustrate and explain the calculation by using equations, rectangular arrays, and/or area models.

Number & Operations in Base Ten **4.NBT.6**

Find whole-number quotients and remainders with up to four-digit dividends and one-digit divisors, using strategies based on place value, the properties of operations, and/or the relationship between multiplication and division. Illustrate and explain the calculation by using equations, rectangular arrays, and/or area models.

Number & Operations - Fractions **4.NF.1**

Explain why a fraction a/b is equivalent to a fraction $(n \times a)/(n \times b)$ by using visual fraction models, with attention to how the number and size of the parts differ even though the two fractions themselves are the same size. Use this principle to recognize and generate equivalent fractions.

Number & Operations - Fractions **4.NF.2**

Compare two fractions with different numerators and different denominators, e.g., by creating common denominators or numerators, or by comparing to a benchmark fraction such as 1/2. Recognize that comparisons are valid only when the two fractions refer to the same whole. Record the results of comparisons with symbols >, =, or <, and justify the conclusions, e.g., by using a visual fraction model.

Number & Operations - Fractions **4.NF.3**

Understand a fraction *a*/*b* with *a* > 1 as a sum of fractions 1/*b*. Understand addition and subtraction of fractions as joining and separating parts referring to the same whole. Decompose a fraction into a sum of fractions with the same denominator in more than one way, recording each decomposition by an equation. Justify decompositions, e.g., by using a visual fraction model. *Examples: 3/8 = 1/8 + 1/8 + 1/8 ; 3/8 = 1/8 + 2/8 ; 2 1/8 = 1 + 1 + 1/8 = 8/8 + 8/8 + 1/8.* Add and subtract mixed numbers with like denominators, e.g., by replacing each mixed number with an equivalent fraction, and/or by using properties of operations and the relationship between addition and subtraction. Solve word problems involving addition and subtraction of fractions referring to the same whole and having like denominators, e.g., by using visual fraction models and equations to represent the problem.

Number & Operations - Fractions **4.NF.4**

Apply and extend previous understandings of multiplication to multiply a fraction by a whole number. Understand a fraction *a*/*b* as a multiple of 1/*b*. *For example, use a visual fraction model to represent 5/4 as the product 5 × (1/4), recording the conclusion by the equation 5/4 = 5 × (1/4).* Understand a multiple of a/b as a multiple of 1/b, and use this understanding to multiply a fraction by a whole number. *For example, use a visual fraction model to express 3 × (2/5) as 6 × (1/5), recognizing this product as 6/5. (In general, n × (a/b) = (n × a)/b.).* Solve word problems involving multiplication of a fraction by a whole number, e.g., by using visual fraction models and equations to represent the problem. *For example, if each person at a party will eat 3/8 of a pound of roast beef, and there will be 5 people at the party, how many pounds of roast beef will be needed? Between what two whole numbers does your answer lie?*

COMMON CORE STATE STANDARDS

Number & Operations - Fractions **4.NF.5**

Express a fraction with denominator 10 as an equivalent fraction with denominator 100, and use this technique to add two fractions with respective denominators 10 and 100.[2] *For example, express 3/10 as 30/100, and add 3/10 + 4/100 = 34/100.*

Number & Operations - Fractions **4.NF.6**

Use decimal notation for fractions with denominators 10 or 100. *For example, rewrite 0.62 as 62/100; describe a length as 0.62 meters; locate 0.62 on a number line diagram.*

Number & Operations - Fractions **4.NF.7**

Compare two decimals to hundredths by reasoning about their size. Recognize that comparisons are valid only when the two decimals refer to the same whole. Record the results of comparisons with the symbols >, =, or <, and justify the conclusions, e.g., by using a visual model.

Measurement & Data **4.MD.1**

Know relative sizes of measurement units within one system of units including km, m, cm; kg, g; lb, oz.; l, ml; hr, min, sec. Within a single system of measurement, express measurements in a larger unit in terms of a smaller unit. Record measurement equivalents in a two-column table. *For example, know that 1 ft is 12 times as long as 1 in. Express the length of a 4 ft snake as 48 in. Generate a conversion table for feet and inches listing the number pairs (1, 12), (2, 24), (3, 36), ...*

Measurement & Data **4.MD.2**

Use the four operations to solve word problems involving distances, intervals of time, liquid volumes, masses of objects, and money, including problems involving simple fractions or decimals, and problems that require expressing measurements given in a larger unit in terms of a smaller unit. Represent measurement quantities using diagrams such as number line diagrams that feature a measurement scale.

COMMON CORE STATE STANDARDS

Measurement & Data **4.MD.3**

Apply the area and perimeter formulas for rectangles in real world and mathematical problems. *For example, find the width of a rectangular room given the area of the flooring and the length, by viewing the area formula as a multiplication equation with an unknown factor.*

Measurement & Data **4.MD.4**

Make a line plot to display a data set of measurements in fractions of a unit (1/2, 1/4, 1/8). Solve problems involving addition and subtraction of fractions by using information presented in line plots. *For example, from a line plot find and interpret the difference in length between the longest and shortest specimens in an insect collection.*

Measurement & Data **4.MD.5**

Recognize angles as geometric shapes that are formed wherever two rays share a common endpoint, and understand concepts of angle measurement: An angle is measured with reference to a circle with its center at the common endpoint of the rays, by considering the fraction of the circular arc between the points where the two rays intersect the circle. An angle that turns through 1/360 of a circle is called a "one-degree angle," and can be used to measure angles. An angle that turns through n one-degree angles is said to have an angle measure of n degrees.

Measurement & Data **4.MD.6**

Measure angles in whole-number degrees using a protractor. Sketch angles of specified measure.

Measurement & Data **4.MD.7**

Recognize angle measure as additive. When an angle is decomposed into non-overlapping parts, the angle measure of the whole is the sum of the angle measures of the parts. Solve addition and subtraction problems to find unknown angles on a diagram in real world and mathematical problems, e.g., by using an equation with a symbol for the unknown angle measure.

Geometry **4.G.1**

Draw points, lines, line segments, rays, angles (right, acute, obtuse), and perpendicular and parallel lines. Identify these in two-dimensional figures.

Geometry **4.G.2**

Classify two-dimensional figures based on the presence or absence of parallel or perpendicular lines, or the presence or absence of angles of a specified size. Recognize right triangles as a category, and identify right triangles.

Geometry **4.G.3**

Recognize a line of symmetry for a two-dimensional figure as a line across the figure such that the figure can be folded along the line into matching parts. Identify line-symmetric figures and draw lines of symmetry.

MATHEMATICS CHART

LENGTH

Metric	Customary
1 kilometer = 1000 meters	1 yard = 3 feet
1 meter = 100 centimeters	1 foot = 12 inches
1 centimeter = 10 millimeters	

CAPACITY & VOLUME

Metric	Customary
1 liter = 1000 milliliters	1 gallon = 4 quarts
	1 gallon = 128 ounces
	1 quart = 2 pints
	1 pint = 2 cups
	1 cup = 8 ounces

MASS & WEIGHT

Metric	Customary
1 kilogram = 1000 grams	1 ton = 2000 pounds
1 gram = 1000 milligrams	1 pound = 16 ounces

TIME

1 year = 365 days

1 year = 12 months

1 year = 52 weeks

1 week = 7 days

1 day = 24 hours

1 hour = 60 minutes

1 minute = 60 seconds

Name ___________________________

DIAGNOSTIC

Common Core Standard 4.OA.1 – Operations & Algebraic Thinking

☐ **Which equation below shows that 64 is 8 times as many as 8? Be sure to show your work.**

A 4 x 16 = 64

B 32 x 2 = 64

C 64 = 56 + 8

D 64 = 8 x 8

Common Core Standard 4.OA.1– Operations & Algebraic Thinking

☐ **The expression 4 x 7 = 28 shows the number of seats arranged in 4 rows and 7 columns. Which of the following expressions shows the number of seats arranged in 7 rows and 4 columns? Be sure to show your work.**

A 7 x 4 = 28

B 4 + 7 = 11

C 7 + 4 = 11

D 7 x 4 = 74

Common Core Standard 4.OA.1 – Operations & Algebraic Thinking

☐ **Which equation below shows that 54 equals 6 times as many as 9? Be sure to show your work.**

A 6 x 9 = 54

B 54 = 27 x 2

C 45 + 9 = 54

D 9 + 9 + 9 + 9 + 9 = 54

Name ______________________________

DIAGNOSTIC

Common Core Standard 4.OA.1 – Operations & Algebraic Thinking

☐ The expression 2 x 4 = 8 shows the number of wheels of 2 cars. Which of the following expressions also shows the number of wheels of 2 cars? Be sure to show your work.

A $2 \times 2 = 4$

B $4 \times 4 = 4 + 4 + 4 + 4$

C $4 + 2 = 6$

D $4 \times 2 = 8$

Common Core Standard 4.OA.1 – Operations & Algebraic Thinking

☐ Which equation below shows that 36 equals 12 times as many as 3? Be sure to show your work.

A 36 = 9 x 4

B 6 x 6 = 36

C 12 x 3 = 36

D 12 + 24 = 36

Common Core Standard 4.OA.1 – Operations & Algebraic Thinking

☐ The expression 2 x 11 = 22 shows the number of players of 2 soccer teams. Which of the following expressions also shows the number of players of 2 soccer teams? Be sure to show your work.

A $2 + 11 = 13$

B $2 \times 2 = 2 + 2$

C 11 x 2 = 22

D $2 \times 22 = 44$

Name ____________________________

PRACTICE

Common Core Standard 4.OA.1 – Operations & Algebraic Thinking

☐ The expression 5 x 4 = 20 shows the number of legs of 5 dogs. Which of the following expressions also shows the number of legs of 5 dogs? Be sure to show your work.

A 4 × 5 = 20

B 4 + 5 = 9

C 5 + 4 = 20

D 4 x 4 = 4 + 4 + 4 + 4

Common Core Standard 4.OA.1– Operations & Algebraic Thinking

☐ Which equation below shows that 20 is 2 times as many as 10? Be sure to show your work.

A 20 = 10 + 10

B 20 = 5 x 4

C 2 x 10 = 20

D 2 x 10 = 2 + 2 + 2 + 2 + 2 + 2 + 2 + 2 + 2

Common Core Standard 4.OA.1 – Operations & Algebraic Thinking

☐ The expression 4 x 6 = 24 shows the perimeter of a square with a 6 inch long side. Which of the following expressions also shows the perimeter of a square? Be sure to show your work.

A 6 x 4 = 24

B 4 + 6 = 6 + 4

C 6 x 6 = 6 + 6 + 6 + 6 + 6 + 6

D 6 × 4 = 4 + 4 + 4 + 4

Name ___________________________

PRACTICE

Common Core Standard 4.OA.1 – Operations & Algebraic Thinking

☐ Which equation below shows that 55 is 5 times as many as 11? Be sure to show your work.

A 55 = 50 + 5

B 5 x 11 = 5 + 5 + 5 + 5 +5 + 5 + 5 + 5 +5 + 5

C 5 × 11 = 11 × 5

D 5 × 11 = 55

Common Core Standard 4.OA.1 – Operations & Algebraic Thinking

☐ The expression 3 x 6 = 18 shows the number of sides of 3 cubes. Which of the following expressions also shows the number of sides of 3 cubes? Be sure to show your work.

A 6 x 3 = 18

B 3 + 6 = 9

C 3 × 3 = 3 + 3 + 3

D 3 x 18 = 54

Common Core Standard 4.OA.1 – Operations & Algebraic Thinking

☐ Which equation below shows that 63 is 7 times as many as 9? Be sure to show your work.

A 63 = 54 + 9

B 7 × 9 = 7 + 7 + 7 + 7 + 7 + 7 + 7

C 7 × 9 = 9 × 7

D 7 x 9 = 63

Name ______________________

PRACTICE

Common Core Standard 4.OA.1 – Operations & Algebraic Thinking

☐ **Which equation below shows that 49 is 7 times as many as 7? Be sure to show your work.**

A 7 x 1 = 7

B 7 + 7 + 7 + 7 + 7 + 7 = 7 x 7

C 49 = 42 + 7

D 49 = 7 x 7

Common Core Standard 4.OA.1– Operations & Algebraic Thinking

☐ **The expression 5 x 3 = 15 shows the number of vertices of 5 triangles. Which of the following expressions also shows the number of vertices of 5 triangles? Be sure to show your work.**

A 3 x 5 = 15

B 5 x 15 = 15 x 5

C 3 x 15 = 15 + 15 + 15

D 3 + 5 = 8

Common Core Standard 4.OA.1 – Operations & Algebraic Thinking

☐ **Which equation below shows that 28 is 4 times as many as 7? Be sure to show your work.**

A 4 x 7 = 28

B 28 = 14 x 2

C 21 + 7 = 28

D 4 + 4 + 4 + 4 + 4 + 4 = 28

Name ____________________

PRACTICE

Common Core Standard 4.OA.1 – Operations & Algebraic Thinking

☐ **Which equation shows the commutative property of multiplication? Be sure to show your work.**

A (5 × 7) × 3 = 5 × (7 × 3)

B 5 × 7 = 5 + 5 + 5 + 5 + 5 + 5 + 5

C 5 x 7 = 35

D 5 × 7 = 7 × 5

Common Core Standard 4.OA.1 – Operations & Algebraic Thinking

☐ **Which equation below shows that 42 is 6 times as many as 7? Be sure to show your work.**

A 42 = 6 x 7

B 14 x 3 = 42

C 21 x 3 = 42

D 35 + 7 = 42

Common Core Standard 4.OA.1 – Operations & Algebraic Thinking

☐ **The expression 8 x 4 = 32 shows the number of angles of 8 rectangles. Which of the following expressions also shows the number of angles of 8 rectangles? Be sure to show your work.**

A 4 x 8 = 32

B 8 + 4 = 12

C 8 x 8 = 64

D 4 x 4 = 16

Name ________________________

ASSESSMENT

Common Core Standard 4.OA.1 – Operations & Algebraic Thinking

☐ The expression 8 x 5 = 40 shows the number of seats in 5 cars. Which of the following expressions also shows the number of seats in 5 cars? Be sure to show your work.

A 5 + 8 = 13

B 5 x 8 = 40

C 5 x 5 = 5 + 5 + 5 + 5 + 5

D 8 + 8 = 16

Common Core Standard 4.OA.1– Operations & Algebraic Thinking

☐ Which equation below shows that 72 is 8 times as many as 9? Be sure to show your work.

A 72 = 8 x 9

B 54 = 27 x 2

C 14 x 4 = 72

D 72 = 36 x 2

Common Core Standard 4.OA.1 – Operations & Algebraic Thinking

☐ The expression 4 x 6 = 24 shows the number of players in 4 volleyball teams. Which of the following expressions also shows the number of players in 4 volleyball teams? Be sure to show your work.

A 4 + 6 = 6 + 4

B 6 x 4 = 24

C 4 x 4 = 16

D 6 x 6 = 6 + 6 + 6 + 6 + 6 + 6

Name ____________________________

ASSESSMENT

Common Core Standard 4.OA.1 – Operations & Algebraic Thinking

☐ **Which equation below shows that 25 is 5 times as many as 5? Be sure to show your work.**

A $25 = 20 + 5$

B $5 \times 5 = 25$

C $2 \times 12.5 = 25$

D $5 \times 5 = 5 + 5 + 5 + 5 + 5$

Common Core Standard 4.OA.1 – Operations & Algebraic Thinking

☐ **The expression 5 x 9 = 45 shows the number of apple trees in the orchard arranged in 5 rows and 9 columns. Which of the following expressions also shows the number of apple trees? Be sure to show your work.**

A $9 \times 5 = 45$

B $9 + 5 = 5 + 9$

C $5 \times 5 = 5 + 5 + 5 + 5 + 5$

D $9 \times 9 = 81$

Common Core Standard 4.OA.1 – Operations & Algebraic Thinking

☐ **Which equation below shows that 35 is 5 times as many as 7? Be sure to show your work.**

A $35 = 30 + 5$

B $35 = 5 \times 7$

C $2 \times 17.5 = 35$

D $5 \times 5 = 5 + 5 + 5 + 5 + 5$

Name ________________________

DIAGNOSTIC

Common Core Standard 4.OA.2 – Operations & Algebraic Thinking

☐ Deonna has 36 pairs of shoes. She only has 6 storage boxes. How many equal pairs of shoes must Deonna put in each box to store them away? How many shoes in total are in each box? Be sure to show your work.

A 4 pairs of shoes in a box with 8 shoes in total

B 6 pairs of shoes in a box with 12 shoes in total

C 6 pairs of shoes in a box with 24 shoes in total

D 5 pairs of shoes in a box with 10 shoes in total

Common Core Standard 4.OA.2– Operations & Algebraic Thinking

☐ Arin, Heather, and Aubrey each have 12 pieces of lollipops. How many lollipops do they have in total? Be sure to show your work.

A 15 lollipops

B 4 lollipops

C 36 lollipops

D 30 lollipops

Common Core Standard 4.OA.2 – Operations & Algebraic Thinking

☐ Coach Stanford wants to create some football teams. There are 44 players who are divided evenly onto 4 teams. How many players are on each team? Be sure to show your work.

A 40 players

B 11 players

C 48 players

D 12 players

Name ______________________

DIAGNOSTIC

Common Core Standard 4.OA.2 – Operations & Algebraic Thinking

☐ Alex bought some bananas at the grocery store. He divided the bananas equally into 4 bags. He has 60 bananas. How many bananas are in each bag? Be sure to show your work.

A 64 bananas

B 56 bananas

C 14 bananas

D 15 bananas

Common Core Standard 4.OA.2 – Operations & Algebraic Thinking

☐ Kacy's mother is throwing Kacy a birthday party. She is inviting 10 of Kacy's friends to the party. Her mother has 20 juice boxes. How many juice boxes will each of Kacy's friends receive? Be sure to show your work.

A 1 juice box

B 2 juice boxes

C 20 juice boxes

D 100 juice boxes

Common Core Standard 4.OA.2 – Operations & Algebraic Thinking

☐ There are 60 minutes in 1 hour. How many minutes are there in 24 hours? Be sure to show your work.

A 25 minutes

B 84 minutes

C 36 minutes

D 1,440 minutes

Name ____________________________

PRACTICE

Common Core Standard 4.OA.2 – Operations & Algebraic Thinking

☐ Tyson, Michael, and Mitch go on camping trip. The trip costs ninety dollars. The cost is divided equally amoung the boys. How much did each boy pay for the trip? If the trip was for 3 days, how much did it cost each day? Be sure to show your work.

A $25; $8.30 per day

B $30; $10 per day

C $20; $6.66 per day

D $35; $11.66 per day

Common Core Standard 4.OA.2– Operations & Algebraic Thinking

☐ Marium has 7 baskets in her closet. Each basket holds 35 rings. How many rings are there in total? Be sure to show your work.

A 5 rings

B 28 rings

C 245 rings

D 238 rings

Common Core Standard 4.OA.2 – Operations & Algebraic Thinking

☐ McKayla writes 10 pages in an hour in her diary. How many pages can she write in 15 hours? Be sure to show your work.

A 5 pages

B 150 pages

C 25 pages

D 120 pages

Name ____________________

PRACTICE

Common Core Standard 4.OA.2 – Operations & Algebraic Thinking

☐ Katherine has 10 boxes of Christmas ornaments with a total of 60 ornaments. How many ornaments were in each box? Be sure to show your work.

A 6 ornaments

B 50 ornaments

C 70 ornaments

D 5 ornaments

Common Core Standard 4.OA.2 – Operations & Algebraic Thinking

☐ There are 120 ping pong balls in 12 packages. How many ping pong balls are in each package? Be sure to show your work.

A 25 balls

B 10 balls

C 12 balls

D 45 balls

Common Core Standard 4.OA.2 – Operations & Algebraic Thinking

☐ LeAnn saves $24 per month. How much money will she save in 6 months? Be sure to show your work.

A $40

B $144

C $168

D $120

Name ___________________________

PRACTICE

Common Core Standard 4.OA.2 – Operations & Algebraic Thinking

☐ Sarah bought 7 small bags of sugar. Each bag contains 4 grams of sugar. How many grams of sugar did Sarah buy? Be sure to show your work.

A 28 grams

B 21 grams

C 35 grams

D 11 grams

Common Core Standard 4.OA.2– Operations & Algebraic Thinking

☐ Mrs. Smythe made 30 cupcakes to give to her students. If there are 15 students in her classroom, how many cupcakes should she give to each student? Be sure to show your work.

A 15 cupcakes

B 3 cupcakes

C 2 cupcakes

D 4 cupcakes

Common Core Standard 4.OA.2 – Operations & Algebraic Thinking

☐ The Night-Lite Candle Store has 100 candles. On Saturday 20 customers visited the store to purchase candles. If the candles are divided equally among the customers, how many candles could each person purchase? Be sure to show your work.

A 4 candles

B 5 candles

C 200 candles

D 80 candles

Name ______________________

PRACTICE

Common Core Standard 4.OA.2 – Operations & Algebraic Thinking

☐ Craig buys 10 packages of gum. Each package holds 25 sticks of gum. How many sticks of gum did Craig buy in all? Be sure to show your work.

A 230 sticks of gum

B 35 sticks of gum

C 15 sticks of gum

D 250 sticks of gum

Common Core Standard 4.OA.2 – Operations & Algebraic Thinking

☐ Dior has 4 cats. Each cat has 6 kittens. How many kittens does Dior have in total? Be sure to show your work.

A 10 kittens

B 18 kittens

C 30 kittens

D 24 kittens

Common Core Standard 4.OA.2 – Operations & Algebraic Thinking

☐ Adam sells 20 liters of juice per day at the local state fair. How many liters of juice does Adam sell in a week? Be sure to show your work.

A 27 liters of juice

B 140 liters of juice

C 100 liters of juice

D 25 liters of juice

Name ___________________________

ASSESSMENT

Common Core Standard 4.OA.2 – Operations & Algebraic Thinking

☐ Russell wants to save $56 in the next 8 weeks. How much does he need to save per week to achieve his goal? How much per day? Be sure to show your work.

A $7 per week; $1 per day

B $14 per week; $2 per day

C $6 per week: $.50 per day

D $12 per week; $1.50 per day

Common Core Standard 4.OA.2– Operations & Algebraic Thinking

☐ Brinkley Elementary is going on a field trip to the zoo. There will be 5 buses going on the trip. The seating capacity of each bus is 25 people and there are 120 students altogether. If there is an equal number of students on each bus, how many students will be on each bus? Be sure to show your work.

A 24 students

B 30 students

C 6 students

D 20 students

Common Core Standard 4.OA.2 – Operations & Algebraic Thinking

☐ Raul has a collection of baseball cards that he wants to sell. He sold 24 baseball cards to 6 of his friends. How many cards did he sell to each of his friends equally? Be sure to show your work.

A 18 cards

B 12 cards

C 5 cards

D 4 cards

Name ____________________________

ASSESSMENT

Common Core Standard 4.OA.2 – Operations & Algebraic Thinking

☐ Jorge saves $30 per day. How much money did he save in 20 days? Be sure to show your work.

A $50

B $600

C $100

D $500

Common Core Standard 4.OA.2 – Operations & Algebraic Thinking

☐ Lillit has 50 flowers. She wants to put the collection of flowers into five vases. How many flowers will go in each vase? Be sure to show your work.

A 25 flowers

B 10 flowers

C 12 flowers

D 45 flowers

Common Core Standard 4.OA.2 – Operations & Algebraic Thinking

☐ There are 7 days in a week. How many days are there in 7 weeks? Be sure to show your work.

A 14 days

B 42 days

C 49 days

D 35 days

Name ___________________________

DIAGNOSTIC

Common Core Standard 4.OA.3 – Operations & Algebraic Thinking

☐ Keisha, Tonya, Brittney, Samatha, and Carol go to school together. They each brought 4 books to share. Keisha, Tonya, and Carol lost 1 book each. How many books do they have now? Be sure to show your work.

A 5 books

B 13 books

C 17books

D 3 books

Common Core Standard 4.OA.3 – Operations & Algebraic Thinking

☐ There are 9 sandwiches in each of the 4 lunchboxes. Mitchell puts 3 more sandwiches in each of the lunchboxes. How many sandwiches are there in all? Be sure to show your work.

A 48

B 540

C 19

D 40

Common Core Standard 4.OA.3 – Operations & Algebraic Thinking

☐ Five times a number plus 15 is equal to 40. Find the number. Be sure to show your work.

A 35

B 6

C 8

D 5

Name ___________________________

DIAGNOSTIC

Common Core Standard 4.OA.3 – Operations & Algebraic Thinking

☐ Maria reads 4 pages per day of her library book. How many pages does she read in a week? Be sure to show your work.

A 11 pages

B 20 pages

C 28 pages

D 30 pages

Common Core Standard 4.OA.3 – Operations & Algebraic Thinking

☐ Chuck bought 15 baseballs and 11 footballs. The cost of each baseball is $2, and the cost of each football is $4. How much did he pay for all the baseballs and footballs? Be sure to show your work.

A $192.00

B $74.00

C $74.25

D $32.00

Common Core Standard 4.OA.3 – Operations & Algebraic Thinking

☐ Simon's allowance is three dollars per day. How much allowance will Simon have in 30 days? Be sure to show your work.

A $30.00

B $50.00

C $90.00

D $60.00

Name ___________________________

PRACTICE

Common Core Standard 4.OA.3 – Operations & Algebraic Thinking

☐ Sydney has 2 bracelets, Caroline has 7 bracelets, and Shana has 5 more bracelets than Caroline. How many bracelets does Shana have? Be sure to show your work.

A 2

B 35

C 12

D 28

Common Core Standard 4.OA.3 – Operations & Algebraic Thinking

☐ Andy, Jackson, and Jonathan take a total of 48 minutes to finish their homework. How much time did it take each to complete his work, if each spent the same amount of time? Be sure to show your work.

A 144 minutes

B 16 minutes

C 51 minutes

D 45 minutes

Common Core Standard 4.OA.3 – Operations & Algebraic Thinking

☐ FairView Park has 12 picnic tables. If there are 8 people sitting at each picnic table, how many people in all can sit at the picnic tables? Be sure to show your work.

A 96 people

B 20 people

C 88 people

D 108 people

Name ___________________________

PRACTICE

Common Core Standard 4.OA.3 – Operations & Algebraic Thinking

☐ Connor buys 18 packages of gum. Each package holds 10 sticks of gum. How many sticks of gum did Connor buy? Be sure to show your work.

A 200 sticks of gum

B 28 sticks of gum

C 8 sticks of gum

D 180 sticks of gum

Common Core Standard 4.OA.3 – Operations & Algebraic Thinking

☐ Robert's father owns a business. He works 8 hours per day, every day; however, he works only 3 hours on 10 days out of each month. How many hours will Robert's father work in the month of November? Be sure to show your work.

A 210 hours

B 270 hours

C 278 hours

D 190 hours

Common Core Standard 4.OA.3 – Operations & Algebraic Thinking

☐ Lori wants to sew 7 teddy bears every day for a charity event. How many teddy bears will she sew in a typical month? Be sure to show your work.

A 196 teddy bears

B 210 teddy bears

C 280 teddy bears

D 248 teddy bears

Name ________________________

PRACTICE

Common Core Standard 4.OA.3 – Operations & Algebraic Thinking

☐ Thomas puts forty books on each shelf of a cabinet. There are four shelves in the cabinet. How many books does Thomas put in the cabinet in total? Be sure to show your work.

A 160 books

B 120 books

C 44 books

D 10 books

Common Core Standard 4.OA.3 – Operations & Algebraic Thinking

☐ Jacob went shopping for some new T-shirts. He bought 3 new T-shirts and he already had 5 T-shirts. How many T-shirts does he have now? Be sure to show your work.

A 12 T-shirts

B 2 T-shirts

C 15 T-shirts

D 8 T-shirts

Common Core Standard 4.OA.3 – Operations & Algebraic Thinking

☐ Stanley has 40 sticks of gum. He gives 12 sticks of gum to Rick, 15 sticks of gum to Josh, and 5 sticks of gum to Trish. How many sticks of gum did Stanley have left? Be sure to show your work.

A 7 sticks of gum

B 8 sticks of gum

C 6 sticks of gum

D 9 sticks of gum

Name ____________________________

PRACTICE

Common Core Standard 4.OA.3 – Operations & Algebraic Thinking

☐ An average person can eat 2 slices of pizza per day. How many slices of pizzas could a person eat in 13 days? Be sure to show your work.

A 26 slices of pizza

B 15 slices of pizza

C 11 slices of pizza

D 30 slices of pizza

Common Core Standard 4.OA.3 – Operations & Algebraic Thinking

☐ There are 20 baseball bats in each of the 13 bags. Joe puts 10 more baseball bats in each bag. How many baseball bats are there in all? Be sure to show your work.

A 370 baseball bats

B 490 baseball bats

C 53 baseball bats

D 390 baseball bats

Common Core Standard 4.OA.3 – Operations & Algebraic Thinking

☐ Chanise buys 20 pairs of socks on sale. Chanise gives two pairs of socks to her sister and 3 pairs to her cousin. How many pairs of socks does Chanise have left? Be sure to show your work.

A 17 pairs of socks

B 15 pairs of socks

C 23 pairs of socks

D 60 pairs of socks

Name ___________________________

ASSESSMENT

Common Core Standard 4.OA.3 – Operations & Algebraic Thinking

☐ In Blake's neighborhood there are 14 houses on Lakebrook Street. Seven of those houses have 2 cars each parked in the garage and the remaining houses have 3 cars each. How many cars are parked on Lakebrook Street in all? Be sure to show your work.

A 70 cars

B 35 cars

C 9 cars

D 45 cars

Common Core Standard 4.OA.3 – Operations & Algebraic Thinking

☐ Henry, Carly, Jessica, Jack, Steve, Randy, and Vance are going to play dodge ball together. They all brought 2 balls each. Carly and Vance lost 1 ball each. How many balls do they have now? Be sure to show your work.

A 8 balls

B 12 balls

C 6 balls

D 10 balls

Common Core Standard 4.OA.3 – Operations & Algebraic Thinking

☐ The cost of 1 chocolate pie is $12. If Rania purchased 15 pies for her school, how much money did she spend on pies? Be sure to show your work.

A $27

B $192

C $180

D $168

Name ___________________________

ASSESSMENT

Common Core Standard 4.OA.3 – Operations & Algebraic Thinking

☐ Gerald buys 5 peaches each day, Tuesday through Thursday. He buys 6 peaches on each of the remaining days of the week. How many total peaches did Gerald buy in seven days? Be sure to show your work.

A 37 peaches

B 39 peaches

C 40 peaches

D 11 peaches

Common Core Standard 4.OA.3 – Operations & Algebraic Thinking

☐ Charlotte has 12 friendship bracelets in each of her 3 drawers. Charlotte put 5 more friendship bracelets in 2 of the drawers. How many friendship bracelets are there in all? Be sure to show your work.

A 22 bracelets

B 46 bracelets

C 460 bracelets

D 105 bracelets

Common Core Standard 4.OA.3 – Operations & Algebraic Thinking

☐ Amber paid 80 dollars for an easy-bake oven. What was the original price of the easy-bake oven if she received a $12 discount? Be sure to show your work.

A $65.00

B $68.00

C $90.00

D $92.00

Name ___________________________

DIAGNOSTIC

Common Core Standard 4.OA.4 – Operations & Algebraic Thinking

☐ Find the correct answer for the following problem. Be sure to show your work.

$96 \div 4 = \square$

Common Core Standard 4.OA.4 – Operations & Algebraic Thinking

☐ Look at the numbers below. What numbers are multiples of 15?

20, 30, 36, 45, 55, 65, 75, 78, 85

A 30, 45, 55, 75

B 30, 45, 75

C 45, 55, 65, 75, 85

D 30, 45, 75, 85

Common Core Standard 4.OA.4 – Operations & Algebraic Thinking

☐ Find the correct answer for the following problem. Be sure to show your work.

$72 \div 18 = \square$

Name ____________________________

DIAGNOSTIC

Common Core Standard 4.OA.4 – Operations & Algebraic Thinking

☐ Which set of numbers below are factors of 69 from smallest to greatest?

A 3, 21, 23, 69

B 3, 23, 43

C 3, 23, 69

D 21, 23, 69

Common Core Standard 4.OA.4 – Operations & Algebraic Thinking

☐ Find the correct answer for the following problem. Be sure to show your work.

$$7\overline{)91}$$

Common Core Standard 4.OA.4 – Operations & Algebraic Thinking

☐ Look at the numbers below. What numbers are multiples of 12?

12, 24, 30, 34, 48, 50, 60, 72, 88

A 12, 24, 30, 48, 60, 72

B 12, 24, 48, 60, 72

C 12, 30, 48, 60, 72

D 24, 34, 48, 60, 72, 88

Name ____________________

PRACTICE

Common Core Standard 4.OA.4 – Operations & Algebraic Thinking

☐ **Find the correct answer for the following problem. Be sure to show your work.**

96 ÷ 6 = ☐

Common Core Standard 4.OA.4 – Operations & Algebraic Thinking

☐ **Look at the numbers below. What numbers are multiples of 11?**

15, 22, 31, 33, 40, 45, 52, 62, 70, 77, 80

A 31, 45, 77, 80

B 22, 33, 45, 77

C 22, 31, 33, 77

D 22, 33, 77

Common Core Standard 4.OA.4 – Operations & Algebraic Thinking

☐ **Find the correct answer for the following problem. Be sure to show your work.**

$3\overline{)81}$

Name ___________________________

PRACTICE

Common Core Standard 4.OA.4 – Operations & Algebraic Thinking

☐ Which set of numbers below are factors of 90 from smallest to greatest?

A 3, 5, 6, 9, 10, 20

B 4, 5, 6, 9, 10, 15

C 9, 18, 27, 36, 45, 54

D 9, 10, 15, 18, 30, 45

Common Core Standard 4.OA.4 – Operations & Algebraic Thinking

☐ Find the correct answer for the following problem. Be sure to show your work.

$$6\overline{)84}$$

Common Core Standard 4.OA.4 – Operations & Algebraic Thinking

☐ Look at the numbers below. What numbers are factors of 51?

3, 4, 11, 17, 24, 37

A 3, 11, 17, 37

B 3, 17

C 3, 11, 17

D 3, 17, 24

Name ___________________________

PRACTICE

Common Core Standard 4.OA.4 – Operations & Algebraic Thinking

☐ Find the correct answer for the following problem. Be sure to show your work.

$$9\overline{)72}$$

Common Core Standard 4.OA.4 – Operations & Algebraic Thinking

☐ Look at the numbers below. What numbers are multiples of 10?

20, 30, 36, 45, 55, 60, 75, 78, 85

A 30, 45, 55, 75

B 20, 30, 60

C 45, 55, 65, 75, 85

D 30, 45, 75, 85

Common Core Standard 4.OA.4 – Operations & Algebraic Thinking

☐ Find the correct answer for the following problem. Be sure to show your work.

56 ÷ 8 = ☐

Name ______________________

PRACTICE

Common Core Standard 4.OA.4 – Operations & Algebraic Thinking

☐ Find all the numbers below that are a multiple of 9.

26, 36, 45, 50, 62, 69, 75, 81, 87

A 36, 45, 69, 81

B 26, 36, 45, 69, 81

C 36, 45, 81

D 36, 45, 75

Common Core Standard 4.OA.4 – Operations & Algebraic Thinking

☐ Find the correct answer for the following problem. Be sure to show your work.

88 ÷ 8 = ☐

Common Core Standard 4.OA.4 – Operations & Algebraic Thinking

☐ Find all the numbers below that are a multiple of 4.

7, 12, 16, 19, 22, 30, 35, 40

A 12, 16, 22, 40

B 12, 16, 40

C 16, 35, 40

D 16, 40

Name ___________________________

ASSESSMENT

Common Core Standard 4.OA.4 – Operations & Algebraic Thinking

☐ **Find the correct answer for the following problem. Be sure to show your work.**

$$7\overline{)84}$$

Common Core Standard 4.OA.4 – Operations & Algebraic Thinking

☐ **Look at the numbers below. What numbers are factors of 16?**

1, 2, 3, 4, 8, 10, 20, 16, 30

A 1, 2, 3, 4, 8, 16

B 1, 2, 4, 8, 16

C 1, 2, 4, 8, 10, 16

D 2, 3, 8, 10, 16

Common Core Standard 4.OA.4 – Operations & Algebraic Thinking

☐ **Find the correct answer for the following problem. Be sure to show your work.**

90 ÷ 5 = ☐

Name ___________________________

ASSESSMENT

Common Core Standard 4.OA.4 – Operations & Algebraic Thinking

☐ Find all the numbers below that are a multiple of 10.

11, 20, 29, 35, 40, 51, 60, 69

A 11, 29, 35, 69

B 20, 40, 51, 60

C 20, 40, 60

D 20, 40, 69

Common Core Standard 4.OA.4 – Operations & Algebraic Thinking

☐ Find the correct answer for the following problem. Be sure to show your work.

48 ÷ 3 = ☐

Common Core Standard 4.OA.4 – Operations & Algebraic Thinking

☐ Find the correct answer for the following problem. Be sure to show your work.

98 ÷ 14 = ☐

Name ________________________

DIAGNOSTIC

Common Core Standard 4.OA.5 – Operations & Algebraic Thinking

☐ **Find the missing numbers in the pattern sequence below.**

5, 13, ☐, 29,☐, 45, ☐

A 14, 30, 46

B 20, 37, 52

C 21, 37, 53

D 20, 30, 50

Common Core Standard 4.OA.5 – Operations & Algebraic Thinking

☐ **Find the missing shapes in the pattern sequence below.**

△◺♡ ? ◺ ?

A △◺♡◺◺♡

C △◺♡♡◺△

B △◺♡△◺♡

D △◺♡△◺△

Common Core Standard 4.OA.5 – Operations & Algebraic Thinking

☐ **Find the next number by using the following rule.**

Rule: Multiply by 2 then add 1.

2, 5, 11, 23, 47, ☐

A 94

B 95

C 93

D 50

Name ____________________________

DIAGNOSTIC

Common Core Standard 4.OA.5 – Operations & Algebraic Thinking

☐ **Find the missing shapes in the pattern sequence below.**

⇔ ⇩ ⇦ ? ? ⇦

A ⇔ ⇩ ⇦ ⇔ ⇦ ⇦

B ⇔ ⇩ ⇦ ⇩ ⇔ ⇦

C ⇔ ⇩ ⇦ ⇩ ⇩ ⇦

D ⇔ ⇩ ⇦ ⇔ ⇩ ⇦

Common Core Standard 4.OA.5 – Operations & Algebraic Thinking

☐ **Find the number by using the following rule.**

Rule: Multiply by 3 then add 3.

5, 18, 57, 174, ☐

A 180

B 525

C 174

D 535

Common Core Standard 4.OA.5 – Operations & Algebraic Thinking

☐ **Find the missing numbers in the pattern sequence below.**

4, ☐, 10, 13, 16, 19, ☐, ☐

A 7, 22, 25

B 5, 20, 21

C 6, 37, 40

D 6, 21, 24

Name ______________________

PRACTICE

Common Core Standard 4.OA.5 – Operations & Algebraic Thinking

☐ **Find the missing numbers in the pattern sequence below.**

6, 11, 16, 21, ☐, 31, ☐, ☐

A 25, 34, 38

B 26, 36, 41

C 22, 32, 33

D 23, 33, 36

Common Core Standard 4.OA.5 – Operations & Algebraic Thinking

☐ **Find the missing shapes in the pattern sequence below.**

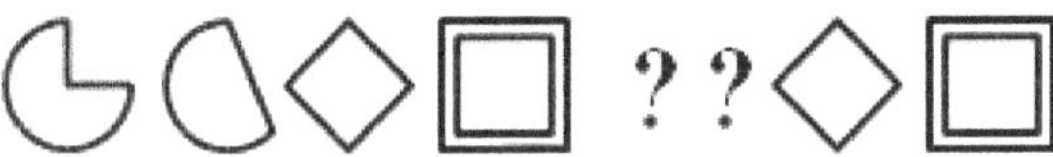

A

C

B

D

Common Core Standard 4.OA.5 – Operations & Algebraic Thinking

☐ **Find the next number by using the following rule.**

Rule: Multiply by 1 then add 5.

4, 9, 14, 19, 24, ☐

A 28

B 39

C 29

D 40

Name ____________________

PRACTICE

Common Core Standard 4.OA.5 – Operations & Algebraic Thinking

☐ **Find the missing shapes in the pattern sequence below.**

? ?

A

B

C

D

Common Core Standard 4.OA.5 – Operations & Algebraic Thinking

☐ **Find the number by using the following rule.**

Rule: Subtract 2 then multiply by 4.

7, 20, 72, 280, ☐

A 286

B 284

C 552

D 1,112

Common Core Standard 4.OA.5 – Operations & Algebraic Thinking

☐ **Find the missing numbers in the pattern sequence below.**

15, 13, ☐, ☐, 7, ☐, 3

A 15, 9, 5

B 11, 8, 5

C 12, 10, 4

D 11, 9, 5

Name ___________________________ **PRACTICE**

Common Core Standard 4.OA.5 – Operations & Algebraic Thinking

☐ **Find the missing shapes in the pattern sequence below.**

A

B

C

D

Common Core Standard 4.OA.5 – Operations & Algebraic Thinking

☐ **Find the number by using the following rule.**

Rule: Add 6 then divide by 3.

84, 30, 12, 6, ☐

A 4

B 2

C 12

D 15

Common Core Standard 4.OA.5 – Operations & Algebraic Thinking

☐ **Find the missing numbers in the pattern sequence below.**

3, 4, 6, 9, ☐, 18, ☐

A 24, 48

B 16, 40

C 13, 24

D 30, 48

Name ______________________

PRACTICE

Common Core Standard 4.OA.5 – Operations & Algebraic Thinking

☐ Find the missing numbers in the pattern sequence below.

9, 12, ☐, ☐, 21, ☐, 27

A 13, 14, 22

B 15, 18, 24

C 15, 19, 24

D 15, 18, 23

Common Core Standard 4.OA.5 – Operations & Algebraic Thinking

☐ Find the missing shapes in the pattern sequence below.

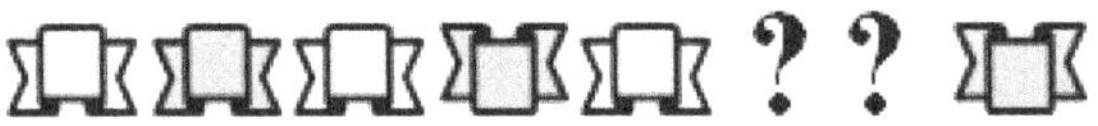

? ?

A

B

C

D

Common Core Standard 4.OA.5 – Operations & Algebraic Thinking

☐ Find the next number by using the following rule.

Rule: Multiply by 2 then add 3.

5, 13, 29, 61, 125, ☐

A 256

B 250

C 126

D 253

Name ____________________________

ASSESSMENT

Common Core Standard 4.OA.5 – Operations & Algebraic Thinking

☐ **Find the missing shapes in the pattern sequence below.**

A

B

C

D

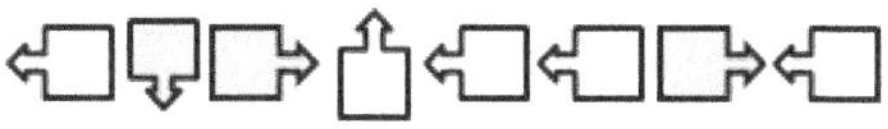

Common Core Standard 4.OA.5 – Operations & Algebraic Thinking

☐ **Find the number by using the following rule.**

Rule: Subtract 2 then multiply by 4.

3, 4, 8, 24, 88, ☐

A 344

B 244

C 360

D 21

Common Core Standard 4.OA.5 – Operations & Algebraic Thinking

☐ **Find the missing numbers in the pattern sequence below.**

6, 12, 18, ☐, 30, ☐, ☐

A 24, 36, 48

B 24, 36, 42

C 19, 31, 32

D 24, 30, 36

Name ____________________

ASSESSMENT

Common Core Standard 4.OA.5 – Operations & Algebraic Thinking

☐ **Find the missing numbers in the pattern sequence below.**

72, 60, 48, ☐, 24, ☐

A 40, 20

B 47, 23

C 34, 12

D 36, 12

Common Core Standard 4.OA.5 – Operations & Algebraic Thinking

☐ **Find the missing shapes in the pattern sequence below.**

◎ ○ ◎ ? ○ ?

A ◎○◎◎○◎

C ◎○◎◎○◎

B ◎○◎◎○◎

D ◎○◎○○◎

Common Core Standard 4.OA.5 – Operations & Algebraic Thinking

☐ **Find the next number by using the following rule.**

Rule: Multiply by 3 then add 6.

5, 21, 69, 213, 645, ☐

A 1953

B 654

C 1290

D 1,941

Name ____________________________

DIAGNOSTIC

Common Core Standard 4.NBT.1 – Number & Operations in Base Ten

☐ **What is the correct answer for the value below?**

8 thousands = ☐ tens

A 8

B 8000

C 80

D 800

Common Core Standard 4.NBT.1 – Number & Operations in Base Ten

☐ **What is the correct answer for the value below?**

☐ hundreds = 400 ones

A 400

B 4

C 40

D 4000

Common Core Standard 4.NBT.1 – Number & Operations in Base Ten

☐ **What is the correct answer for the value below?**

16 thousands = ☐ hundreds

A 160

B 1600

C 16

D 16000

Name ____________________

DIAGNOSTIC

Common Core Standard 4.NBT.1 – Number & Operations in Base Ten

☐ What is the correct answer for the value below?

☐ hundreds = 200 tens

A 20

B 200

C 2000

D 10

Common Core Standard 4.NBT.1 – Number & Operations in Base Ten

☐ What is the correct answer for the value below?

150 tens = ☐ ones

A 15

B 150

C 1500

D 15000

Common Core Standard 4.NBT.1 – Number & Operations in Base Ten

☐ What is the correct answer for the value below?

☐ thousands = 9000 ones

A 90

B 900

C 9

D 9000

Name ____________________

PRACTICE

Common Core Standard 4.NBT.1 – Number & Operations in Base Ten

☐ What is the correct answer for the value below?

☐ thousands = 400 tens

A 400

B 4000

C 40

D 4

Common Core Standard 4.NBT.1 – Number & Operations in Base Ten

☐ What is the correct answer for the value below?

6 hundreds = ☐ ones

A 6000

B 60

C 6

D 600

Common Core Standard 4.NBT.1 – Number & Operations in Base Ten

☐ What is the correct answer for the value below?

21 thousands = ☐ hundreds

A 2100

B 210

C 21

D 21000

Name ____________________

PRACTICE

Common Core Standard 4.NBT.1 – Number & Operations in Base Ten

☐ What is the correct answer for the value below?

20 thousands = ☐ tens

A 200

B 20

C 2000

D 10

Common Core Standard 4.NBT.1 – Number & Operations in Base Ten

☐ What is the correct answer for the value below?

☐ ones = 3 ones

A 300

B 3

C 3000

D 30

Common Core Standard 4.NBT.1 – Number & Operations in Base Ten

☐ What is the correct answer for the value below?

☐ hundreds = 4500 tens

A 45000

B 450

C 4500

D 45

Name ________________________

PRACTICE

Common Core Standard 4.NBT.1 – Number & Operations in Base Ten

☐ **What is the correct answer for the value below?**

☐ thousands = 5000 tens

A 500

B 50000

C 50

D 5000

Common Core Standard 4.NBT.1 – Number & Operations in Base Ten

☐ **What is the correct answer for the value below?**

8 hundreds = ☐ tens

A 8000

B 80

C 8

D 800

Common Core Standard 4.NBT.1 – Number & Operations in Base Ten

☐ **What is the correct answer for the value below?**

230 hundreds = ☐ tens

A 2300

B 230

C 23

D 23000

Name ______________________

PRACTICE

Common Core Standard 4.NBT.1 – Number & Operations in Base Ten

☐ What is the correct answer for the value below?

☐ thousands = 2000 hundreds

A 20000

B 20

C 200

D 10

Common Core Standard 4.NBT.1 – Number & Operations in Base Ten

☐ What is the correct answer for the value below?

☐ tens = 3000 ones

A 30

B 3

C 3000

D 300

Common Core Standard 4.NBT.1 – Number & Operations in Base Ten

☐ What is the correct answer for the value below?

☐ tens = 5500 ones

A 55000

B 550

C 5500

D 55

Name ______________________

ASSESSMENT

Common Core Standard 4.NBT.1 – Number & Operations in Base Ten

☐ What is the correct answer for the value below?

☐ ones = 70 hundreds

A 700

B 70000

C 70

D 7000

Common Core Standard 4.NBT.1 – Number & Operations in Base Ten

☐ What is the correct answer for the value below?

34 thousands = ☐ hundreds

A 34000

B 340

C 34

D 3400

Common Core Standard 4.NBT.1 – Number & Operations in Base Ten

☐ What is the correct answer for the value below?

100 hundreds = ☐ tens

A 100

B 10

C 10000

D 1000

Name ________________________

ASSESSMENT

Common Core Standard 4.NBT.1 – Number & Operations in Base Ten

☐ **What is the correct answer for the value below?**

☐ thousands = 600 tens

A 60000

B 600

C 60

D 6

Common Core Standard 4.NBT.1 – Number & Operations in Base Ten

☐ **What is the correct answer for the value below?**

☐ tens = 670 ones

A 67000

B 670

C 6700

D 67

Common Core Standard 4.NBT.1 – Number & Operations in Base Ten

☐ **What is the correct answer for the value below?**

☐ tens = 980 thousands

A 980000

B 98000

C 9800

D 980

Name ____________________________

DIAGNOSTIC

Common Core Standard 4.NBT.2 – Number & Operations in Base Ten

☐ **Which answer below best represents the number 553 in expanded form?**

A Five hundred, fifty-three

B 500 + 50 + 3

C 5 hundreds, 5 tens, 3 ones

D 5 + 5 + 3

Common Core Standard 4.NBT.2 – Number & Operations in Base Ten

☐ **Round and compare the place values for the numbers that are underlined below using “>, <, or =”.**

$$4\underline{8}0 \; \square \; 5\underline{6}1$$

A >

B <

C =

D None of the above

Common Core Standard 4.NBT.2 – Number & Operations in Base Ten

☐ **Find the place value of the number that is underlined below.**

$$4\underline{3}60$$

A Ones

B Hundreds

C Tens

D Thousands

Name ____________________________

DIAGNOSTIC

Common Core Standard 4.NBT.2 – Number & Operations in Base Ten

☐ **Which answer below best represents the number 391 as a number name?**

A 3 + 9 + 1

B 300 + 90 + 1

C 3 hundreds, 9 tens, 1 ones

D Three hundred, ninety-one

Common Core Standard 4.NBT.2 – Number & Operations in Base Ten

☐ **Round and compare the place values for the numbers that are underlined below using “>, <, or =”.**

763 ☐ 397

A =

B <

C >

D None of the above

Common Core Standard 4.NBT.2 – Number & Operations in Base Ten

☐ **Which answer below best describes the number 769 as a number of hundreds, tens, and ones?**

A 7 + 6 + 9

B 700 + 60 + 9

C 7 hundreds, 6 tens, 9 ones

D Seven hundred, sixty-nine

Name ____________________

PRACTICE

Common Core Standard 4.NBT.2 – Number & Operations in Base Ten

☐ **Which answer below best represents the number 5438 as a number name?**

A Five thousand, 4 hundred, thirty-eight

B 5 + 4 + 3 + 8

C 5 thousands, 4 hundreds, 3 tens, 8 ones

D 5000 + 400 + 30 + 8

Common Core Standard 4.NBT.2 – Number & Operations in Base Ten

☐ **Find the place value of the number that is underlined below.**

372

A Ones

B Hundreds

C Tens

D Thousands

Common Core Standard 4.NBT.2 – Number & Operations in Base Ten

☐ **Round and compare the place values for the numbers that are underlined below using ">, <, or =".**

8712 ☐ 9623

A >

B <

C =

D None of the above

Name ______________________________

PRACTICE

Common Core Standard 4.NBT.2 – Number & Operations in Base Ten

☐ **Which answer below best represents the number 1364 in expanded form?**

A One thousand, Three hundred, sixty-four

B 1000 +300 + 60 + 4

C 1 thousands, 3 hundreds, 6 tens, 4 ones

D 1 + 3 + 6 + 4

Common Core Standard 4.NBT.2 – Number & Operations in Base Ten

☐ **Round and compare the place values for the numbers that are underlined below using “>, <, or =”.**

955 ☐ 963

A =

B <

C >

D None of the above

Common Core Standard 4.NBT.2 – Number & Operations in Base Ten

☐ **Which answer below best describes the number 830 as a number of hundreds, tens, and ones?**

A 8 + 3 + 0

B 800 + 30 + 0

C 8 hundreds, 3 tens, 0 ones

D Eight hundred, thirty

Name ___________________________

PRACTICE

Common Core Standard 4.NBT.2 – Number & Operations in Base Ten

☐ **Which answer below best describes the number 449 in expanded form?**

A Four hundred, forty-nine

B 4 + 4 + 9

C 4 hundreds, 4 tens, 9 ones

D 400 + 40 + 9

Common Core Standard 4.NBT.2 – Number & Operations in Base Ten

☐ **Round and compare the place values for the numbers that are underlined below using ">, <, or =".**

$$8\underline{8}6 \ \square \ 8\underline{3}9$$

A <

B =

C >

D None of the above

Common Core Standard 4.NBT.2 – Number & Operations in Base Ten

☐ **Find the place value of the number that is underlined below.**

$$\underline{7}35$$

A Tens

B Thousands

C Ones

D Hundreds

Name ____________________

PRACTICE

Common Core Standard 4.NBT.2 – Number & Operations in Base Ten

☐ **Which answer below best represents the number 1864 as a number of thousands, hundreds, tens, and ones?**

A 1000 + 800 + 60 + 4

B 1 +8 + 6 + 4

C 1 thousands, 8 hundreds, 6 tens, 4 ones

D One thousand, eight hundred, sixty-four

Common Core Standard 4.NBT.2 – Number & Operations in Base Ten

☐ **Find the place value of the number that is underlined below.**

5236

A Tens

B Thousands

C Ones

D Hundreds

Common Core Standard 4.NBT.2 – Number & Operations in Base Ten

☐ **Round and compare the place values for the numbers that are underlined below using ">, <, or =".**

444 ☐ 454

A <

B =

C >

D None of the above

Name ______________________

ASSESSMENT

Common Core Standard 4.NBT.2 – Number & Operations in Base Ten

☐ **Which answer below best describes the number 315 as a number name?**

A 3 + 1 + 5

B Three hundred, fifteen

C 3 hundreds, 1 tens, 5 ones

D 300 + 10 + 5

Common Core Standard 4.NBT.2 – Number & Operations in Base Ten

☐ **Round and compare the place values for the numbers that are underlined below using ">, <, or =".**

194 ☐ 143

A =

B <

C >

D None of the above

Common Core Standard 4.NBT.2 – Number & Operations in Base Ten

☐ **Which answer below best represents the number 6836 as a number of thousands, hundreds, tens, and ones?**

A 6 + 8 + 3 + 6

B 6000 + 800 + 30 + 6

C 6 thousands, 8 hundreds, 3 tens, 6 ones

D Six thousand, Eight hundred, thirty-six

Name ______________________

ASSESSMENT

Common Core Standard 4.NBT.2 – Number & Operations in Base Ten

☐ **Which answer below best describes the number 999 in expanded form?**

A 900 + 90 + 9

B 9 + 9 + 9

C 9 hundreds, 9 tens, 9 ones

D Nine hundred, ninety-nine

Common Core Standard 4.NBT.2 – Number & Operations in Base Ten

☐ **Find the place value of the number that is underlined below.**

71<u>4</u>5

A Ones

B Hundreds

C Tens

D Thousands

Common Core Standard 4.NBT.2 – Number & Operations in Base Ten

☐ **Which answer below best represents the number 712 as a number name?**

A 700 + 10 + 2

B 7 + 1 + 2

C 7 hundreds, 1 tens, 2 ones

D Seven hundred, twelve

Name ___________________________

DIAGNOSTIC

Common Core Standard 4.NBT.3 – Number & Operations in Base Ten

☐ **Round 274 to hundreds.**

A 200

B 250

C 300

D 500

Common Core Standard 4.NBT.3 – Number & Operations in Base Ten

☐ **Find correct answer for the missing digits below.**

___ thousands + ___ hundreds + ___ tens + 4 ones = 6354

A 6 thousands, 3 hundreds, 5 tens, 4 ones

B 6 hundreds, 3 tens, 54 ones

C 6 thousands, 354 ones

D 6 thousands, 35 hundred, 4 ones

Common Core Standard 4.NBT.3 – Number & Operations in Base Ten

☐ **Which group of numbers is in order from greatest to least?**

A	1,637,537	1,636, 419	1,637,020	1,636,342
B	1,637,537	1,637,020	1,636,419	1,636,342
C	1,636,342	1,636,419	1,637,020	1,637,537
D	1,637,537	1,637,020	1,636,342	1,636,419

Name ________________________

DIAGNOSTIC

Common Core Standard 4.NBT.3 – Number & Operations in Base Ten

☐ Round 2,384 to tens.

A 2,300

B 2,400

C 2,380

D 2,390

Common Core Standard 4.NBT.3 – Number & Operations in Base Ten

☐ Which numeral has a larger digit in the hundreds place than in the tens place?

A 356,281

B 1,375,290

C 27,192

D 6,437

Common Core Standard 4.NBT.3 – Number & Operations in Base Ten

☐ What is the place value of the 8 in 8,502,734?

A 8 thousand

B 8 hundred thousand

C 8 million

D 8 hundred million

Name ______________________

PRACTICE

Common Core Standard 4.NBT.3 – Number & Operations in Base Ten

☐ Round 526 to hundreds.

A 0

B 1000

C 600

D 500

Common Core Standard 4.NBT.3 – Number & Operations in Base Ten

☐ Find correct answer for the missing digits below.

4 hundreds + ___ tens + ___ ones = 458

A 4 hundreds, 58 ones

B 4 hundreds, 58 tens

C 4 hundreds, 5 tens, 8 ones

D Four hundred, fifty-eight

Common Core Standard 4.NBT.3 – Number & Operations in Base Ten

☐ A movie theater kept a record of the number of tickets they sold. They sold 5,390 tickets in January, 5,178 tickets in February, 5,199 tickets in March, and 5,096 tickets in April. Which group below shows the number of tickets sold in order from greatest to least?

A	5,390	5,096	5,178	5,199
B	5,096	5,178	5,199	5,390
C	5,390	5,199	5,178	5,096
D	5,390	5,178	5,199	5,096

Name ________________________

PRACTICE

Common Core Standard 4.NBT.3 – Number & Operations in Base Ten

☐ Round 28,125 to ten thousands.

A 20,000

B 30,000

C 50,000

D 100,000

Common Core Standard 4.NBT.3 – Number & Operations in Base Ten

☐ It is time for school pictures. The students must line up in order from the tallest to the shortest. April is 48 inches tall, Brad is 56 inches tall, Callie is 50 inches tall, and David is 55 inches tall. In which order should the students line up?

A Brad, David, Callie, April

B April, Callie, David, Brad

C April, Brad, Callie, David

D Brad, April, Callie, David

HEIGHT OF STUDENTS

Student	Height in Inches
April	48 in
Brad	56 in
Callie	50 in
David	55 in

Common Core Standard 4.NBT.3 – Number & Operations in Base Ten

☐ Find correct answer for the missing digits below.

9 thousands + ___ hundreds + ___ tens + ____ ones = 9458

A 4 hundreds, 58 ones

B 4 hundreds, 58 tens

C 4 hundreds, 5 tens, 8 ones

D Four hundred, fifty-eight

Name ____________________

PRACTICE

Common Core Standard 4.NBT.3 – Number & Operations in Base Ten

☐ **Which number has an 8 in the thousands place and a 6 in the ones place?**

A 483,566

B 528,616

C 637,586

D 738,862

Common Core Standard 4.NBT.3 – Number & Operations in Base Ten

☐ **Which group of numbers is in order from greatest to least?**

A	3,744,560	3,744,428	3,744,508	3,744,499
B	3,744,428	3,744,499	3,744,508	3,744,560
C	3,744,560	3,744,508	3,744,428	3,744,499
D	3,744,560	3,744,508	3,744,499	3,744,428

Common Core Standard 4.NBT.3 – Number & Operations in Base Ten

☐ **Round 2,693,204 to millions.**

A 2,000,000

B 2,500,000

C 3,000,000

D 5,000,000

Name ____________________ **PRACTICE**

Common Core Standard 4.NBT.3 – Number & Operations in Base Ten

☐ What is the place value of the 4 in 842,093?

A thousands

B ten thousands

C millions

D hundred thousands

Common Core Standard 4.NBT.3 – Number & Operations in Base Ten

☐ Find correct answer for the missing digits below.

7 ten thousands + ___ thousands + 9 hundreds + 9 tens + ___ ones = 73,993

A 73 thousands, 9 hundreds, 9 tens, 9 ones

B 7 ten thousands, 3 thousands, 9 hundreds, 9 tens, 3 ones

C 7 thousands, 9 hundreds, 9 tens, 3 ones

D Seventy-three thousand, nine hundred, ninety-three

Common Core Standard 4.NBT.3 – Number & Operations in Base Ten

☐ The Farmer Dairy Company has kept a record of their sales every ten years. In 1990 their sales were $168,499; $180,982 in 1980; $120,001 In 1970; and $108,955 in 1960. If they put the sales totals in order from the worst year to the best year, which order would be correct?

SALES

Year	Sales in Dollars
1990	$168,499
1980	$180,982
1970	$120,001
1960	$108,955

A $168,499 $180,982 $120,001 $108,955

B $180,982 $168,499 $120,001 $108,955

C $108,955 $168,499 $120,001 $180,982

D $108,955 $120,001 $168,499 $180,982

Name ___________________________

ASSESSMENT

Common Core Standard 4.NBT.3 – Number & Operations in Base Ten

☐ **Which number has a 4 in the ten thousands place and a 5 in the hundred thousands place?**

A 5,424,501

B 3,543,459

C 5,745,365

D 6,534,354

Common Core Standard 4.NBT.3 – Number & Operations in Base Ten

☐ **Which group of numbers is in order from greatest to least?**

A	2,452,319	2,452,261	2,452,225	2,452,201
B	2,452,261	2,452,225	2,452,319	2,452,201
C	2,452,201	2,452,225	2,452,261	2,452,319
D	2,452,319	2,452,225	2,452,261	2,452,201

Common Core Standard 4.NBT.3 – Number & Operations in Base Ten

☐ **Round 3,294,182 to hundred thousands.**

A 3,200,000

B 3,300,000

C 3,500,000

D 5,000,000

Name ____________________________

ASSESSMENT

Common Core Standard 4.NBT.3 – Number & Operations in Base Ten

☐ **What is the place value of the 8 in 8,030,274?**

A Millions

B Hundred thousands

C Hundred millions

D Ten thousands

Common Core Standard 4.NBT.3 – Number & Operations in Base Ten

☐ **Find correct answer for the missing digits below.**

___ thousands + ___ hundreds + 2 tens + ___ ones = 4729

A 4 thousands, 7 hundreds, 29 tens

B Four thousand, seven hundred, twenty-nine

C 47 thousands, 2 tens, 9 ones

D 4 thousands, 7 hundreds, 2 tens, 9 ones

Common Core Standard 4.NBT.3 – Number & Operations in Base Ten

☐ **A city in Florida listed its population figures for four years. If the figures are arranged in order from smallest number of people to the largest number of people, which order of years would be correct?**

A 1999 2000 2001 2002

B 2000 2001 2002 1999

C 1999 2002 2001 2000

D 2000 2002 2001 1999

Year	Population
1999	327,580
2000	326,977
2001	327,009
2002	327,050

Name ___________________________

DIAGNOSTICS

Common Core Standard 4.NBT.4 – Number & Operations in Base Ten

☐ The Christmas parade is Saturday. Mr. Black believes that many people will buy cookies from his bakery while at the parade. In order to get ready for Saturday his bakery baked 456 cookies on Wednesday. On Thursday he baked 321 cookies, and on Friday he baked 478 cookies. How many cookies did he bake on those 3 days? Be sure to show your work.

Common Core Standard 4.NBT.4 – Number & Operations in Base Ten

☐ What is the difference in the number of pages between a telephone book with 2,010 pages and a telephone book with 67 pages? Be sure to show your work.

Common Core Standard 4.NBT.4 – Number & Operations in Base Ten

☐ A city built a toll bridge across a river. The total number of vehicles that crossed the river last year was 6,473. If 3,799 vehicles crossed from January to May, how many vehicles used the toll bridge after May? Be sure to show your work.

Name ___________________________

DIAGNOSTICS

Common Core Standard 4.NBT.4 – Number & Operations in Base Ten

☐ Carter Elementary spent $2,086 on new books for the library. The librarian spent $95 on additional shelves for the new books. How much was spent altogether? Be sure to show your work.

Common Core Standard 4.NBT.4 – Number & Operations in Base Ten

☐ A county fair had 2,852 people in attendance on Friday, 4,199 people on Saturday, and 3,005 people on Sunday. What was the total number of people who attended the fair on those 3 days? Be sure to show your work.

Common Core Standard 4.NBT.4 – Number & Operations in Base Ten

☐ What is the difference between the distance of 1,700 miles that Beverly's family traveled on their vacation and the distance of 99 miles that Cameron's family traveled last weekend? Be sure to show your work.

Name ________________________

PRACTICE

Common Core Standard 4.NBT.4 – Number & Operations in Base Ten

☐ A city had 115 entries in the Flower parade, 68 entries in the Easter parade, and 101 entries in the Fourth of July parade. What was the total number of entries in the 3 parades? Be sure to show your work.

Common Core Standard 4.NBT.4 – Number & Operations in Base Ten

☐ Carley's class collected 4,954 cans last year. If they collected 1,976 cans before January, how many cans were collected after January? Be sure to show your work.

Common Core Standard 4.NBT.4 – Number & Operations in Base Ten

☐ Adelina has saved $192 to buy school clothes for her sister and herself. When she and her sister went shopping, they found that they needed $351, including tax, to buy the clothes they had chosen. How much more money does Adelina need to buy the school clothes? Be sure to show your work.

Name ________________________

PRACTICE

Common Core Standard 4.NBT.4 – Number & Operations in Base Ten

☐ Jonesville has a population of 4,257,388 people. Lake City has a population of 7,125,210 people. How much larger is Lake City than Jonesville? Be sure to show your work.

Common Core Standard 4.NBT.4 – Number & Operations in Base Ten

☐ A grocery store sold 1,328 pounds of poultry during Thanksgiving. This was 449 pounds more than they sold last year. How many pounds of poultry did they sell last year? Be sure to show your work.

Common Core Standard 4.NBT.4 – Number & Operations in Base Ten

☐ A cafeteria baked 2,175 cookies and 712 muffins. After the third and fourth grade classes had eaten lunch, there were 594 cookies and 274 muffins left. How many cookies did the third and fourth grade classes eat? Be sure to show your work.

Name ___________________________

PRACTICE

Common Core Standard 4.NBT.4 – Number & Operations in Base Ten

☐ A group of fourth grade classes had a recycling contest. Ms. Herman's class collected 523 cans. Mr. Zola's class collected 2,578 cans. What was the total number of cans collected by the two classes? Be sure to show your work.

Common Core Standard 4.NBT.4 – Number & Operations in Base Ten

☐ A library is having a reading contest. Ricardo has read 2,446 pages this month, Rebekah has read 658 pages, and Mark has read 805 pages. How many pages have the three students read altogether this month? Be sure to show your work.

Common Core Standard 4.NBT.4 – Number & Operations in Base Ten

☐ The population of Halleyville was 5,291. Last year, the population increased by 89 people. What is the total population of Halleyville now? Be sure to show your work.

Name ________________________

PRACTICE

Common Core Standard 4.NBT.4 – Number & Operations in Base Ten

☐ A bakery baked 3,155 loaves of bread, 2,821 packages of rolls, and 1,088 packages of cookies. How many items did the bakery bake altogether? Be sure to show your work.

Common Core Standard 4.NBT.4 – Number & Operations in Base Ten

☐ A local club sold raffle tickets at Thanksgiving. Mr. Florence sold 199 tickets, Mr. Tucker sold 263 tickets, and Mr. Simpson sold 77 tickets. How many tickets did the three men sell? Be sure to show your work.

Common Core Standard 4.NBT.4 – Number & Operations in Base Ten

☐ Three towns have trash collected each week. Centerville collects 2,534 tons of trash on Monday, Bakertown collects 5,387 tons of trash on Tuesday, and Highland collects 1,284 tons of trash on Thursday. What is the total amount of trash collected from all three towns? Be sure to show your work.

Name ___________________________

ASSESSEMENT

Common Core Standard 4.NBT.4 – Number & Operations in Base Ten

☐ A new building in Betina's hometown is 1,207 feet tall. The building next to it is 897 feet tall. If the buildings were stacked on top of each other, how tall would they be altogether? Be sure to show your work.

Common Core Standard 4.NBT.4 – Number & Operations in Base Ten

☐ Jessica has saved $129 from her allowance. She wants to buy a boom box that costs $200, including tax. How much more money does Jessica need in order to buy the boom box? Be sure to show your work.

Common Core Standard 4.NBT.4 – Number & Operations in Base Ten

☐ Mrs. White bought a new dining room suite. The table cost $1,042, the chairs were $599, and the china cabinet was $755. How much did she spend altogether? Be sure to show your work.

Name ________________________

ASSESSEMENT

Common Core Standard 4.NBT.4 – Number & Operations in Base Ten

☐ **Madeline's father raises chickens for a poultry company. Last year he sold 1,258,304 chickens to a poultry company. This year he sold 1,786,135. How many fewer chickens did he sell last year than this year? Be sure to show your work.**

Common Core Standard 4.NBT.4 – Number & Operations in Base Ten

☐ **Mr. Vasquez bought a new car. The car cost $7,563. He added a CD player that cost $348 and a sunroof that cost $874. How much did Mr. Vasquez spend altogether for the car? Be sure to show your work.**

Common Core Standard 4.NBT.4 – Number & Operations in Base Ten

☐ **Blaine was born in 1990. His great-grandfather was born 112 years before Blaine. In what year was his great-grandfather born? Be sure to show your work.**

Name ______________________

DIAGNOSTIC

Common Core Standard 4.NBT.5 – Number & Operations in Base Ten

☐ **Solve the problem below. Be sure to show your work.**

$$\begin{array}{r} 569 \\ \underline{\times 6} \end{array}$$

Common Core Standard 4.NBT.5 – Number & Operations in Base Ten

☐ **Find the product using the blocks below. Be sure to show your work.**

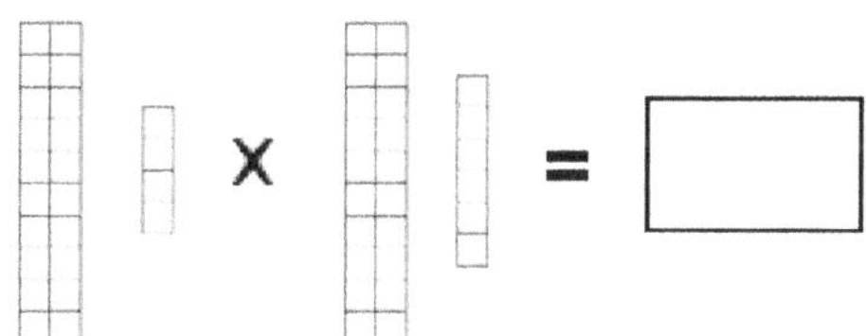

Common Core Standard 4.NBT.5 – Number & Operations in Base Ten

☐ **Solve the problem below. Be sure to show your work.**

$$\begin{array}{r} 62 \\ \underline{\times 15} \end{array}$$

Name ___________________________

DIAGNOSTIC

Common Core Standard 4.NBT.5 – Number & Operations in Base Ten

☐ Find the product using the blocks below. Be sure to show your work.

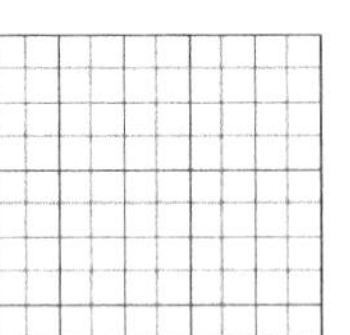 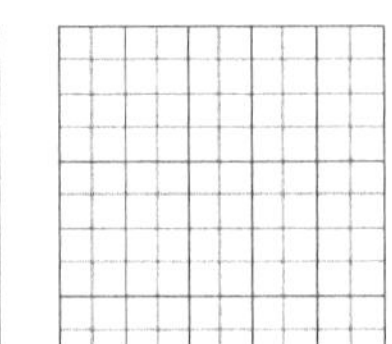 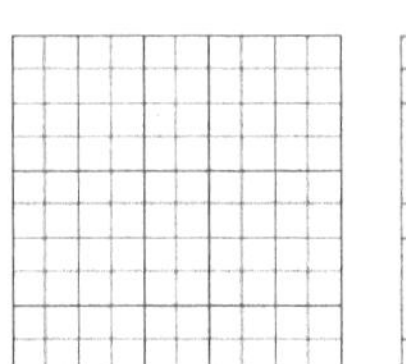 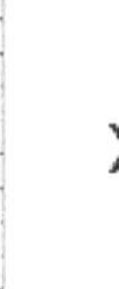 X = 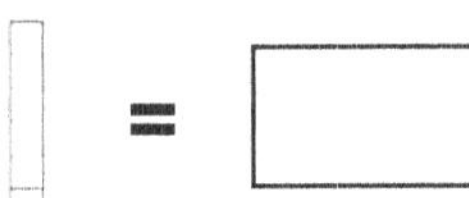

Common Core Standard 4.NBT.5 – Number & Operations in Base Ten

☐ Solve the problem below. Be sure to show your work.

$$\begin{array}{r} 63 \\ \underline{\times 17} \end{array}$$

Common Core Standard 4.NBT.5 – Number & Operations in Base Ten

☐ Find the factor using the blocks below. Be sure to show your work.

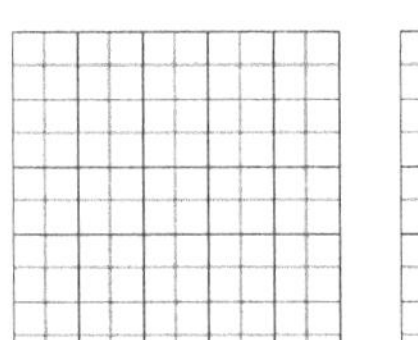 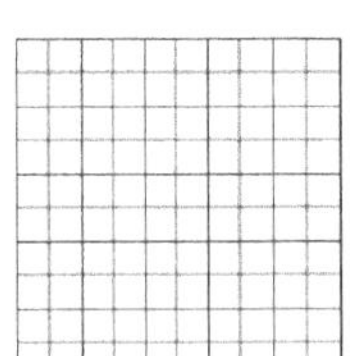 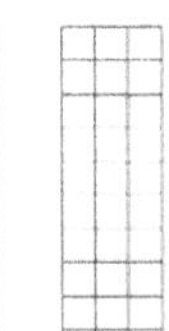 ☐ X ☐ = 1,840

Name ____________________________

PRACTICE

Common Core Standard 4.NBT.5 – Number & Operations in Base Ten

☐ Find the product using the blocks below. Be sure to show your work.

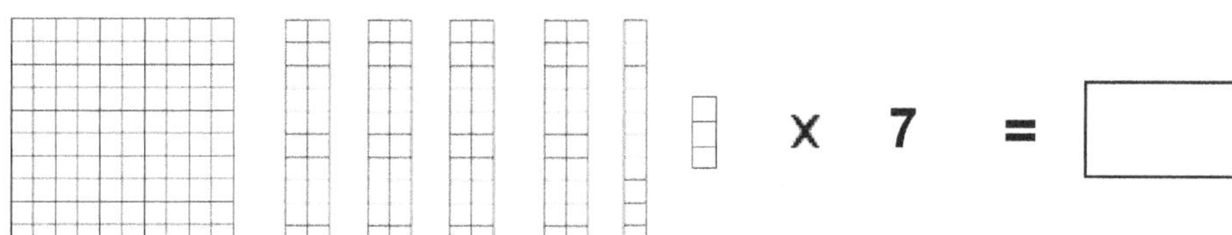

Common Core Standard 4.NBT.5 – Number & Operations in Base Ten

☐ Solve the problem below. Be sure to show your work.

$$\begin{array}{r} 29 \\ \underline{\times 19} \end{array}$$

Common Core Standard 4.NBT.5 – Number & Operations in Base Ten

☐ Solve the problem below. Be sure to show your work.

$$\begin{array}{r} 1{,}275 \\ \underline{\times \ \square} \\ 7{,}650 \end{array}$$

Name ___________________________

PRACTICE

Common Core Standard 4.NBT.5 – Number & Operations in Base Ten

☐ **Solve the problem below. Be sure to show your work.**

$$\begin{array}{r} 38 \\ \times\ 69 \\ \hline \end{array}$$

Common Core Standard 4.NBT.5 – Number & Operations in Base Ten

☐ **Find the product using the blocks below. Be sure to show your work.**

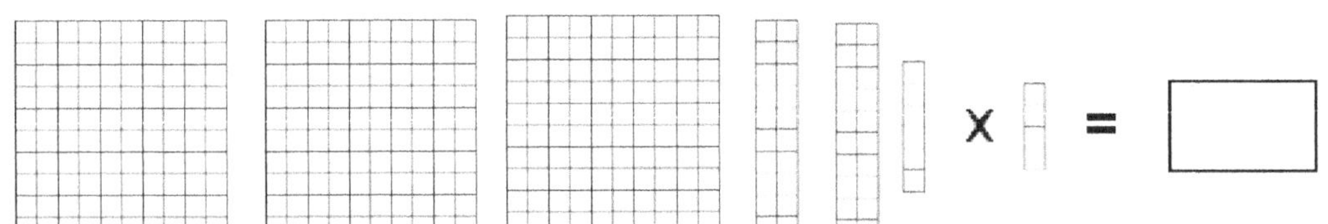

Common Core Standard 4.NBT.5 – Number & Operations in Base Ten

☐ **Solve the problem below. Be sure to show your work.**

$$\begin{array}{r} 95 \\ \times\ 63 \\ \hline \end{array}$$

Name ______________________

PRACTICE

Common Core Standard 4.NBT.5 – Number & Operations in Base Ten

☐ **Find the product using the blocks below. Be sure to show your work.**

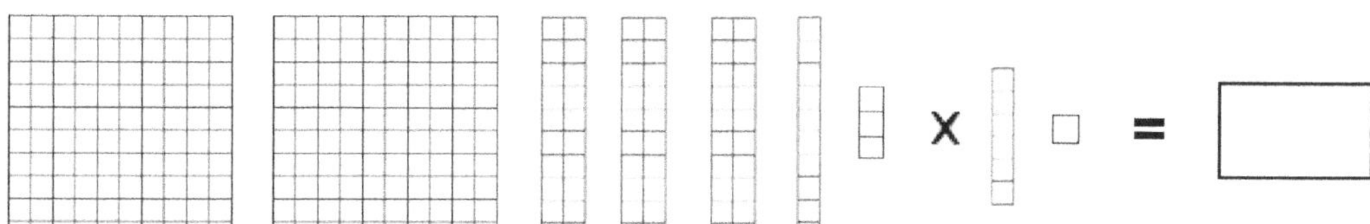

Common Core Standard 4.NBT.5 – Number & Operations in Base Ten

☐ **Solve the problem below. Be sure to show your work.**

$$\begin{array}{r} 192 \\ \underline{\times \ \ 7} \end{array}$$

Common Core Standard 4.NBT.5 – Number & Operations in Base Ten

☐ **Find the factor using the blocks below. Be sure to show your work.**

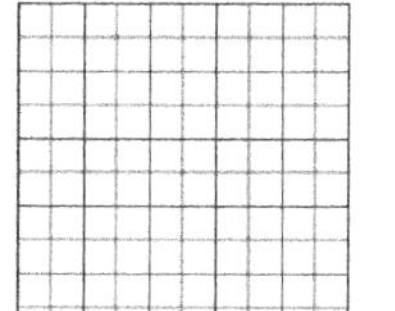 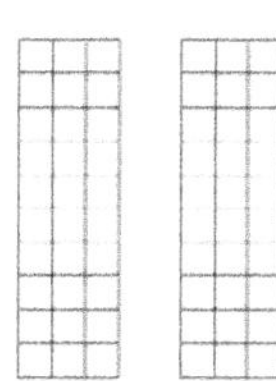 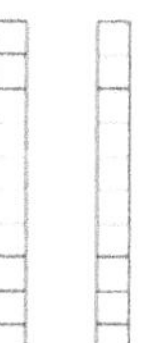 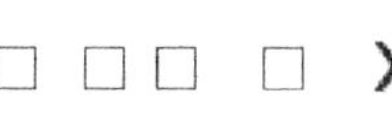  X ☐ = **1,044**

Name ___________________________

PRACTICE

Common Core Standard 4.NBT.5 – Number & Operations in Base Ten

☐ Solve the problem below. Be sure to show your work.

$$\begin{array}{r} 35 \\ \underline{\times\ 42} \end{array}$$

Common Core Standard 4.NBT.5 – Number & Operations in Base Ten

☐ Solve the problem below. Be sure to show your work.

$$\begin{array}{r} 5,279 \\ \underline{\times 8} \end{array}$$

Common Core Standard 4.NBT.5 – Number & Operations in Base Ten

☐ Solve the problem below. Be sure to show your work.

$$\begin{array}{r} \square \\ \underline{\times 62} \\ 2,356 \end{array}$$

Name ______________________

ASSESSMENT

Common Core Standard 4.NBT.5 – Number & Operations in Base Ten

☐ Solve the problem below. Be sure to show your work.

$$\begin{array}{r} 1{,}325 \\ \underline{\times\ 4} \end{array}$$

Common Core Standard 4.NBT.5 – Number & Operations in Base Ten

☐ Find the product using the blocks below. Be sure to show your work.

X = ☐

Common Core Standard 4.NBT.5 – Number & Operations in Base Ten

☐ Solve the problem below. Be sure to show your work.

$$\begin{array}{r} 77 \\ \underline{\times\ 77} \end{array}$$

Name ____________________________

ASSESSMENT

Common Core Standard 4.NBT.5 – Number & Operations in Base Ten

☐ **Find the factor using the blocks below. Be sure to show your work.**

☐ x 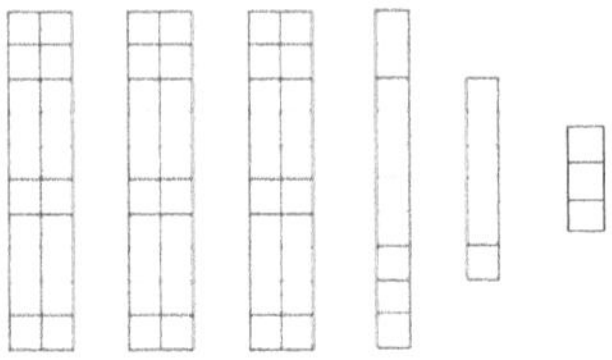 = **711**

Common Core Standard 4.NBT.5 – Number & Operations in Base Ten

☐ **Solve the problem below. Be sure to show your work.**

$$\begin{array}{r} 93 \\ \underline{\times\ 99} \end{array}$$

Common Core Standard 4.NBT.5 – Number & Operations in Base Ten

☐ **Solve the problem below. Be sure to show your work.**

$$\begin{array}{r} 4{,}347 \\ \underline{\times\ \square} \\ 26{,}082 \end{array}$$

Name ____________________

DIAGNOSTIC

Common Core Standard 4.NBT.6 – Number & Operations in Base Ten

☐ Complete the problem below. Be sure to show your work.

325 ÷ 5 = ☐

Common Core Standard 4.NBT.6 – Number & Operations in Base Ten

☐ Complete the problem below. Be sure to show your work.

$4\overline{)1{,}260}$

Common Core Standard 4.NBT.6 – Number & Operations in Base Ten

☐ Complete the problem below. Be sure to show your work.

742 divided by 7 equals ____.

Name ___________________________

DIAGNOSTIC

Common Core Standard 4.NBT.6 – Number & Operations in Base Ten

☐ Issac wants to place 280 mini erasers into 20 bags. How many mini erasers will he put in each bag? Be sure to show your work.

Common Core Standard 4.NBT.6 – Number & Operations in Base Ten

☐ Complete the problem below. Be sure to show your work.

9,650 ÷ 5 = ☐

Common Core Standard 4.NBT.6 – Number & Operations in Base Ten

☐ Jeremy's family drove from Los Angeles to New York City for their summer vacation trip. His family drove 2886 miles in 6 days. How many miles did they drive each day? Be sure to show your work.

Name ____________________

PRACTICE

Common Core Standard 4.NBT.6 – Number & Operations in Base Ten

☐ Complete the problem below. Be sure to show your work.

7,216 ÷ 4 = ☐

Common Core Standard 4.NBT.6 – Number & Operations in Base Ten

☐ Complete the problem below. Be sure to show your work.

1,274 / 7 = ☐

Common Core Standard 4.NBT.6 – Number & Operations in Base Ten

☐ Rahul made 56 liters of lemonade for his class. If he has 8 containers, how much lemonade can he put in each container equally? Be sure to show your work.

Name ____________________

PRACTICE

Common Core Standard 4.NBT.6 – Number & Operations in Base Ten

☐ **Complete the problem below. Be sure to show your work.**

$$4{,}290 \div 6 = \square$$

Common Core Standard 4.NBT.6 – Number & Operations in Base Ten

☐ **Complete the problem below. Be sure to show your work.**

$$8\overline{)8{,}448}$$

Common Core Standard 4.NBT.6 – Number & Operations in Base Ten

☐ **Complete the problem below. Be sure to show your work.**

$$3{,}429 \,/\, 9 = \square$$

Name ____________________

PRACTICE

Common Core Standard 4.NBT.6 – Number & Operations in Base Ten

☐ Safe Travel Airlines can carry 567 passengers from Erie to Philadelphia. There are 9 airplanes at Safe Travel Airlines. How many passengers can fit equally on each plane? Be sure to show your work.

Common Core Standard 4.NBT.6 – Number & Operations in Base Ten

☐ Complete the problem below. Be sure to show your work.

$$4{,}085 \div 5 = \square$$

Common Core Standard 4.NBT.6 – Number & Operations in Base Ten

☐ At Mabelvale Elementary there are 788 students and each student is given a school t-shirt. The shirts come in either blue, red, black, or white. The shirts were equally distributed to each students. How many blue shirts were given? Be sure to show your work.

Name ____________________

PRACTICE

Common Core Standard 4.NBT.6 – Number & Operations in Base Ten

☐ **Complete the problem below. Be sure to show your work.**

$$6{,}744 \div 8 = \square$$

Common Core Standard 4.NBT.6 – Number & Operations in Base Ten

☐ **Complete the problem below. Be sure to show your work.**

$$9\overline{)6{,}498}$$

Common Core Standard 4.NBT.6 – Number & Operations in Base Ten

☐ **Complete the problem below. Be sure to show your work.**

$$4{,}312 / 7 = \square$$

Name ____________________________

ASSESSMENT

Common Core Standard 4.NBT.6 – Number & Operations in Base Ten

☐ Bright Minds book store has 556 books in stock. Exactly half of them are soft cover books. How many soft cover books does Bright Minds book store have? Be sure to show your work.

Common Core Standard 4.NBT.6 – Number & Operations in Base Ten

☐ Complete the problem below. Be sure to show your work.

$$6{,}921 \div 3 = \square$$

Common Core Standard 4.NBT.6 – Number & Operations in Base Ten

☐ Clean Yards mowed and raked 315 yards last week. The company operates from Monday to Friday. How many yards did they mow and rake each day? Be sure to show your work.

Name ____________________________

ASSESSMENT

Common Core Standard 4.NBT.6 – Number & Operations in Base Ten

☐ Complete the problem below. Be sure to show your work.

$1{,}089 \div 9 = \square$

Common Core Standard 4.NBT.6 – Number & Operations in Base Ten

☐ Complete the problem below. Be sure to show your work.

$2{,}555 / 5 = \square$

Common Core Standard 4.NBT.6 – Number & Operations in Base Ten

☐ Complete the problem below. Be sure to show your work.

1,760 divided by 5 equals ____.

Name ______________________________

DIAGNOSTIC

Common Core Standard 4.NF.1 – Number & Operations - Fractions

☐ **Look at the shaded parts of the circles. Which statement shows these fraction models?**

A 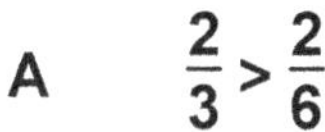 $\frac{2}{3} > \frac{2}{6}$

B  $\frac{1}{3} = \frac{2}{6}$

C 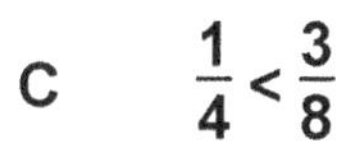 $\frac{1}{4} < \frac{3}{8}$

D  $\frac{1}{3} > \frac{4}{6}$

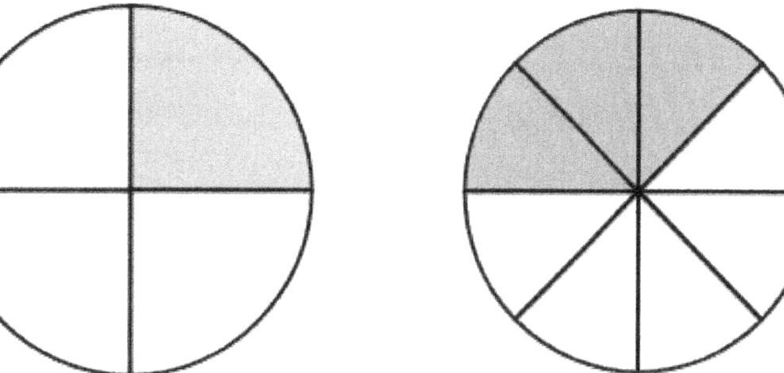

Common Core Standard 4.NF.1 – Number & Operations - Fractions

☐ **Which of the models is equivalent to $\frac{1}{2}$?**

A

C

B

D

Common Core Standard 4.NF.1 – Number & Operations - Fractions

☐ **Which model does *not* show an equivalent fraction for $\frac{1}{4}$?**

A

C 

B 

D 

Name ____________________

DIAGNOSTIC

Common Core Standard 4.NF.1 – Number & Operations - Fractions

☐ Look at the shadeded figure below. Which fraction is equivalent to $\frac{2}{8}$?

A $\frac{1}{4}$

B $\frac{2}{4}$

C $\frac{4}{8}$

D $\frac{12}{16}$

Common Core Standard 4.NF.1 – Number & Operations - Fractions

☐ Which of the models is equivalent to $\frac{2}{3}$?

A 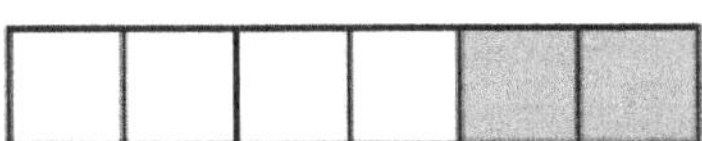

C 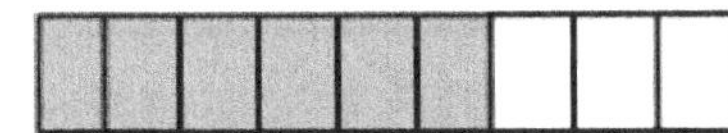

B

D

Common Core Standard 4.NF.1 – Number & Operations - Fractions

☐ Which model does *not* show an equivalent fraction for $\frac{2}{3}$?

A 

C 

B 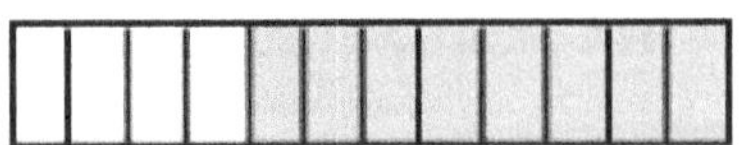

D 

Name ____________________________

PRACTICE

Common Core Standard 4.NF.1 – Number & Operations - Fractions

☐ The figures are shaded to show equivalent fractions. Which fraction is equivalent to $\frac{3}{5}$?

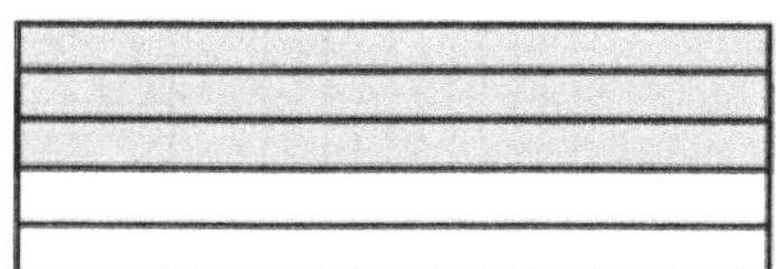

A $\frac{4}{6}$

B $\frac{4}{10}$

C $\frac{6}{4}$

D $\frac{6}{10}$

Common Core Standard 4.NF.1 – Number & Operations - Fractions

☐ Which of the models is equivalent to $\frac{3}{5}$?

A

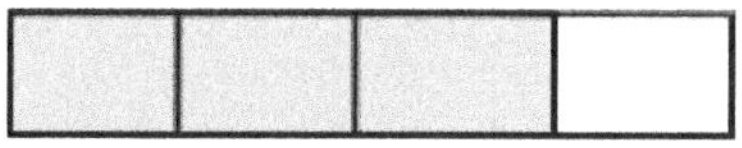

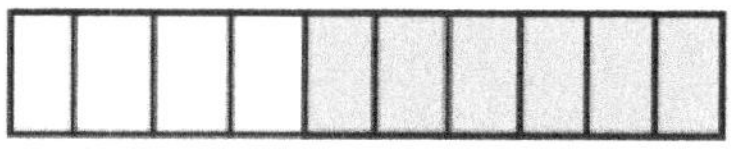

B

C

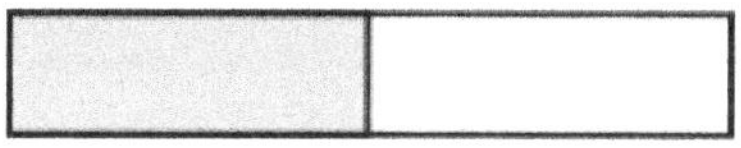

D

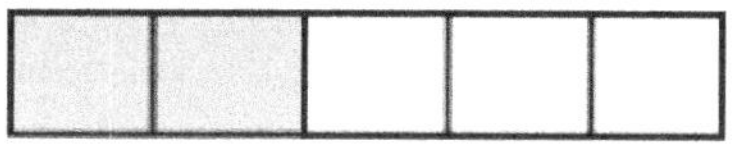

Common Core Standard 4.NF.1 – Number & Operations - Fractions

☐ Which model does *not* show an equivalent fraction for $\frac{1}{6}$?

A

B

C

D

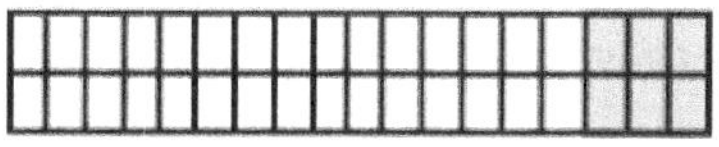

Name ____________________

PRACTICE

Common Core Standard 4.NF.1 – Number & Operations - Fractions

☐ Look at the shaded parts of the models. Which models show $\frac{2}{10} = \frac{1}{5}$?

A 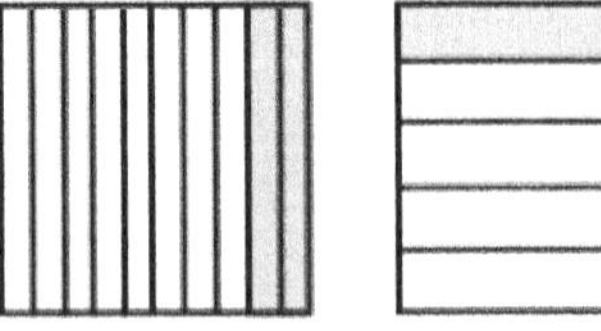

C 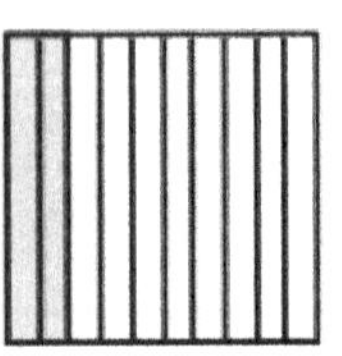 

B 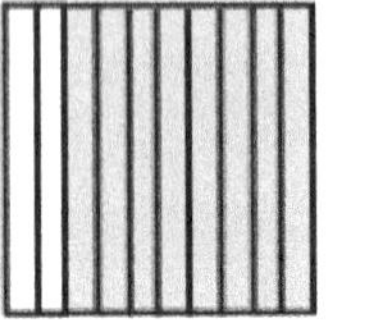

D 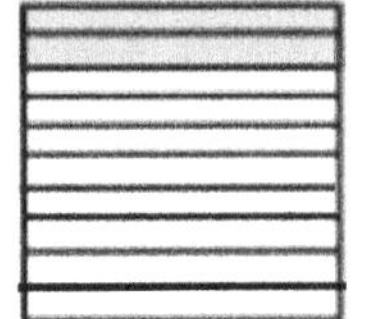 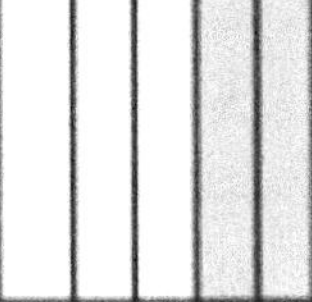

Common Core Standard 4.NF.1 – Number & Operations – Fractions

☐ The figures are shaded to show equivalent fractions. Which fraction is equivalent to $\frac{6}{7}$?

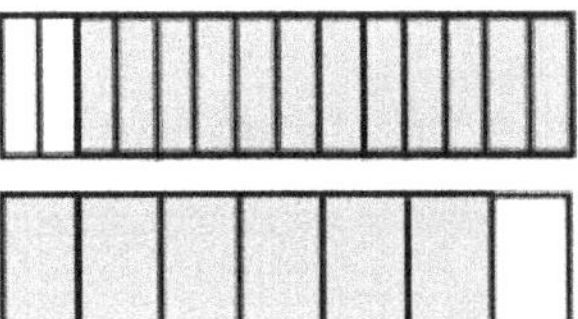

A $\frac{6}{14}$

B $\frac{12}{14}$

C $\frac{6}{12}$

D $\frac{1}{7}$

Common Core Standard 4.NF.1 – Number & Operations – Fractions

☐ Which model does *not* show an equivalent fraction for $\frac{3}{4}$?

A 

C 

B 

D 

Name ______________________

PRACTICE

Common Core Standard 4.NF.1 – Number & Operations - Fractions

☐ **The figures are shaded to show equivalent fractions. Which fraction is equivalent to $\frac{2}{5}$?**

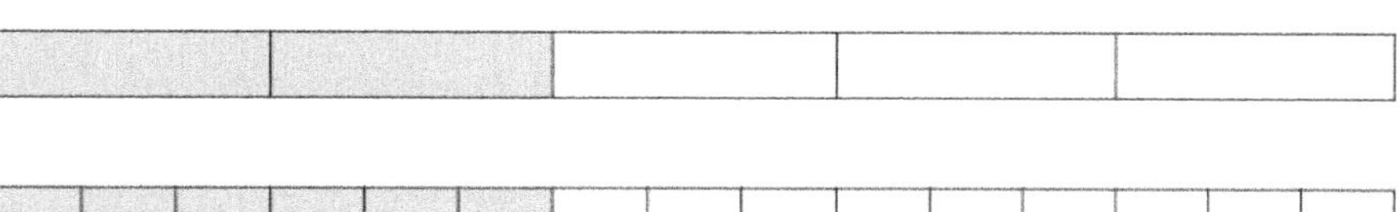

A $\frac{4}{6}$

B $\frac{15}{6}$

C $\frac{6}{15}$

D $\frac{6}{10}$

Common Core Standard 4.NF.1 – Number & Operations - Fractions

☐ **Which of the models is equivalent to $\frac{3}{9}$?**

A

B

C

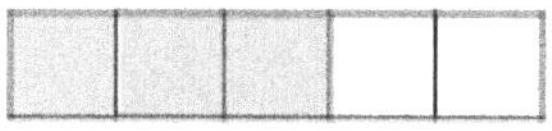

D

Common Core Standard 4.NF.1 – Number & Operations - Fractions

☐ **Which model does *not* show an equivalent fraction for $\frac{12}{16}$?**

A

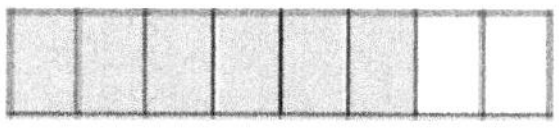

B

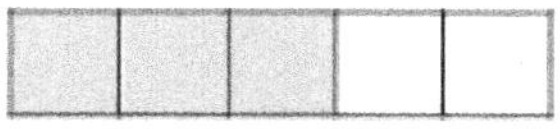

C

D

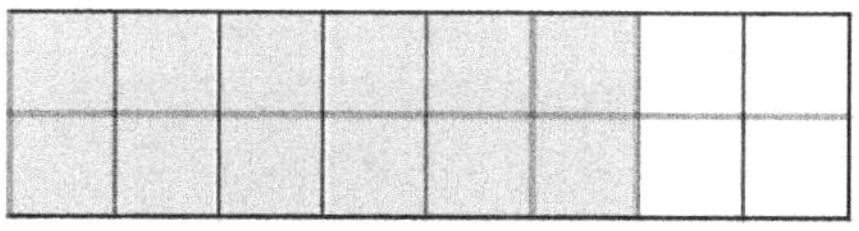

Name ___________________________

PRACTICE

Common Core Standard 4.NF.1 – Number & Operations - Fractions

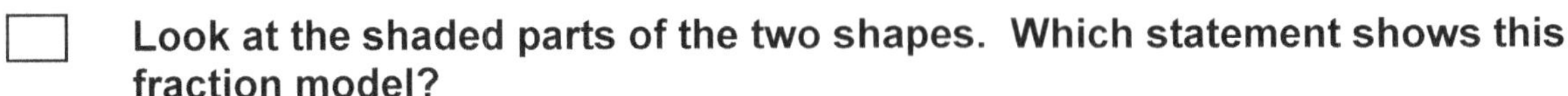

☐ **Look at the shaded parts of the two shapes. Which statement shows this fraction model?**

A $\frac{1}{3} > \frac{3}{9}$

B $\frac{1}{3} < \frac{3}{9}$

C $\frac{1}{3} = \frac{3}{9}$

D $\frac{1}{3} > \frac{4}{12}$

Common Core Standard 4.NF.1 – Number & Operations - Fractions

☐ **Which of the models is equivalent to $\frac{1}{4}$?**

A 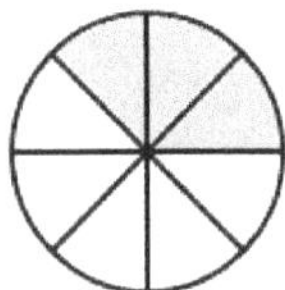

C 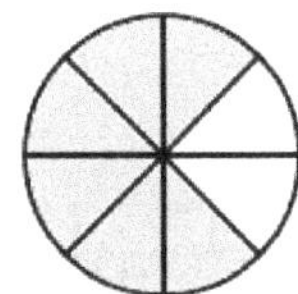

B 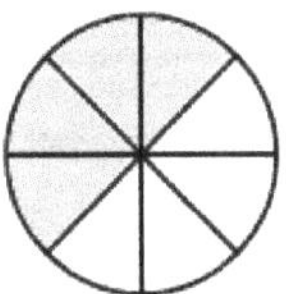

D 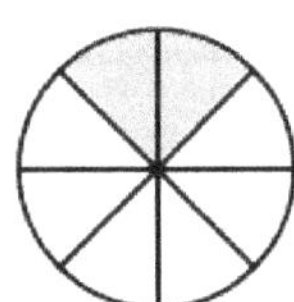

Common Core Standard 4.NF.1 – Number & Operations - Fractions

☐ **Which model shows an equivalent fraction for $\frac{1}{8}$?**

A 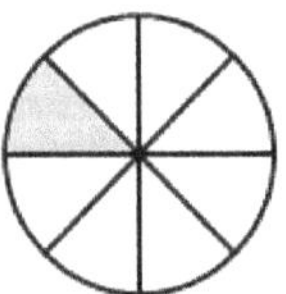

C 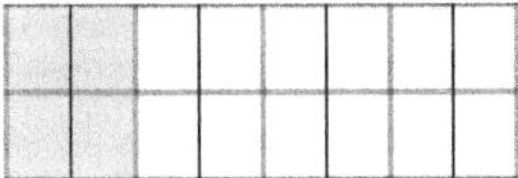

B 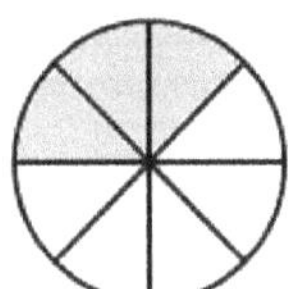

D 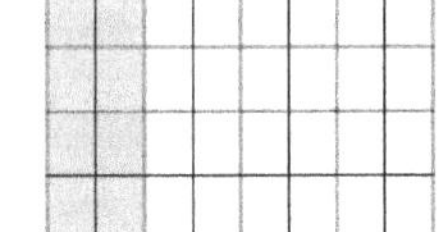

Name ____________________

ASSESSEMENT

Common Core Standard 4.NF.1 – Number & Operations - Fractions

☐ **Look at the shaded parts of the objects below. Which statement shows this fraction model?**

A 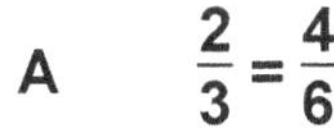 $\frac{2}{3} = \frac{4}{6}$

B $\frac{2}{3} < \frac{4}{6}$

C $\frac{1}{4} < \frac{2}{8}$

D $\frac{2}{3} > \frac{4}{6}$

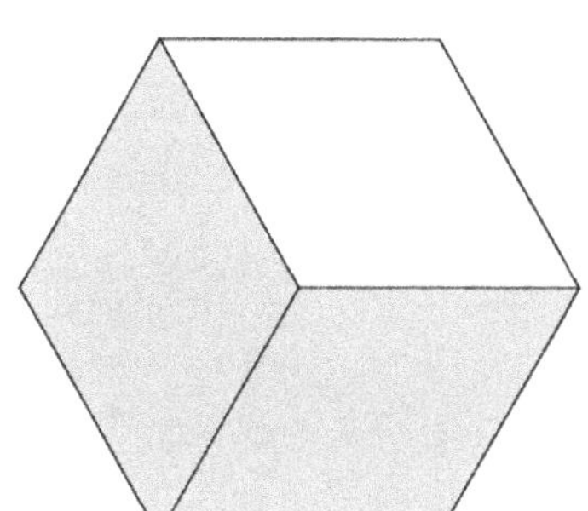

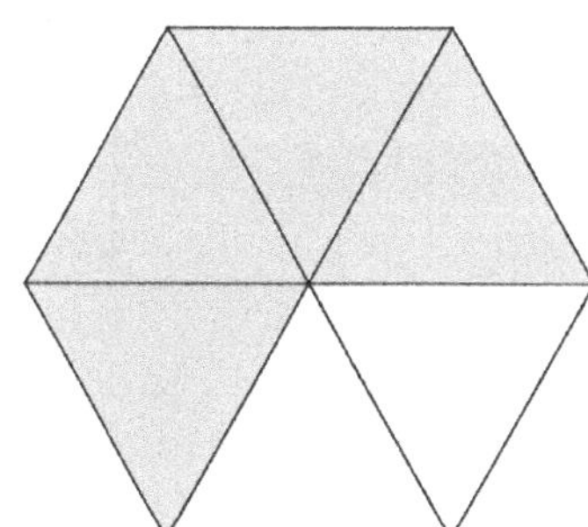

Common Core Standard 4.NF.1 – Number & Operations - Fractions

☐ **Which of the models is equivalent to $\frac{9}{12}$?**

A

C

B

D

Common Core Standard 4.NF.1 – Number & Operations - Fractions

☐ **Which model does *not* show an equivalent fraction for $\frac{4}{16}$?**

A 

C 

B 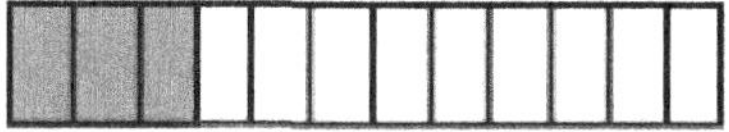

D

Name ________________________

ASSESSMENT

Common Core Standard 4.NF.1 – Number & Operations - Fractions

☐ The figures are shaded to show equivalent fractions. Which fraction is equivalent to $\frac{2}{18}$?

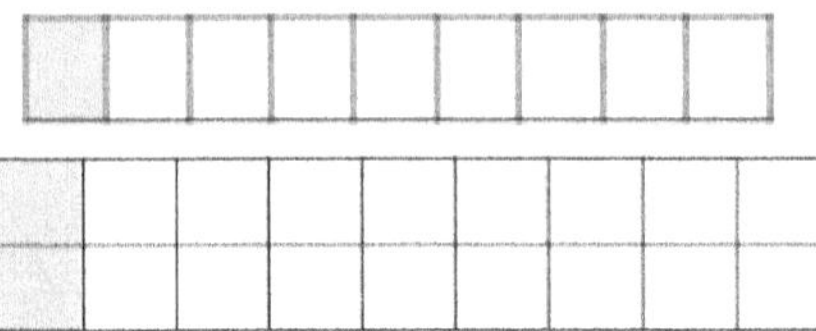

A $\frac{1}{6}$

B $\frac{1}{9}$

C $\frac{1}{7}$

D $\frac{14}{16}$

Common Core Standard 4.NF.1 – Number & Operations - Fractions

☐ Which of the models is equivalent to $\frac{2}{3}$?

A

B

C

D

Common Core Standard 4.NF.1 – Number & Operations - Fractions

☐ Which model shows an equivalent fraction for $\frac{15}{21}$?

A

B

C

D

Name ____________________

DIAGNOSTIC

Common Core Standard 4.NF.2 – Number & Operations - Fractions

☐ **Look at the shaded parts of the models. Which models show $\frac{1}{4} < \frac{3}{9}$?**

A 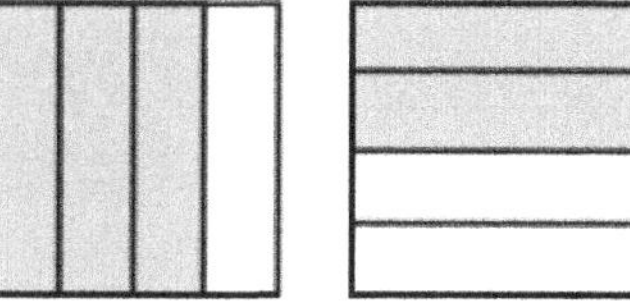

C 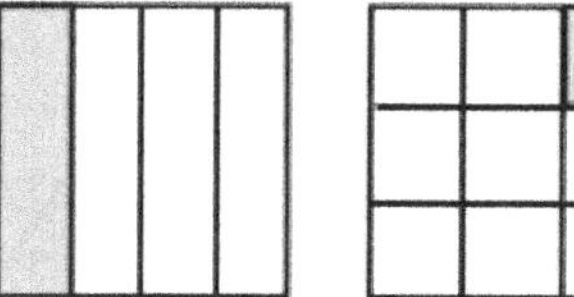

B 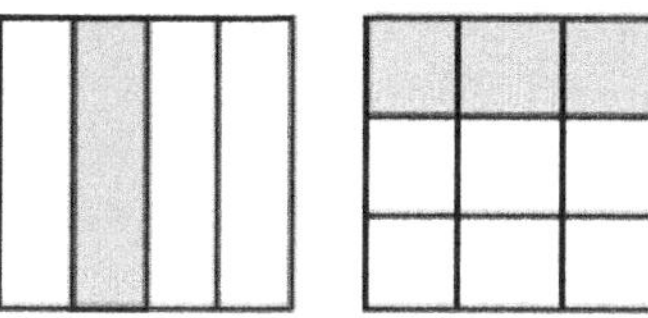

D 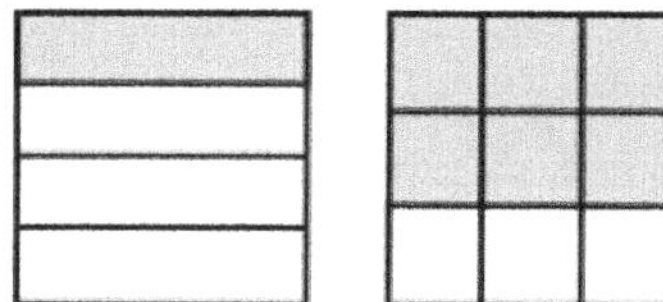

Common Core Standard 4.NF.2 – Number & Operations – Fractions

☐ **Which statement is true?**

A 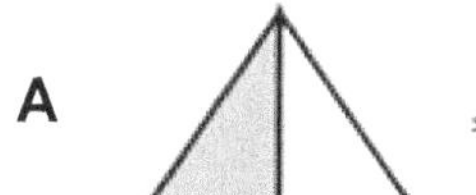 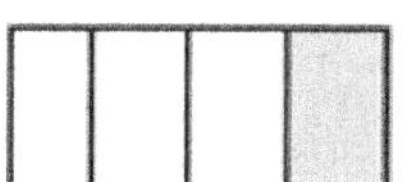

C  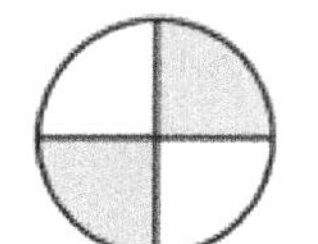 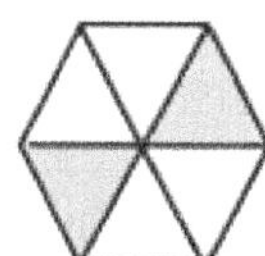

B 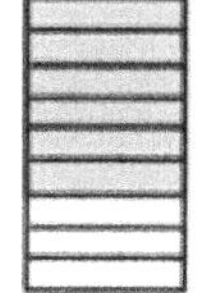 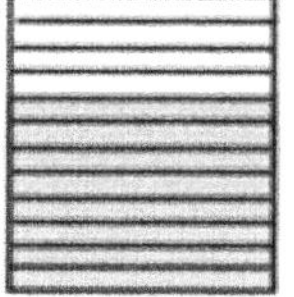

D 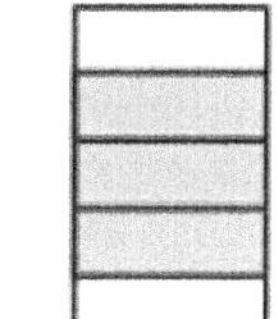 

Common Core Standard 4.NF.2 – Number & Operations – Fractions

☐ **Look at the shaded parts of the figures. Which statement shows the fraction model?**

A $\frac{9}{12} = \frac{1}{9}$

B $\frac{9}{18} > \frac{1}{2}$

C $\frac{9}{18} = \frac{1}{2}$

D $\frac{9}{18} < \frac{1}{4}$

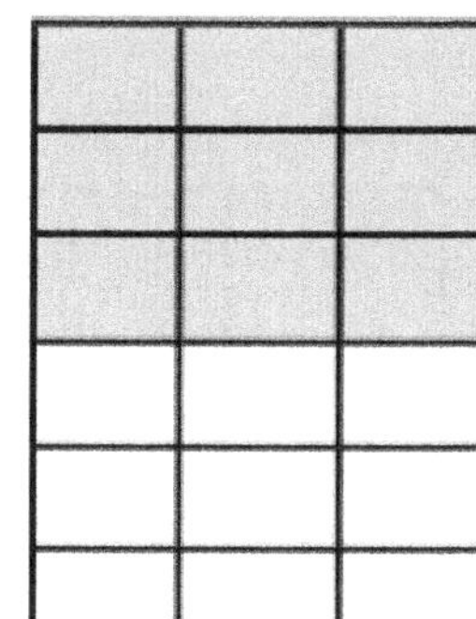

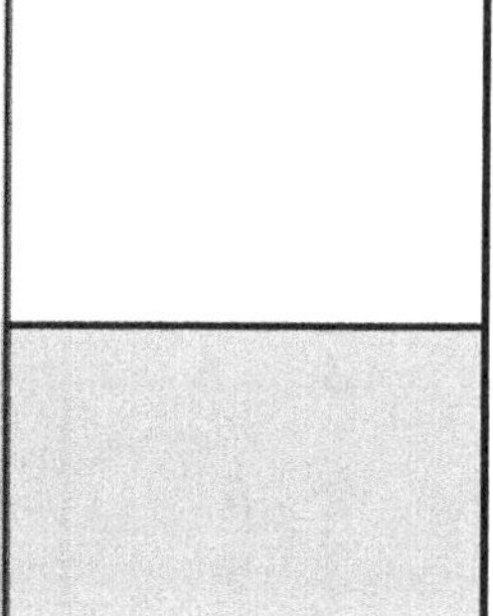

Name ____________________________

DIAGNOSTIC

Common Core Standard 4.NF.2 – Number & Operations - Fractions

☐ If ⬭ = $\frac{1}{4}$, △ = $\frac{1}{2}$, □ = $\frac{1}{8}$, and ☆ = $\frac{1}{3}$, which of the following would be in the correct order from *greatest* to *least*?

A ☆ ⬭ □ △

B ⬭ △ □ ☆

C △ ☆ ⬭ □

D △ ⬭ ☆ □

Common Core Standard 4.NF.2 – Number & Operations – Fractions

☐ **Which statement is true?**

A 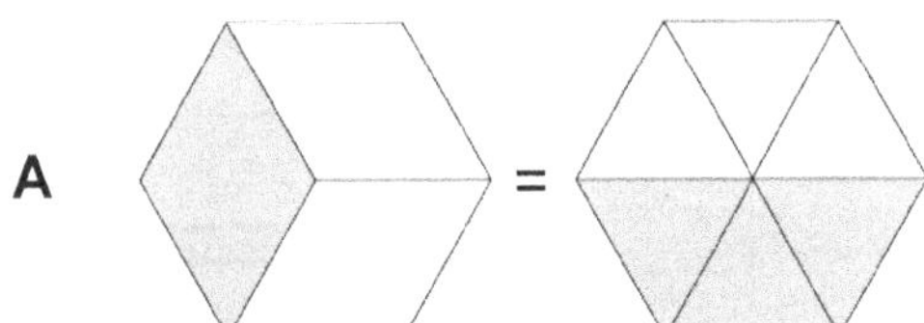

C 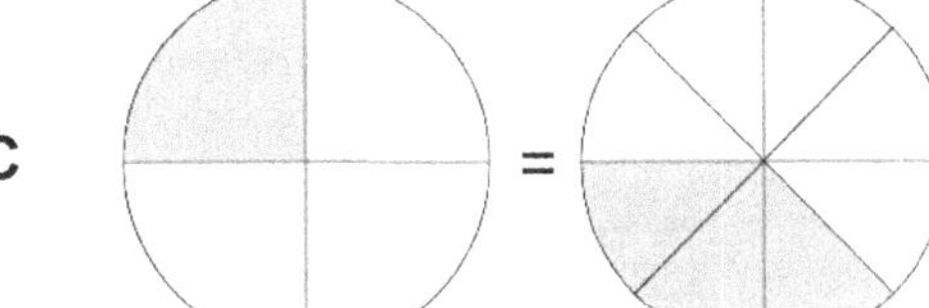

B

D

Common Core Standard 4.NF.2 – Number & Operations – Fractions

☐ **The models are shaded to show that:**

A $\frac{2}{3} < \frac{1}{6}$

B $\frac{1}{3} = \frac{1}{6}$

C $\frac{2}{3} < \frac{5}{6}$

D $\frac{2}{3} > \frac{5}{6}$

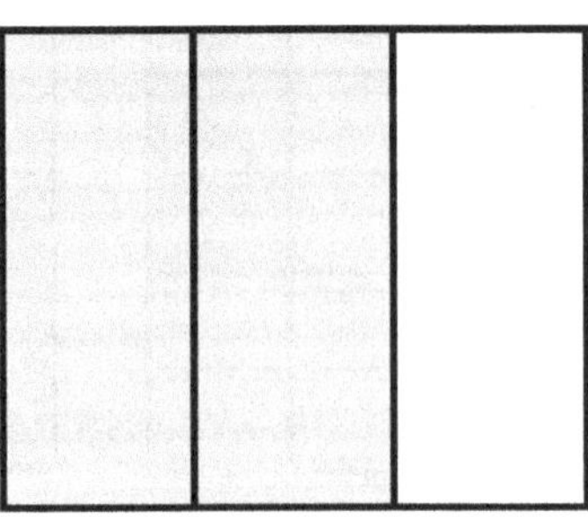

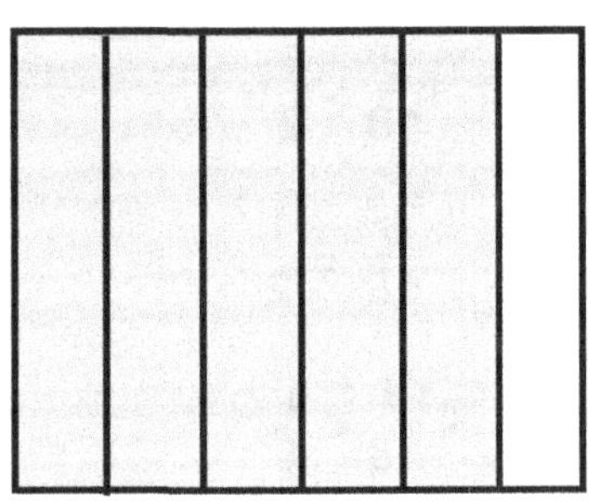

Name ______________________

PRACTICE

Common Core Standard 4.NF.2 – Number & Operations – Fractions

☐ **Which statement is true?**

A  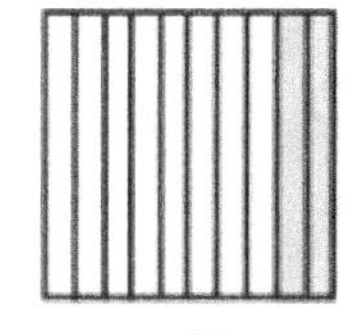 = 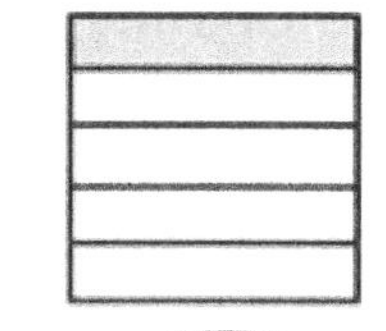

C  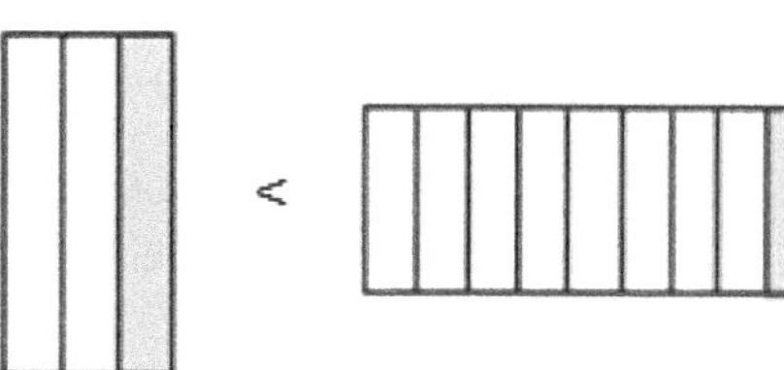

B 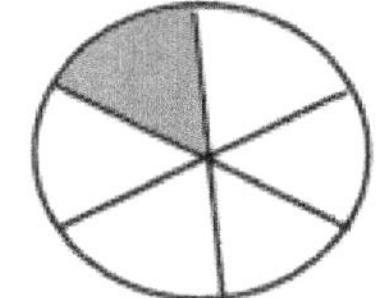 = 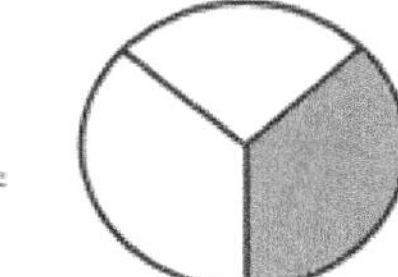

D  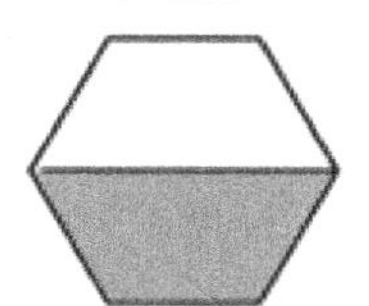 > 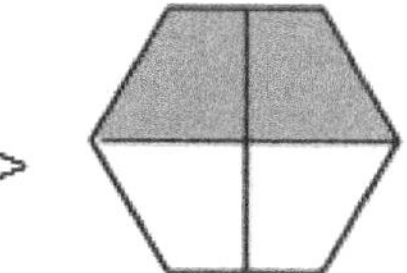

Common Core Standard 4.NF.2 – Number & Operations – Fractions

☐ Molly's grandmother makes delicious cornbread. Her recipe uses $\frac{3}{4}$ cup of cornmeal, $\frac{1}{2}$ cup of flour, and $\frac{2}{3}$ cup of milk. Which list of fractions shows the ingredients Molly's grandmother uses in order from least to greatest?

A $\frac{1}{2}, \frac{2}{3}, \frac{3}{4}$

B $\frac{3}{4}, \frac{1}{2}, \frac{2}{3}$

C $\frac{2}{3}, \frac{3}{4}, \frac{1}{2}$

D $\frac{3}{4}, \frac{2}{3}, \frac{1}{2}$

Common Core Standard 4.NF.2 – Number & Operations – Fractions

☐ Madison and Trent are having a discussion about fractions. Trent believes $\frac{2}{10}$ is less than $\frac{1}{3}$. Which models can he use to prove his belief is true?

A 1 and 4

B 1 and 3

C 3 and 4

D 2 and 4

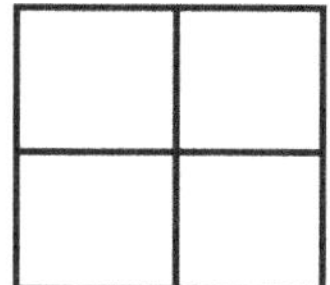

Name ____________________

PRACTICE

Common Core Standard 4.NF.2 – Number & Operations – Fractions

☐ Mariah, Jamie, and Destiny each bought a candy bar. Mariah ate $\frac{1}{2}$ of her candy bar. Jamie ate $\frac{1}{3}$ of hers, and Destiny ate $\frac{5}{8}$ of her candy bar. Which grouping below shows who has eaten the candy bars in order from the greatest to the least?

A Destiny, Jamie, Mariah

B Destiny, Mariah, Jamie

C Mariah, Destiny, Jamie

D Jamie, Mariah, Destiny

Common Core Standard 4.NF.2 – Number & Operations – Fractions

☐ A city's basketball teams have both boys and girls on each team. The Dribblers are made up of $\frac{6}{10}$ girls, and the Racers are made up of $\frac{5}{12}$ girls. Which statement is a correct comparison of the number of girls on each team?

A $\frac{6}{10} > \frac{5}{12}$

B $\frac{6}{10} < \frac{5}{12}$

C $\frac{5}{12} = \frac{6}{10}$

D $\frac{6}{12} = \frac{5}{10}$

Dribblers

Racers

Common Core Standard 4.NF.2 – Number & Operations – Fractions

☐ An art teacher is checking the supply of tempera paint. She has $\frac{3}{4}$ of a gallon of orange paint, $\frac{1}{2}$ of a gallon of yellow paint, and $\frac{1}{8}$ of a gallon of white paint. If she places the containers in order from the least amount of paint to the greatest amount of paint, which of the following would be correct?

A Orange, yellow, white

B Yellow, white, orange

C White, orange, yellow

D White, yellow, orange

Name ___________________________

PRACTICE

Common Core Standard 4.NF.2 – Number & Operations – Fractions

☐ **Look at the figures. Which grouping shows the shaded portions of the figures in order from least to greatest?**

A $\frac{5}{8}, \frac{3}{8}, \frac{3}{4}$

B $\frac{3}{8}, \frac{5}{8}, \frac{3}{4}$

C $\frac{3}{4}, \frac{3}{8}, \frac{5}{8}$

D $\frac{3}{8}, \frac{3}{4}, \frac{5}{8}$

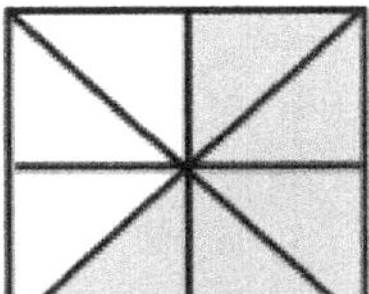
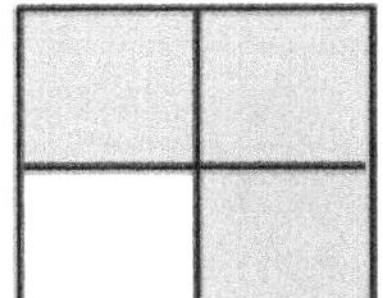
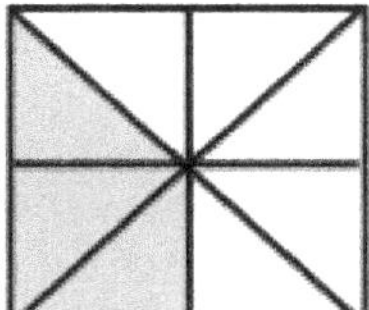

Common Core Standard 4.NF.2 – Number & Operations – Fractions

☐ **Mr. Johnson's students are studying fractions in their math class. Which models can the class use to show that $\frac{2}{6}$ is less than $\frac{2}{3}$?**

A 2 and 4

B 2 and 3

C 1 and 4

D 1 and 3

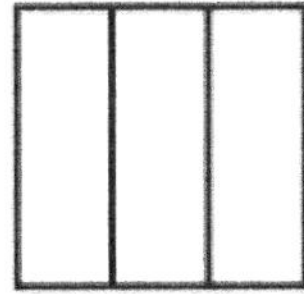
1

2
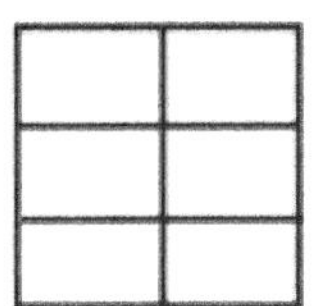
3
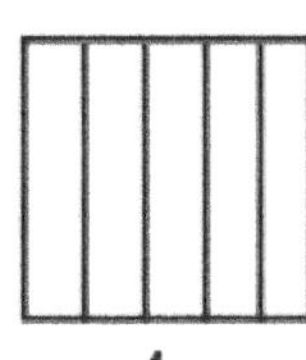
4

Common Core Standard 4.NF.2 – Number & Operations – Fractions

☐ **A band is selling fruit for the holidays. They have sold $\frac{3}{4}$ of the boxes of apples, $\frac{1}{2}$ of the boxes of oranges, and $\frac{7}{8}$ of the boxes of grapefruit. If the boxes of fruit are lined up in order from the least amount of fruit sold to the greatest amount of fruit sold, which order would be correct?**

A Apples, oranges, grapefruit

B Oranges, apples, grapefruit

C Oranges, grapefruit, apples

D Grapefruit, apples, oranges

Name ___________________________

PRACTICE

Common Core Standard 4.NF.2 – Number & Operations – Fractions

☐ **Mrs. Blocker's class bought 3 pizzas. Jasmine's group ate $\frac{3}{4}$ of their pizza. Blake's group ate $\frac{7}{8}$ of their pizza, and Yolanda's group ate $\frac{1}{8}$ of their pizza. Which answer below shows the order from greatest to the least amount of pizza eaten by each group?**

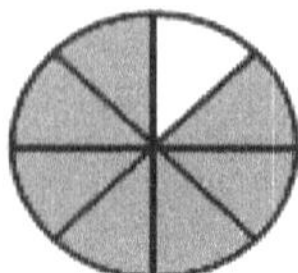 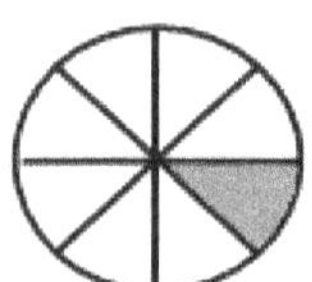 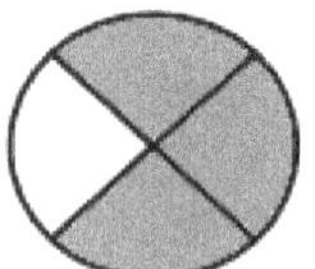

A Yolanda, Jasmine, Blake

B Blake, Yolanda, Jasmine

C Blake, Jasmine, Yolanda

D Jasmine, Yolanda, Blake

Common Core Standard 4.NF.2 – Number & Operations – Fractions

☐ **The 2 shapes are shaded to show that:**

A $\frac{7}{8} > \frac{3}{4}$

B $\frac{1}{4} < \frac{1}{8}$

C $\frac{3}{4} = \frac{7}{8}$

D $\frac{1}{8} > \frac{1}{4}$

$\frac{1}{8}$	$\frac{1}{8}$	$\frac{1}{8}$	$\frac{1}{8}$	$\frac{1}{8}$	$\frac{1}{8}$	$\frac{1}{8}$	$\frac{1}{8}$

$\frac{1}{4}$	$\frac{1}{4}$	$\frac{1}{4}$	$\frac{1}{4}$

Common Core Standard 4.NF.2 – Number & Operations – Fractions

☐ **Which statement can be used to show a comparison of $\frac{6}{8}$ and $\frac{5}{15}$?**

A $\frac{5}{15}$ is greater than $\frac{6}{8}$

B $\frac{6}{8}$ is less than $\frac{5}{15}$

C $\frac{5}{15}$ is equal to $\frac{6}{8}$

D $\frac{6}{8}$ is greater than $\frac{5}{15}$

Name ____________________

ASSESSMENT

Common Core Standard 4.NF.2 – Number & Operations – Fractions

☐ Which of the following best represents $\frac{15}{40} > \frac{4}{16}$?

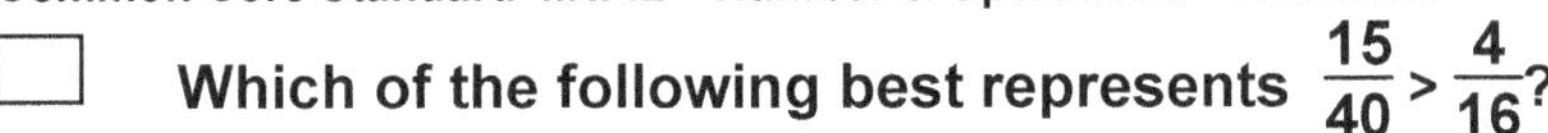

A 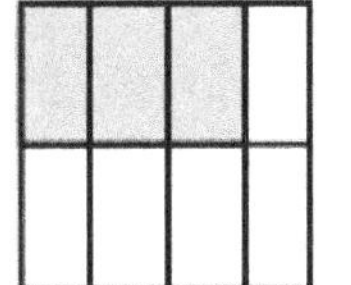 > 

C 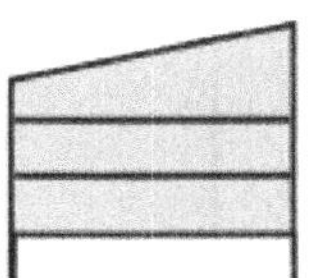 >

B 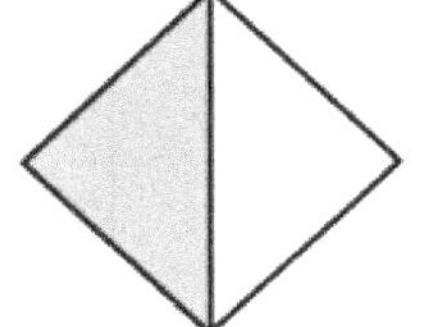 >

D  > 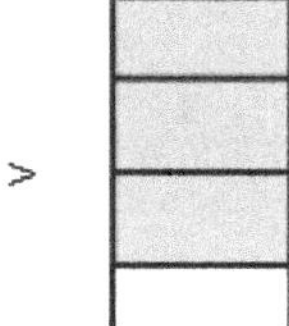

Common Core Standard 4.NF.2 – Number & Operations – Fractions

☐ The models are shaded to show that:

A $\frac{1}{2} < \frac{1}{5}$

B $\frac{1}{2} < \frac{3}{5}$

C $\frac{1}{2} = \frac{3}{5}$

D $\frac{2}{5} > \frac{1}{2}$

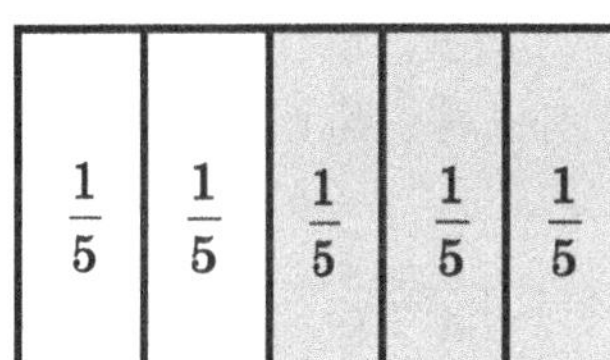

Common Core Standard 4.NF.2 – Number & Operations – Fractions

☐ Which statement can be used to show a comparison of $\frac{3}{12}$ and $\frac{2}{8}$?

A $\frac{3}{12}$ is greater than $\frac{2}{8}$

B $\frac{2}{8}$ is less than $\frac{3}{12}$

C $\frac{2}{8}$ is equal to $\frac{3}{12}$

D $\frac{3}{12}$ is less than $\frac{2}{8}$

Name ____________________

ASSESSMENT

Common Core Standard 4.NF.2 – Number & Operations – Fractions

☐ **Which statement is true?**

A 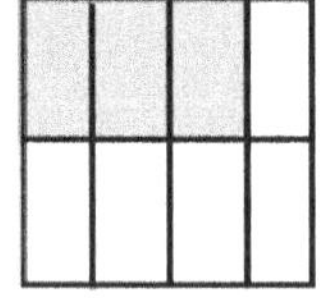 < 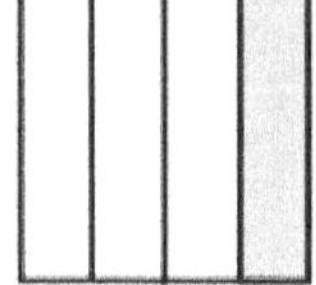

C 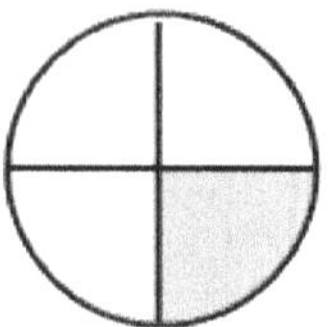 =

B 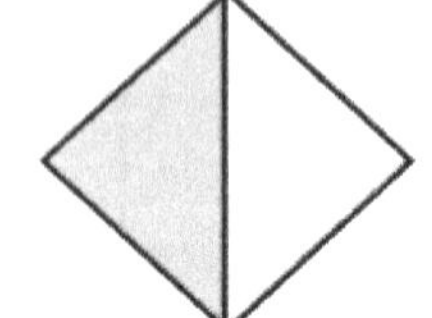 =

D 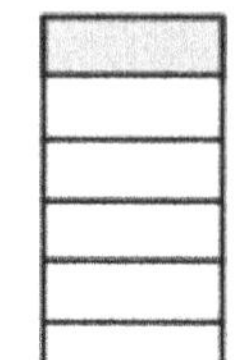 > 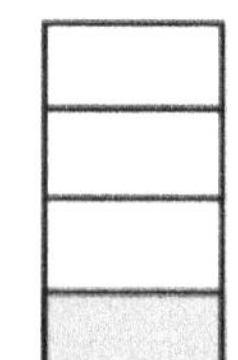

Common Core Standard 4.NF.2 – Number & Operations – Fractions

☐ **Look at the shaded parts of the circles. Which statement shows the fraction model?**

A $\frac{1}{3} = \frac{5}{8}$

B $\frac{3}{4} > \frac{5}{8}$

C $\frac{3}{4} = \frac{3}{8}$

D $\frac{1}{4} > \frac{5}{8}$

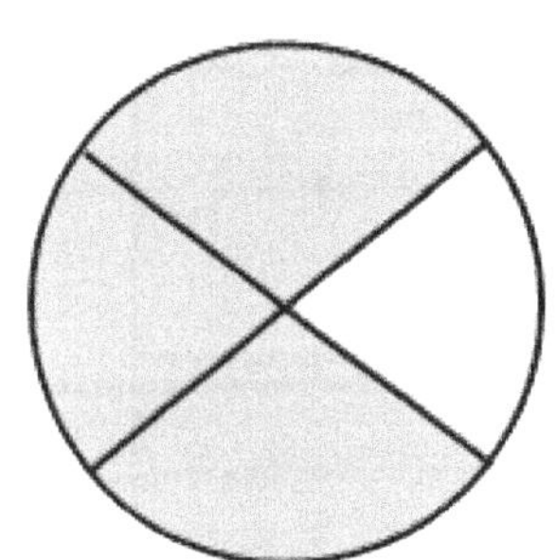 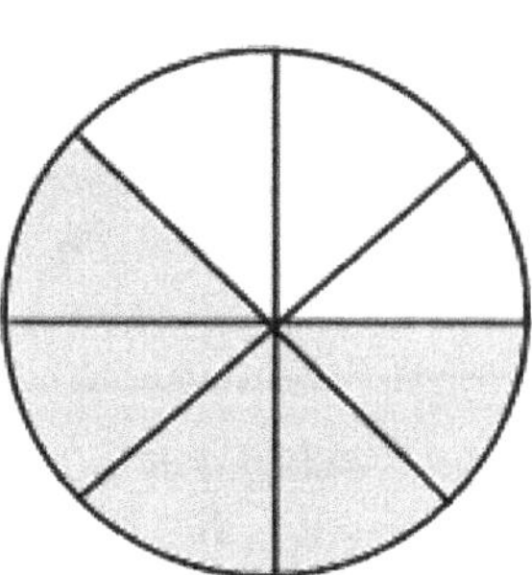

Common Core Standard 4.NF.2 – Number & Operations – Fractions

☐ **Look at the shaded parts of the figures. Which figures show $\frac{3}{8} > \frac{1}{4}$?**

A 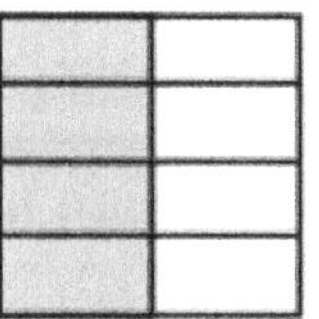

C 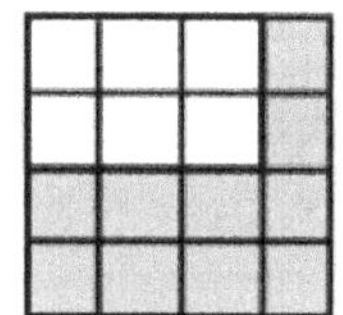 

B 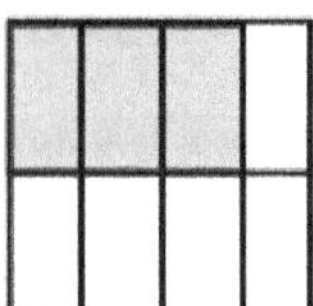

D 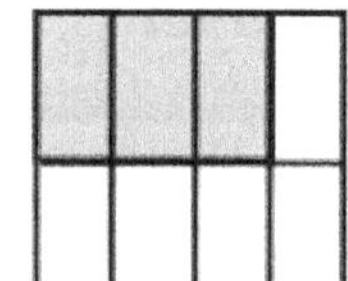 

Name ___________________________

DIAGNOSTIC

Common Core Standard 4.NF.3 – Number & Operations – Fractions

☐ **Theodore Roosevelt Elementary 3rd and 4th grade students are creating a chalk picture in front of the school. The third grade students colored ¼ of the picture and the fourth grade students colored ¼ of the picture. How much did the third and fourth grade student color on the picture all together? Be sure to show your work.**

A $\frac{1}{4}$

B $\frac{1}{2}$

C $\frac{3}{4}$

D $\frac{2}{8}$

Common Core Standard 4.NF.3 – Number & Operations – Fractions

☐ **Subtract the fractions and simplify your answers. Be sure to show your work.**

$$\frac{8}{16} - \frac{6}{16} = \square$$

A $\frac{1}{16}$

B $\frac{1}{8}$

C $\frac{7}{8}$

D $\frac{1}{4}$

Common Core Standard 4.NF.3 – Number & Operations – Fractions

☐ **Add the fractions and simplify your answers. Be sure to show your work.**

$$\frac{9}{27} + \frac{6}{27} = \square$$

A $\frac{5}{9}$

B $\frac{1}{9}$

C $\frac{1}{3}$

D $\frac{2}{3}$

Name ________________________

DIAGNOSTIC

Common Core Standard 4.NF.3 – Number & Operations – Fractions

☐ Coach Miller's class wanted to play dodge ball. If the gym bag had 1/3 of the total number of balls remaining in it, what is the fraction of bills the class was using to play dodge ball? Be sure to show your work.

A $\frac{1}{3}$

B $\frac{1}{2}$

C $\frac{2}{3}$

D $\frac{3}{8}$

Common Core Standard 4.NF.3 – Number & Operations – Fractions

☐ Add the fractions and simplify your answer. Be sure to show your work.

$$\frac{10}{15} + \frac{7}{15} = \square$$

A $\frac{7}{15}$

B $\frac{1}{10}$

C $\frac{1}{5}$

D $\frac{17}{15}$

Common Core Standard 4.NF.3 – Number & Operations – Fractions

☐ Subtract the fractions and simplify your answer. Be sure to show your work.

$$\frac{19}{29} - \frac{11}{29} = \square$$

A $\frac{8}{29}$

B $\frac{29}{29}$

C $\frac{30}{29}$

D $\frac{7}{29}$

Name ____________________________

PRACTICE

Common Core Standard 4.NF.3 – Number & Operations – Fractions

☐ Jarrell and his brother Makal are working on a jigsaw together. Jarrell has finished one quarter of the jigsaw, and Makal has finished two quarters of the jigsaw. How much of the jigsaw have they finished all together? Be sure to show your work.

A $\frac{1}{4}$

C $\frac{1}{2}$

B $\frac{3}{4}$

D $\frac{2}{3}$

Common Core Standard 4.NF.3 – Number & Operations – Fractions

☐ Add the fractions and simplify your answer. Be sure to show your work.

$$\frac{14}{57} + \frac{27}{57} = \square$$

A $\frac{14}{57}$

C $\frac{42}{57}$

B $\frac{9}{19}$

D $\frac{41}{57}$

Common Core Standard 4.NF.3 – Number & Operations – Fractions

☐ Gary and Beth's mother baked a cake. Gary ate one third of the cake and Beth ate one third of the cake. How much did Gary and Beth eat all together? Be sure to show your work.

A $\frac{2}{3}$

C $\frac{1}{3}$

B $\frac{1}{2}$

D $\frac{1}{9}$

Name ______________________

PRACTICE

Common Core Standard 4.NF.3 – Number & Operations – Fractions

☐ Macy and her friend ran around the track together. Macy ran 6/10's of the track. Her friend ran 9/10's of the track. How much further did Macy's friend run than Macy? Be sure to show your work.

A $\frac{1}{4}$ C $\frac{3}{10}$

B $\frac{3}{2}$ D $\frac{3}{4}$

Common Core Standard 4.NF.3 – Number & Operations – Fractions

☐ Subtract the fractions and simplify your answer. Be sure to show your work.

$$\frac{7}{34} - \frac{3}{34} = \square$$

A $\frac{5}{32}$ C $\frac{5}{17}$

B $\frac{10}{17}$ D $\frac{2}{17}$

Common Core Standard 4.NF.3 – Number & Operations – Fractions

☐ Happy Burger restaurant had $\frac{5}{9}$ ground beef yesterday, but today there is only $\frac{2}{9}$ ground beef left. How much ground beef was used today to make hamburgers? Be sure to show your work.

A $\frac{3}{9}$ C $\frac{7}{18}$

B $\frac{7}{9}$ D $\frac{1}{9}$

Name ______________________________

PRACTICE

Common Core Standard 4.NF.3 – Number & Operations – Fractions

☐ In the morning Carkye and her sister Candice eat breakfast burritos. Carkye ate $3\frac{4}{7}$ breakfast burritos. Her sister Candice ate $2\frac{3}{7}$ breakfast burritos. How many more breakfast burritos did Carkye eat than her sister Candice? Be sure to show your work.

A $1\frac{1}{7}$

B $\frac{17}{7}$

C 1

D $\frac{24}{7}$

Common Core Standard 4.NF.3 – Number & Operations – Fractions

☐ Subtract the fractions and simplify your answer. Be sure to show your work.

$$\frac{24}{54} - \frac{15}{54} = \square$$

A $\frac{1}{9}$

B $\frac{1}{6}$

C $\frac{39}{108}$

D $\frac{39}{54}$

Common Core Standard 4.NF.3 – Number & Operations – Fractions

☐ Henrietta made mashed potatoes for her family. Her brothers ate 4/7 the mashed potatoes and her sisters ate 3/7 of the mashed potatoes. How much more mashed potatoes did her brothers eat than her sisters? Be sure to show your work.

A $\frac{1}{7}$

B $\frac{1}{2}$

C 1

D $\frac{2}{7}$

Name ____________________________

PRACTICE

Common Core Standard 4.NF.3 – Number & Operations – Fractions

☐ At Early Bird coffee shop, 3/8 of the customer's order only tea and 4/8 of the customer's order only coffee. What fraction of the customer's order was only tea and coffee? Be sure to show your work.

A $\frac{1}{8}$

C $\frac{7}{16}$

B $\frac{1}{2}$

D $\frac{7}{8}$

Common Core Standard 4.NF.3 – Number & Operations – Fractions

☐ Add the fractions and simplify your answer. Be sure to show your work.

$$\frac{17}{61} + \frac{33}{61} = \square$$

A $\frac{50}{61}$

C $\frac{25}{61}$

B $\frac{16}{61}$

D $\frac{40}{61}$

Common Core Standard 4.NF.3 – Number & Operations – Fractions

☐ Seth went to the grocery store and bought 4/7 kg of sugar and 2/7 kg of salt. How much sugar and salt did Seth buy at the grocery store all together? Be sure to show your work.

A $\frac{3}{7}$

C $\frac{2}{7}$

B $\frac{1}{7}$

D $\frac{6}{7}$

Name ____________________________

Common Core Standard 4.NF.3 – Number & Operations – Fractions

☐ Prenilla makes 2 friendship bracelets. Her first bracelet took 8/12 of an hour to make. Her second bracelet took 5/12 of an hour to make. How much more time did the first bracelet take to make? Be sure to show your work.

A $\frac{13}{12}$

B $\frac{13}{24}$

C $\frac{1}{4}$

D $\frac{1}{2}$

Common Core Standard 4.NF.3 – Number & Operations – Fractions

☐ Subtract the fractions and simplify your answer. Be sure to show your work.

$$\frac{49}{32} - \frac{41}{32} = \square$$

A $\frac{90}{32}$

B $\frac{1}{4}$

C $\frac{9}{8}$

D $\frac{1}{2}$

Common Core Standard 4.NF.3 – Number & Operations – Fractions

☐ Add the fractions and simplify your answer. Be sure to show your work.

$$\frac{21}{59} + \frac{26}{59} = \square$$

A $\frac{5}{59}$

B $\frac{46}{59}$

C $\frac{47}{118}$

D $\frac{47}{59}$

Name ______________________

ASSESSEMENT

Common Core Standard 4.NF.3 – Number & Operations – Fractions

☐ Sylvester works at a pizza restaurant. He is making a cheese pizza for a customer. He used $\frac{3}{10}$ cups of mozzarella cheese and $\frac{6}{10}$ cups of cheddar cheese. How much cheese did Sylvester use all together on the pizza? Be sure to show your work.

A $\frac{9}{10}$

B $\frac{3}{10}$

C $\frac{9}{20}$

D $\frac{3}{4}$

Common Core Standard 4.NF.3 – Number & Operations – Fractions

☐ Add the fractions and simplify your answer. Be sure to show your work.

$$\frac{54}{81} + \frac{45}{81} = \square$$

A $\frac{1}{9}$

B $\frac{99}{162}$

C $\frac{98}{81}$

D $\frac{11}{9}$

Common Core Standard 4.NF.3 – Number & Operations – Fractions

☐ Subtract the fractions and simplify your answer. Be sure to show your work.

$$\frac{48}{72} - \frac{24}{72} = \square$$

A $\frac{26}{72}$

B 1

C $\frac{1}{3}$

D $\frac{71}{72}$

Name ____________________

DIAGNOSTIC

Common Core Standard 4.NF.4 – Number & Operations – Fractions

☐ **Jose had 6 baseball cards. He gave his friend Sean $\frac{1}{2}$ of his cards. How many cards did Sean get? Be sure to show your work**

A $^{1}/_{12}$ cards

B 6.2 cards

C 3 cards

D $^{7}/_{2}$ cards

Common Core Standard 4.NF.4 – Number & Operations – Fractions

☐ **Multiply the whole number with the fraction below, and simplify your answer. Be sure to show your work.**

$$5 \times {}^{6}/_{2} =$$

A 15

B $^{6}/_{10}$

C $^{11}/_{12}$

D $^{3}/_{5}$

Common Core Standard 4.NF.4 – Number & Operations – Fractions

☐ **Mary drank 6 glasses of water. Each glass was $^{1}/_{3}$ of a cup full when she drank it. How many cups did Mary drink? Be sure to show your work**

A $^{7}/_{3}$ cups

B 2 cups

C 2.1 cups

D $^{1}/_{8}$ cups

Name ____________________________

DIAGNOSTIC

Common Core Standard 4.NF.4 – Number & Operations – Fractions

☐ **Multiply the whole number with the fraction below, and simplify your answer. Be sure to show your work.**

$$3 \times {}^{4}/_{3} =$$

A $^{4}/_{9}$

B $^{7}/_{3}$

C $^{1}/_{2}$

D 4

Common Core Standard 4.NF.4 – Number & Operations – Fractions

☐ **Austin had 12 chips on his plate. After eating $^{1}/_{2}$ of them, he gave the remaining chips to his brother Dallas. How many chips did Dallas get from Austin? Be sure to show your work**

A $^{1}/_{24}$ chips

B 6 chips

C $^{13}/_{2}$ chips

D 6.5 chips

Common Core Standard 4.NF.4 – Number & Operations – Fractions

☐ **Multiply the whole number with the fraction below, and simplify your answer. Be sure to show your work.**

$$0 \times {}^{2}/_{3} =$$

A $^{2}/_{3}$

B 0

C 1.5

D $^{1}/_{3}$

Name ________________________

PRACTICE

Common Core Standard 4.NF.4 – Number & Operations – Fractions

☐ Brett's puppy needed a bath. The bathtub can hold up to 12 liters of water. Brett put 4/6 of the water in the bathtub to bathe his puppy. How many liters of water did Brett put in the bathtub? Be sure to show your work.

A 8 liters

B 2 liters

C 3 liters

D 5 liters

Common Core Standard 4.NF.4 – Number & Operations – Fractions

☐ Multiply the whole number with the fraction below, and simplify your answer. Be sure to show your work.

$$\frac{14}{5} \times 15 =$$

A $\frac{9}{5}$

B 42

C $\frac{2}{5}$

D 23

Common Core Standard 4.NF.4 – Number & Operations – Fractions

☐ If Juanita had 8 shirts to give to charity and she gave $^{1}/_{4}$ of the shirts to her church, how many did she give to her church? Be sure to show your work.

A $^{9}/_{4}$ shirts

B 3 shirts

C $^{1}/_{12}$ shirts

D 2 shirts

Name ________________________

PRACTICE

Common Core Standard 4.NF.4 – Number & Operations – Fractions

☐ **If a glacier moves $^{1}/_{10}$ of a mile in one year, how far will it move in 35 years? Be sure to show your work.**

A 3.6 miles

B $^{6}/_{5}$ miles

C 3.5 miles

D $^{1}/_{18}$ miles

Common Core Standard 4.NF.4 – Number & Operations – Fractions

☐ **Multiply the whole number with the fraction below, and simplify your answer. Be sure to show your work.**

$$\frac{6}{7} \times 14 =$$

A $\frac{5}{7}$

B $\frac{20}{7}$

C 7

D 12

Common Core Standard 4.NF.4 – Number & Operations – Fractions

☐ **Chester sold lemonade on July 4th. If he started out with 8 liters of lemonade and sold 5/8 of the lemonade, how many liters of lemonade did Chester sell? Be sure to show your work.**

A $\frac{5}{2}$ liters

B 5 liters

C 4 liters

D 2 liters

Name ____________________________

PRACTICE

Common Core Standard 4.NF.4 – Number & Operations – Fractions

☐ Mrs. Matthews is making a cake for her class. She has 5 kg of sugar that she will use for her cake. If she uses 2/5 kg of sugar for the cake, how sugar did she use to make the cake? Be sure to show your work.

A 3 kg

C 2 kg

B $^{7}/_{5}$kg

D 5 kg

Common Core Standard 4.NF.4 – Number & Operations – Fractions

☐ Multiply the whole number with the fraction below, and simplify your answer. Be sure to show your work.

$$25 \times \frac{8}{5} =$$

A 133

B $\frac{33}{5}$

C 13

D 40

Common Core Standard 4.NF.4 – Number & Operations – Fractions

☐ Each time the yard is mowed, Tim's lawn mower uses $^{3}/_{5}$ gallons of gas. How much gas is needed to mow the yard 5 times a month? Be sure to show your work.

A $\frac{6}{5}$ gallons

C $\frac{18}{5}$ gallons

B 3 gallons

D $\frac{1}{18}$ gallons

Name ________________________

PRACTICE

Common Core Standard 4.NF.4 – Number & Operations – Fractions

☐ Dylan has 36 lollipops that he wants to give to his friends. If he gives his friends 5/6 of the lollipops, how many did Dylan give? Be sure to show your work.

A 6 lollipops

B $^{6}/_{5}$ lollipops

C 30 lollipops

D 180 lollipops

Common Core Standard 4.NF.4 – Number & Operations – Fractions

☐ Multiply the whole number with the fraction below, and simplify your answer. Be sure to show your work.

$$39 \times \frac{4}{3} =$$

A $\frac{166}{3}$

B $\frac{166}{6}$

C 52

D 51

Common Core Standard 4.NF.4 – Number & Operations – Fractions

☐ Ethan has 21 soccer balls. He gives $\frac{2}{3}$ of them to charity. How many soccer balls did Ethan give to charity? Be sure to show your work.

A 11 soccer balls

B 7 soccer balls

C 12 soccer balls

D 14 soccer balls

Name ________________________

ASSESSEMENT

Common Core Standard 4.NF.4 – Number & Operations – Fractions

☐ Jolita went to the clothing store with her mother. They bought 10 shirts, of which $\frac{1}{5}$ were black. How many black shirts did they buy? Be sure to show your work.

A 2 black shirts

B $^{20}/_{25}$ black shirts

C 3 black shirts

D 4 black shirts

Common Core Standard 4.NF.4 – Number & Operations – Fractions

☐ Multiply the whole number with the fraction below, and simplify your answer. Be sure to show your work.

$$47 \times \frac{5}{5} =$$

A 48

B 47

C 52

D $\frac{52}{5}$

Common Core Standard 4.NF.4 – Number & Operations – Fractions

☐ There are 30 students in Mrs. Villalobos' class. $\frac{1}{10}$ of them did not turn in their homework that was due. How many students did not turn in their homework? Be sure to show your work.

A 3 students

B 4 students

C $^{31}/_{10}$ students

D 5 students

Name ____________________________

ASSESEMENT

Common Core Standard 4.NF.4 – Number & Operations – Fractions

☐ Jefferson wanted to go fishing. He bought 50 worms to fish with at the lake. He used $\frac{4}{8}$ of the worms to catch fish. How many worms did Jackson use to fish with? Be sure to show your work.

A $^{27}/_{4}$ worms

B 23 worms

C 24 worms

D 25 worms

Common Core Standard 4.NF.4 – Number & Operations – Fractions

☐ Multiply the whole number with the fraction below, and simplify your answer. Be sure to show your work.

$$91 \times \frac{3}{7} =$$

A 39

B $\frac{94}{7}$

C 37

D $\frac{88}{7}$

Common Core Standard 4.NF.4 – Number & Operations – Fractions

☐ There are 48 people at the soccer game. $\frac{2}{3}$ are the soccer players parents. How many soccer players parents are at the game? Be sure to show your work.

A 31

B $^{46}/_{3}$

C $^{50}/_{3}$

D 32

Name ____________________

DIAGNOSTIC

Common Core Standard 4.NF.5 – Number & Operations – Fractions

☐ **Add the fractions and simplify your answer. Be sure to show your work.**

$$\frac{9}{10} + \frac{30}{100} = \square$$

A $\frac{6}{5}$

C $\frac{27}{10}$

B $\frac{39}{100}$

D $\frac{39}{110}$

Common Core Standard 4.NF.5 – Number & Operations – Fractions

☐ **Find the value for *X* in the fraction below. Be sure to show your work**

$$\frac{4}{10} = \frac{X}{100}$$

A 4

B 40

C 400

D 4000

Common Core Standard 4.NF.5 – Number & Operations – Fractions

☐ **Add the fractions and simplify your answer. Be sure to show your work.**

$$\frac{5}{10} + \frac{30}{100} = \square$$

A $\frac{35}{110}$

C $\frac{4}{5}$

B $\frac{3}{2}$

D $\frac{35}{100}$

Name ________________________

DIAGNOSTIC

Common Core Standard 4.NF.5 – Number & Operations – Fractions

☐ Find the value for *X* in the fraction below. Be sure to show your work

$$\frac{6}{10} = \frac{X}{100}$$

A 600

B 6

C 6000

D 60

Common Core Standard 4.NF.5 – Number & Operations – Fractions

☐ Add the fractions and simplify your answer. Be sure to show your work.

$$\frac{7}{10} + \frac{70}{100} = \square$$

A $\frac{77}{100}$

C $\frac{77}{110}$

B $\frac{7}{5}$

D $\frac{49}{10}$

Common Core Standard 4.NF.5 – Number & Operations – Fractions

☐ Find the value for *X* in the fraction below. Be sure to show your work.

$$\frac{17}{10} = \frac{X}{100}$$

A 170

B 17

C 1700

D 17000

Name ______________________

PRACTICE

Common Core Standard 4.NF.5 – Number & Operations – Fractions

☐ Add the fractions and simplify your answer. Be sure to show your work.

$$\frac{16}{10} + \frac{42}{100} = \square$$

A $\frac{168}{25}$

B $\frac{29}{55}$

C $\frac{29}{50}$

D $\frac{101}{50}$

Common Core Standard 4.NF.5 – Number & Operations – Fractions

☐ Find the value for *X* in the fraction below. Be sure to show your work.

$$\frac{9}{10} = \frac{X}{100}$$

A 9000

B 900

C 9

D 90

Common Core Standard 4.NF.5 – Number & Operations – Fractions

☐ Add the fractions and simplify your answer. Be sure to show your work.

$$\frac{3}{10} + \frac{20}{100} = \square$$

A $\frac{1}{2}$

B $\frac{5}{11}$

C $\frac{3}{5}$

D $\frac{23}{110}$

Name ______________________

PRACTICE

Common Core Standard 4.NF.5 – Number & Operations – Fractions

☐ Find the value for *X* in the fraction below. Be sure to show your work.

$$\frac{24}{10} = \frac{X}{100}$$

A 240

B 24

C 2400

D 240000

Common Core Standard 4.NF.5 – Number & Operations – Fractions

☐ Add the fractions and simplify your answer. Be sure to show your work.

$$\frac{6}{10} + \frac{30}{100} = \square$$

A $\frac{9}{25}$

B $\frac{9}{10}$

C $\frac{9}{5}$

D $\frac{18}{55}$

Common Core Standard 4.NF.5 – Number & Operations – Fractions

☐ Find the value for *X* in the fraction below. Be sure to show your work.

$$\frac{60}{10} = \frac{X}{100}$$

A 60

B 60000

C 600

D 6000

Name ___________________________

PRACTICE

Common Core Standard 4.NF.5 – Number & Operations – Fractions

☐ Add the fractions and simplify your answer. Be sure to show your work.

$$\frac{12}{10} + \frac{70}{100} = \square$$

A $\frac{42}{5}$

B $\frac{19}{11}$

C $\frac{19}{10}$

D $\frac{31}{55}$

Common Core Standard 4.NF.5 – Number & Operations – Fractions

☐ Find the value for *X* in the fraction below. Be sure to show your work.

$$\frac{15}{10} = \frac{X}{100}$$

A 15

B 1500

C 150000

D 150

Common Core Standard 4.NF.5 – Number & Operations – Fractions

☐ Add the fractions and simplify your answer. Be sure to show your work.

$$\frac{9}{10} + \frac{80}{100} = \square$$

A $\frac{17}{10}$

B $\frac{36}{5}$

C $\frac{89}{100}$

D $\frac{89}{110}$

Name ____________________

PRACTICE

Common Core Standard 4.NF.5 – Number & Operations – Fractions

☐ Find the value for X in the fraction below. Be sure to show your work.

$$\frac{2}{10} = \frac{X}{100}$$

A 200

B 2

C 20

D 2000

Common Core Standard 4.NF.5 – Number & Operations – Fractions

☐ Add the fractions and simplify your answer. Be sure to show your work.

$$\frac{4}{10} + \frac{85}{100} = \square$$

A $\frac{89}{110}$

B $\frac{89}{100}$

C $\frac{17}{5}$

D $\frac{5}{4}$

Common Core Standard 4.NF.5 – Number & Operations – Fractions

☐ Find the value for X in the fraction below. Be sure to show your work.

$$\frac{37}{10} = \frac{X}{100}$$

A 370

B 37

C 3700

D 37000

Name ___________________________

ASSESSMENT

Common Core Standard 4.NF.5 – Number & Operations – Fractions

☐ Find the value for *X* in the fraction below. Be sure to show your work.

$$\frac{172}{10} = \frac{X}{100}$$

A 17,200

B 172

C 1,720

D 172,000

Common Core Standard 4.NF.5 – Number & Operations – Fractions

☐ Add the fractions and simplify your answer. Be sure to show your work.

$$\frac{9}{10} + \frac{29}{100} = \square$$

A $\frac{119}{100}$

B $\frac{19}{50}$

C $\frac{19}{55}$

D $\frac{261}{100}$

Common Core Standard 4.NF.5 – Number & Operations – Fractions

☐ Find the value for *X* in the fraction below. Be sure to show your work

$$\frac{13}{10} = \frac{X}{100}$$

A 1,300

B 130

C 13,000

D 13

Name ____________________

ASSESSMENT

Common Core Standard 4.NF.5 – Number & Operations – Fractions

☐ **Add the fractions and simplify your answer. Be sure to show your work.**

$$\frac{6}{10} + \frac{45}{100} = \square$$

A $\frac{51}{110}$

B $\frac{27}{25}$

C $\frac{21}{20}$

D $\frac{51}{100}$

Common Core Standard 4.NF.5 – Number & Operations – Fractions

☐ **Find the value for *X* in the fraction below. Be sure to show your work.**

$$\frac{7}{10} = \frac{X}{100}$$

A 7000

B 700

C 7

D 70

Common Core Standard 4.NF.5 – Number & Operations – Fractions

☐ **Add the fractions and simplify your answer. Be sure to show your work.**

$$\frac{2}{10} + \frac{64}{100} = \square$$

A $\frac{21}{25}$

B $\frac{33}{50}$

C $\frac{3}{5}$

D $\frac{32}{25}$

Name ______________________

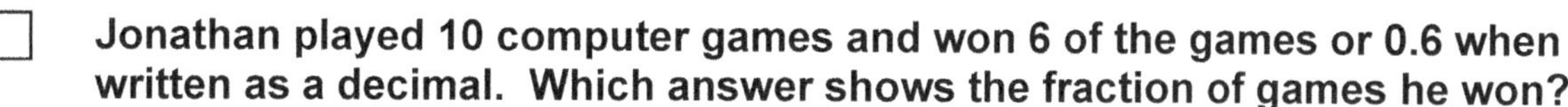

Common Core Standard 4.NF.6 – Number & Operations – Fractions

☐ **Jonathan played 10 computer games and won 6 of the games or 0.6 when written as a decimal. Which answer shows the fraction of games he won?**

A $\frac{4}{10}$

B $\frac{6}{4}$

C $\frac{4}{6}$

D $\frac{6}{10}$

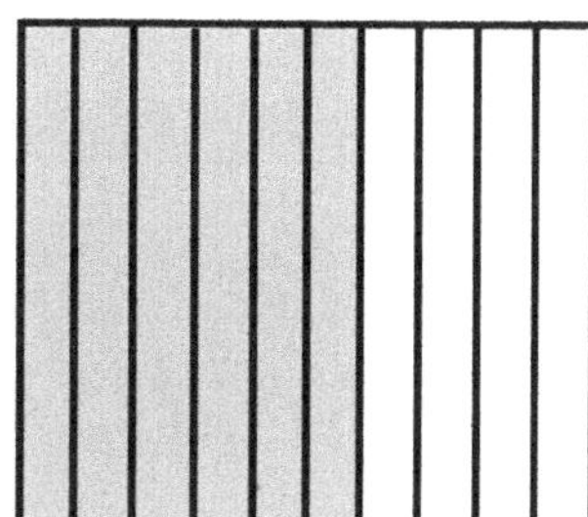

Common Core Standard 4.NF.6 – Number & Operations – Fractions

☐ **Find the answer that best fits the following fraction in decimal format.**

$$\frac{6}{10}$$

A 60

B 0.6

C 0.06

D 6

Common Core Standard 4.NF.6 – Number & Operations – Fractions

☐ **The model is shaded to represent $1\frac{9}{10}$. Which decimal does the model represent?**

A 1.0

B 19.0

C 0.19

D 1.9

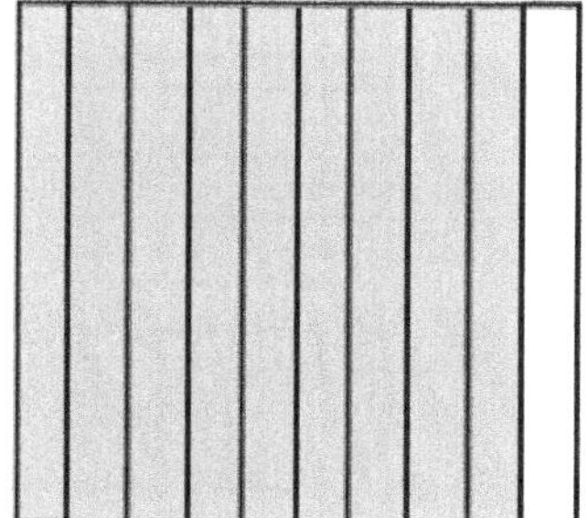

Name ______________________________

DIAGNOSTIC

Common Core Standard 4.NF.6 – Number & Operations – Fractions

☐ **Which model shows that 0.8 is shaded?**

A 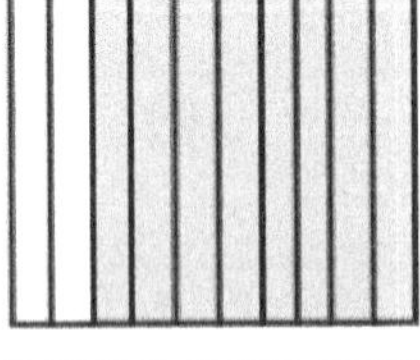 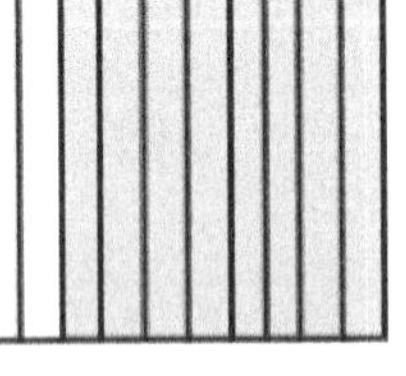

C 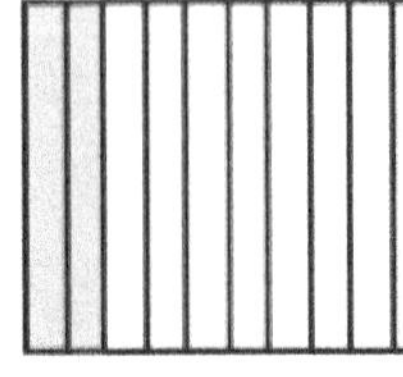

B

D 

Common Core Standard 4.NF.6 – Number & Operations – Fractions

☐ **Find the answer that best fits the following decimal number in fraction format.**

$$0.12 = \square$$

A $\frac{12}{100}$

C $\frac{120}{10}$

B $\frac{12}{10}$

D $\frac{1}{2}$

Common Core Standard 4.NF.6 – Number & Operations – Fractions

☐ **Which model shows that 0.32 is shaded?**

A 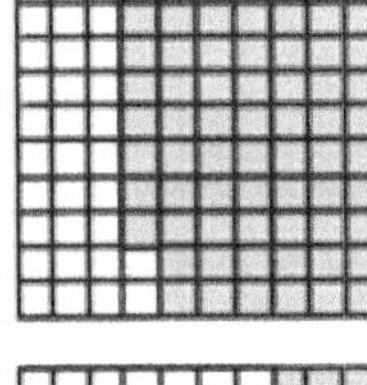

C 

B 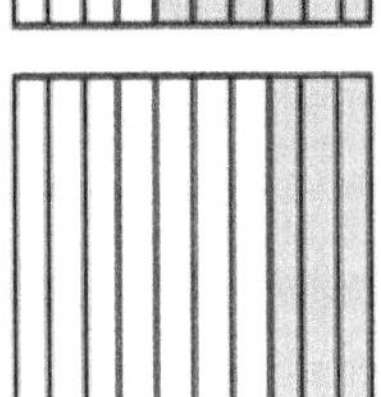

D 

Name ___________________________

PRACTICE

Common Core Standard 4.NF.6 – Number & Operations – Fractions

☐ Lindsey filled a bucket with 2.25 liters of water. Which fraction shows the amount of water she used?

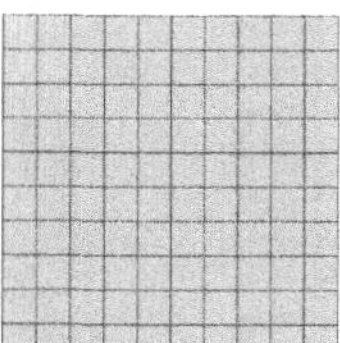 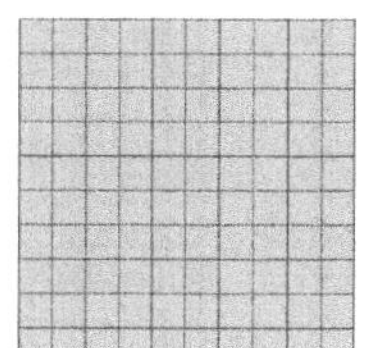 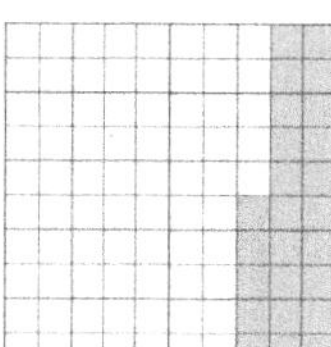

A $\frac{225}{10}$

B $\frac{225}{100}$

C $\frac{25}{10}$

D $\frac{25}{100}$

Common Core Standard 4.NF.6 – Number & Operations – Fractions

☐ Find the answer that best fits the following fraction in decimal format.

$$\frac{5}{100}$$

A 50

B 0.5

C 0.05

D 5

Common Core Standard 4.NF.6 – Number & Operations – Fractions

☐ Kamesha's mother bought her 10 new T-shirts for school. Three of the 10, or $\frac{3}{10}$, of the shirts have polka dots. Which is the correct way to write that amount as a decimal?

A 0.3

B 10.3

C 1.03

D 0.03

Name ______________________

PRACTICE

Common Core Standard 4.NF.6 – Number & Operations – Fractions

☐ **Which decimal tells how much is shaded?**

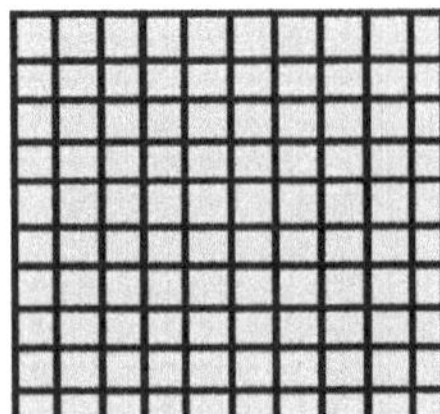
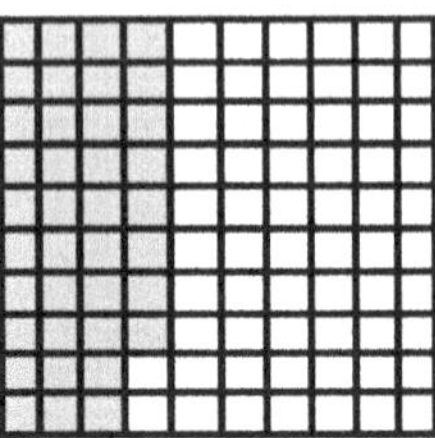

A 1.62

B 0.162

C 162.0

D 1.38

Common Core Standard 4.NF.6 – Number & Operations – Fractions

☐ **Find the answer that best fits the following decimal number in fraction format.**

$$3.48 = \square$$

A $\frac{348}{10}$

B $\frac{348}{1000}$

C $\frac{3}{8}$

D $\frac{348}{100}$

Common Core Standard 4.NF.6 – Number & Operations – Fractions

☐ **Russell spent $\frac{65}{100}$ of a dollar for a candy bar. Which tells how much he spent?**

A $65.00

B $0.65

C $6.50

D $0.065

Name ____________________________ **PRACTICE**

Common Core Standard 4.NF.6 – Number & Operations – Fractions

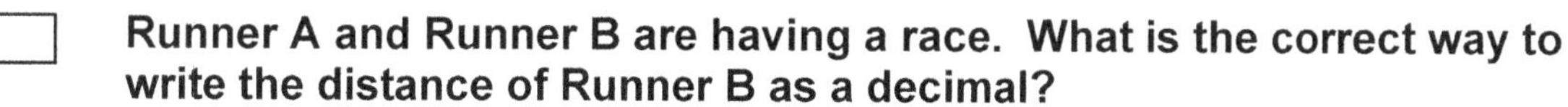

☐ **Runner A and Runner B are having a race. What is the correct way to write the distance of Runner B as a decimal?**

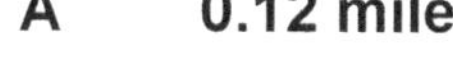

A **0.12 mile**

B **1.20 miles**

C **0.50 mile**

D **1.50 miles**

Runner A — Runner B

0 — $\frac{5}{10}$ mile — 1 mile — $1\frac{5}{10}$ miles — 2 miles

Common Core Standard 4.NF.6 – Number & Operations – Fractions

☐ **Find the answer that best fits the following fraction in decimal format.**

$$\frac{47}{10}$$

A 4.7

B .47

C .047

D 47

Common Core Standard 4.NF.6 – Number & Operations – Fractions

☐ **The model is shaded to represent $1\frac{4}{10}$. Which decimal does the model represent?**

A **1.25**

B **1.4**

C **0.04**

D **1.04**

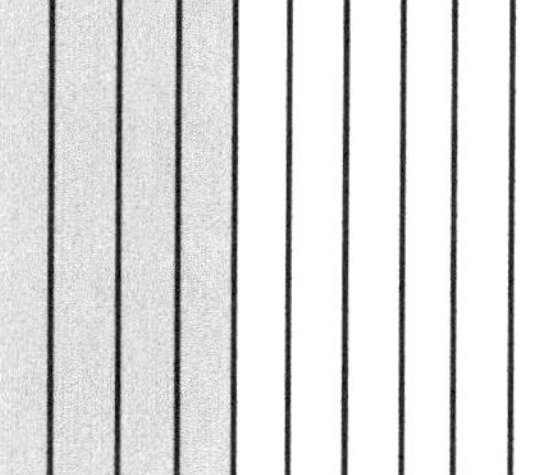

Name ______________________

PRACTICE

Common Core Standard 4.NF.6 – Number & Operations – Fractions

☐ **Which decimal tells how much is shaded?**

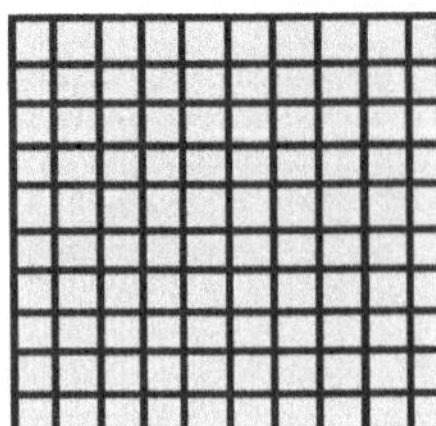 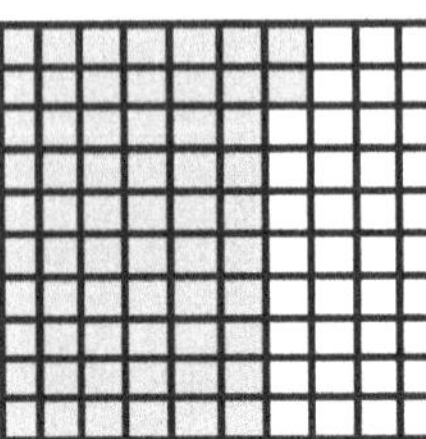

A 1.62

B 0.162

C 162.0

D 1.38

Common Core Standard 4.NF.6 – Number & Operations – Fractions

☐ **Find the answer that best fits the following decimal number in fraction format.**

.79 = ☐

A $\frac{79}{10}$

B $\frac{79}{100}$

C $\frac{9}{7}$

D $\frac{7}{9}$

Common Core Standard 4.NF.6 – Number & Operations – Fractions

☐ **Which model shows that 0.5 is shaded?**

A 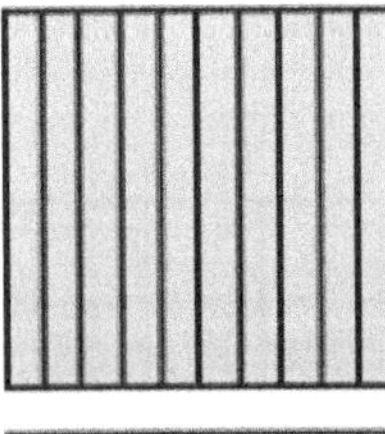

B 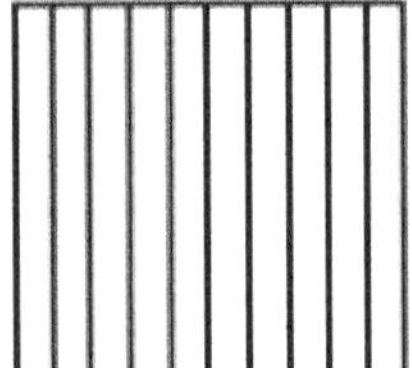

C 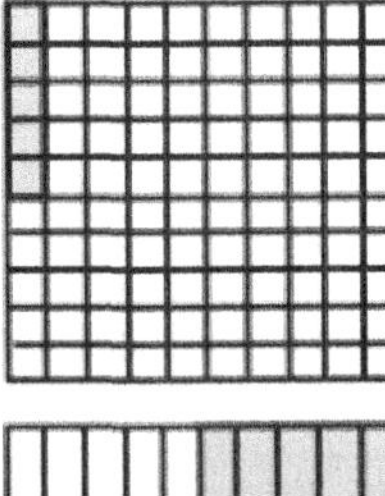

D

Name ______________________________

ASSESSMENT

Common Core Standard 4.NF.6 – Number & Operations – Fractions

☐ **Macey's puppy gained 1.50 pounds last year. What is another way to write the number of pounds her puppy gained?**

A $1\frac{15}{100}$

B $1\frac{1}{50}$

C $1\frac{50}{100}$

D $10\frac{100}{50}$

Common Core Standard 4.NF.6 – Number & Operations – Fractions

☐ **Find the answer that best fits the following fraction in decimal format.**

$$\frac{16}{100}$$

A 16

B 1.6

C .016

D .16

Common Core Standard 4.NF.6 – Number & Operations – Fractions

☐ **Which model shows that 0.74 is shaded?**

A

B

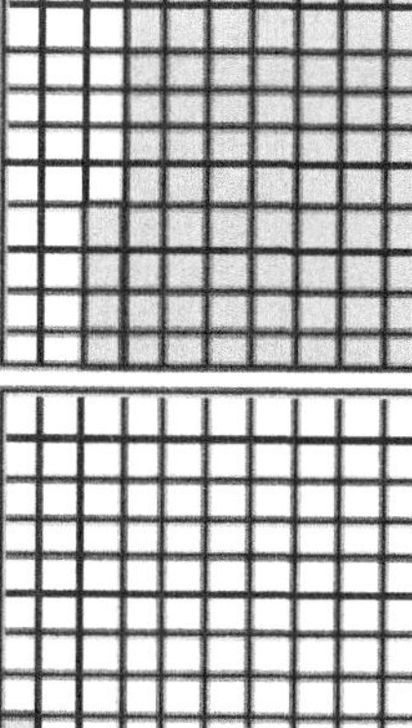

C

D

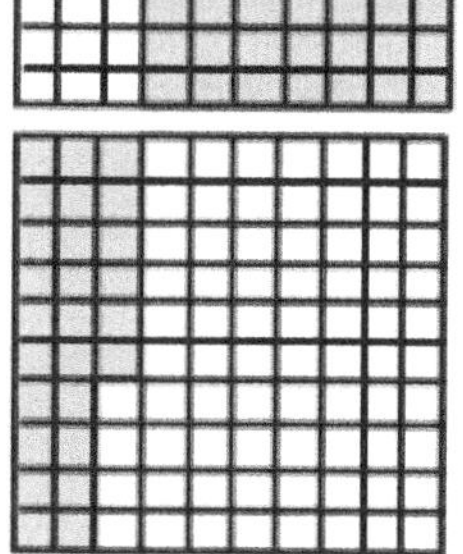

Name ____________________

ASSESSMENT

Common Core Standard 4.NF.6 – Number & Operations – Fractions

☐ **Which decimal tells how much is shaded?**

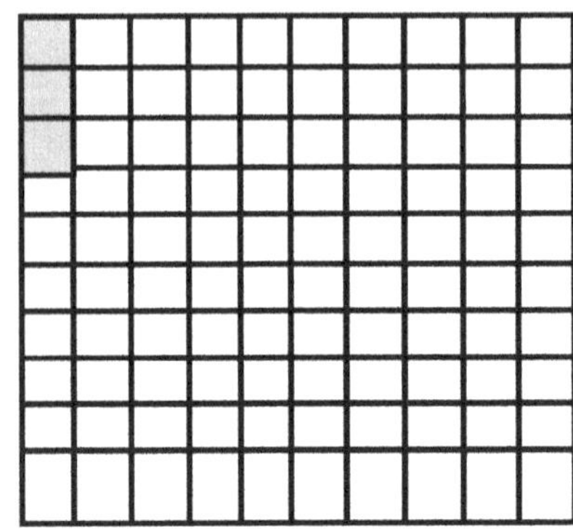

A 3.00

B 0.003

C 0.03

D 0.30

Common Core Standard 4.NF.6 – Number & Operations – Fractions

☐ **Find the answer that best fits the following decimal number in fraction format.**

12.8 = ☐

A $\frac{128}{10}$

B $\frac{128}{1000}$

C $\frac{128}{100}$

D $\frac{12}{8}$

Common Core Standard 4.NF.6 – Number & Operations – Fractions

☐ **Franklin found $\frac{25}{100}$ of a dollar on the sidewalk and $\frac{79}{100}$ of a dollar under his bed. Which answer tells the total amount of money he found?**

A **$0.54**

B **$10.40**

C **$0.94**

D **$1.04**

Name ____________________________

DIAGNOSTIC

Common Core Standard 4.NF.7 – Number & Operations – Fractions

☐ **Find the symbol that best compares the decimals below.**

.12 ☐ .25

A >

B <

C =

D None of the above

Common Core Standard 4.NF.7 – Number & Operations – Fractions

☐ **Which of the following is true?**

A 0.01 is greater than 0.03

B 2.54 is less than 2.45

C 0.06 is greater than 0.60

D 1.02 is less than 1.20

Common Core Standard 4.NF.7 – Number & Operations – Fractions

☐ **Find the decimals that are in order from greatest to least.**

A 0.25, 0.24, 0.273, 0.28, 0.38

B 0.24, 0.25, 0.27, 0.28, 0.38

C 0.38, 0.28, 0.27, 0.25, 0.24

D 0.24, 0.25, 0.28, 0.27, 0.38

Name ______________________________

DIAGNOSTIC

Common Core Standard 4.NF.7 – Number & Operations – Fractions

☐ Find the symbol that best compares the decimals below.

1.28 ☐ 1.29

A <

B >

C =

D None of the above

Common Core Standard 4.NF.7 – Number & Operations – Fractions

☐ Which of the following is NOT true?

A 0.30 is greater than 0.03

B 4.40 is less than 4.04

C 0.09 is greater than 0.06

D 1.00 is less than 1.85

Common Core Standard 4.NF.7 – Number & Operations – Fractions

☐ Find the decimals that are in order from least to greatest.

A 5.28, 6.86, 5.87, 5.24, 5.35

B 5.24, 5.28, 5.87, 5.35, 6.86

C 5.24, 5.28, 5.35, 6.86, 5.87

D 5.24, 5.28, 5.35, 5.87, 6.86

Name ______________________

PRACTICE

Common Core Standard 4.NF.7 – Number & Operations – Fractions

☐ **Find the symbol that best compares the decimals below.**

5.54 ☐ 5.53

A <

B =

C >

D None of the above

Common Core Standard 4.NF.7 – Number & Operations – Fractions

☐ **Which of the following is true?**

A 0.34 is greater than 0.034

B 0.10 is less than 0.01

C 0.17 is greater than 1.7

D 2.0 is less than 0.20

Common Core Standard 4.NF.7 – Number & Operations – Fractions

☐ **Find the decimals that are in order from greatest to least.**

A 2.26, 2.25, 2.24, 2.20, 2.09

B 2.26, 2.24, 2.25, 2.20, 2.09

C 2.25, 2.24, 2.26, 2.20, 2.09

D 2.09, 2.20, 2.24, 2.25, 2.26

Name ___________________________ **PRACTICE**

Common Core Standard 4.NF.7 – Number & Operations – Fractions

☐ **Find the symbol that best compares the decimals below.**

.93 ☐ .99

A <

B =

C >

D None of the above

Common Core Standard 4.NF.7 – Number & Operations – Fractions

☐ **Which of the following is true?**

A 1.57 is greater than 1.58

B 0.69 is less than 0.68

C 0.40 is equal to 0.4

D 3.3 is less than 3.1

Common Core Standard 4.NF.7 – Number & Operations – Fractions

☐ **Find the decimals that are in order from least to greatest.**

A 1.04, 1.00, 0.79, 0.64, 0.78

B 0.64, 0.78, 0.79, 1.00, 1.04

C 0.78, 0.79, 0.64, 1.00, 1.04

D 0.78, 0.64, 0.79, 1.04, 1.00

Name ____________________

PRACTICE

Common Core Standard 4.NF.7 – Number & Operations – Fractions

☐ **Find the symbol that best compares the decimals below.**

0.53 ☐ 0.3

A   <

B   >

C   =

D   None of the above

Common Core Standard 4.NF.7 – Number & Operations – Fractions

☐ **Which of the following is NOT true?**

A   5.43 is less than 5.44

B   .49 is greater than .48

C   0.98 is equal to .98

D   .43 is greater than 0.43

Common Core Standard 4.NF.7 – Number & Operations – Fractions

☐ **Find the decimals that are in order from greatest to least.**

A   1.56, 1.34, 1.46, 1.26, 1.20

B   1.56, 1.46, 1.34, 1.26, 1.20

C   1.20, 1.26, 1.34, 1.46, 1.56

D   1.20, 1.26, 1.34, 1.56, 1.46

Name ___________________________

PRACTICE

Common Core Standard 4.NF.7 – Number & Operations – Fractions

☐ **Find the symbol that best compares the decimals below.**

1.97 ☐ 1.96

A <

B =

C >

D None of the above

Common Core Standard 4.NF.7 – Number & Operations – Fractions

☐ **Which of the following is true?**

A 0.76 is equal to .075

B 0.38 is greater than .8

C 9.48 is less than 9.30

D 6.42 is greater than 6.41

Common Core Standard 4.NF.7 – Number & Operations – Fractions

☐ **Find the decimals that are in order from least to greatest.**

A 1.22, 1.23, 1.59, 1.58, 1.68

B 1.68, 1.59, 1.58, 1.23, 1.22

C 1.22, 1.23, 1.58, 1.59, 1.68

D 1.68, 1.59, 1.58, 1.22, 1.23

Name ___________________________

ASSESSMENT

Common Core Standard 4.NF.7 – Number & Operations – Fractions

☐ **Find the symbol that best compares the decimals below.**

03.68 ☐ 3.68

A <

B >

C =

D None of the above

Common Core Standard 4.NF.7 – Number & Operations – Fractions

☐ **Which of the following is true?**

A 3.33 is greater than 03.33

B .87 is greater than .88

C 0.75 is equal to .75

D .97 is less than 0.97

Common Core Standard 4.NF.7 – Number & Operations – Fractions

☐ **Find the decimals that are in order from greatest to least.**

A 3.00, 3.28, 3.41, 3.56, 3.98

B 3.98, 3.56, 3.41, 3.28, 3.00

C 3.00, 3.28, 3.56, 3.41, 3.98

D 3.98, 3.41, 3.56, 3.28, 3.00

Name ____________________________

ASSESSMENT

Common Core Standard 4.NF.7 – Number & Operations – Fractions

☐ Find the symbol that best compares the decimals below.

3.87 ☐ 4.87

A <

B =

C >

D None of the above

Common Core Standard 4.NF.7 – Number & Operations – Fractions

☐ Which of the following is true?

A .74 is greater than .73

B 345.97 is greater than 355.98

C 0.7 is greater than 00.83

D 9.59 is equal to 9.58

Common Core Standard 4.NF.7 – Number & Operations – Fractions

☐ Find the decimals that are in order from least to greatest.

A .56, .41, .39, .37, .35

B .56, .41, .37, .39, .35

C .56, .41, .37, .35, .39

D .35, .37, .39, .41, .56

Name ___________________________

DIAGNOSTIC

Common Core Standard 4.MD.1 – Measurement & Data

☐ What is the best estimate of the weight of an adult rabbit?

A 30 pounds

B 30 kilograms

C 30 tons

D 30 ounces

Common Core Standard 4.MD.1 – Measurement & Data

☐ Which is the best estimate of the capacity of a bottle of soda?

A 2000 cups

B 2000 milliliters

C 2000 quarts

D 2000 gallons

Common Core Standard 4.MD.1 – Measurement & Data

☐ Megan read her book for her upcoming homework assignment. She read for 5 hours. How many minutes did Megan read?

A 30 minutes

B 300 minutes

C 350 minutes

D 240 minutes

Name ___________________________

DIAGNOSTIC

Common Core Standard 4.MD.1 – Measurement & Data

☐ **Eva picked a flower for her mother. Which of the following units would be the most appropriate for measuring the height of the flower?**

A Liter

B Kilogram

C Centimeter

D Meter

Common Core Standard 4.MD.1 – Measurement & Data

☐ **Joshua is 10 years old. How many months old is Joshua?**

A 10 months

B 120 months

C 100 months

D 110 months

Common Core Standard 4.MD.1 – Measurement & Data

☐ **Which of the following objects would most likely be on the scale if the object weighs 2 ounces?**

A Bag of oranges

B Gallon jug of milk

C Jelly sandwich

D Car

Name ____________________________

PRACTICE

Common Core Standard 4.MD.1 – Measurement & Data

☐ **Which container could hold 2 liters of liquid?**

A B C D

Common Core Standard 4.MD.1 – Measurement & Data

☐ **Mr. Campos took his Boy Scout troop out for a camping trip. They were gone for 5 days. How many hours were the scouts gone?**

A 120 hours

B 60 hours

C 5 hours

D 120 minutes

Common Core Standard 4.MD.1 – Measurement & Data

☐ **Which of the following units would be appropriate for measuring the height of a windmill?**

A Meter

B Inch

C Liter

D Kilometer

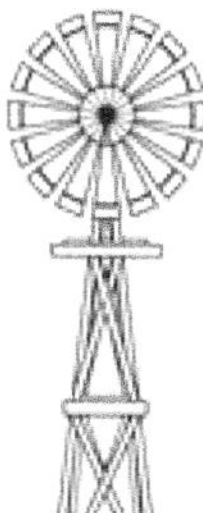

Name ____________________________

PRACTICE

Common Core Standard 4.MD.1 – Measurement & Data

☐ Which object could hold one pint of soda?

A B C D

Common Core Standard 4.MD.1 – Measurement & Data

☐ Kristine is making punch for her party. If she makes 12 pints of punch, how many quarts of punch will she make?

A 5 quarts

B 8 quarts

C 12 quarts

D 6 quarts

Common Core Standard 4.MD.1 – Measurement & Data

☐ Which of the following units would be the most appropriate for measuring the weight of the boy and girl?

A Ounce

B Meter

C Kilogram

D Millimeter

Name ______________________

PRACTICE

Common Core Standard 4.MD.1 – Measurement & Data

☐ Kyle read about an animal whose mass was 500 kilograms. Which of the following did Kyle most likely read about?

A Adult male deer

B Adult female dog

C Adult male lion

D Adult female horse

Common Core Standard 4.MD.1 – Measurement & Data

☐ Hector's family went on a trip over the weekend. They traveled 80,000 meters on their trip, how many kilometers did they travel?

A 120 kilometers

B 128 kilometers

C 80 kilometers

D 40 kilometers

Common Core Standard 4.MD.1 – Measurement & Data

☐ Which of the following units would be the most appropriate for measuring the length of a tennis court?

A Liter

B Feet

C Miles

D Kilometer

Name ___________________________

PRACTICE

Common Core Standard 4.MD.1 – Measurement & Data

☐ **Which container could have a capacity of 1 pint of ice cream?**

A B C D

Common Core Standard 4.MD.1 – Measurement & Data

☐ **Which of the following options is the best estimate of the weight of a large sack of potatoes?**

A 5 ounces

B 5 liters

C 5 pounds

D 5 meters

Common Core Standard 4.MD.1 – Measurement & Data

☐ **What is the best estimate of the weight of a bicycle?**

A 8 meters

B 8 ounces

C 8 pounds

D 8 kilometer

Name ____________________________

ASSESSMENT

Common Core Standard 4.MD.1 – Measurement & Data

☐ If the scale shows a weight of 3 grams, which of the objects is most likely to be on the scale?

A B C D

Common Core Standard 4.MD.1 – Measurement & Data

☐ Kesha's pet rabbit and cat weigh exactly the same. Which of the following could be the weight of the rabbit and cat?

A 50 kilograms

B 6 kilograms

C 100 kilograms

D 75 kilograms

Common Core Standard 4.MD.1 – Measurement & Data

☐ What is the best estimate of the height of a bicycle?

A 1 meter

B 1 ounce

C 1 pound

D 1 kilometer

Name ___________________________

ASSESSMENT

Common Core Standard 4.MD.1 – Measurement & Data

☐ **Adam's grandmother sent him to the store to buy 2 pounds of apples. Which of the following scales shows the amount of apples he should buy?**

A B C D

Common Core Standard 4.MD.1 – Measurement & Data

☐ **Which object is most likely to have a capacity of 2 gallons?**

A Lake

B Container of lemonade

C Bottle of medicine

D Book

Common Core Standard 4.MD.1 – Measurement & Data

☐ **Which object is most likely to have a capacity of 2 liters?**

A Washing machine

B Shoe

C Dose of medicine

D Bottle of soda

Name ___________________________

DIAGNOSTIC

Common Core Standard 4.MD.2 – Measurement & Data

☐ **Madison Middle School spent $2,086 on new books for test preparation. The teacher spent $95 on addition aids for students. How much did the school and the teacher spent altogether? Be sure to show your work.**

A $2,071

B $2,081

C $2,181

D $1,991

Common Core Standard 4.MD.2 – Measurement & Data

☐ **Miranda gets on the school bus at 7:30AM. She wakes up 45 minutes before she gets on the bus. What time did Miranda wake up? Be sure to show your work.**

A 8:15AM

B 6:45AM

C 7:45AM

D 6:15AM

Common Core Standard 4.MD.2 – Measurement & Data

☐ **Bret climbed a tree that is 12 feet 9 inches tall. His brother climbed a tree that is 10 feet 3 inches tall. How much taller was the tree Bret climbed than the tree his brother climbed? Be sure to show your work.**

A 22 feet 12 inches

B 22 feet 6 inches

C 2 feet 6 inches

D 8 inches

Name ___________________________

DIAGNOSTIC

Common Core Standard 4.MD.2 – Measurement & Data

☐ Matthew left school at 3:10 PM to go to a hobby club meeting. The meeting started at 3:30 PM. The meeting lasted 45 minutes. If his mother came to pick him up just as the meeting was ending, what time did she get there? Be sure to show your work.

A 3:55 PM

B 4:15 PM

C 4:00 PM

D 4:30 PM

Common Core Standard 4.MD.2 – Measurement & Data

☐ Pedro bought some supplies at the school store. Pencils cost $.35 each, erasers are $.11 each, and crayons cost $.59 per box. If Pedro buys 1 box of crayons and 2 erasers, how much will he spend? Be sure to show your work.

A $1.05

B $.70

C $.81

D $.57

Common Core Standard 4.MD.2 – Measurement & Data

☐ Michele weighs 79 pounds, her sister weighs 76 pounds. How much more does Michele weigh than her sister in ounces? Be sure to show your work.

A 13 oz.

B 33 oz.

C 33 oz.

D 48 oz.

Name ____________________

PRACTICE

Common Core Standard 4.MD.2 – Measurement & Data

☐ Stella went to the grocery store with her mother. They paid $3.87 for sugar, $5.15 for cereal, and $3.39 for milk. Stella's mother had $37.58 before purchasing these items. How much money does her mother have after the purchases? Be sure to show your work.

A $23.17

B $25.17

C $12.41

D $37.58

Common Core Standard 4.MD.2 – Measurement & Data

☐ Cliff went to a park to play basketball at 9:20AM. He got home 2 hours and 30 minutes later. What time did he get home? Be sure to show your work.

A 11:50AM

B 11:20AM

C 9:50AM

D 11:30AM

Common Core Standard 4.MD.2 – Measurement & Data

☐ Bill's father is 6 feet 4 inches tall. His mother is 5 feet 3 inches tall. How much taller is his father than his mother? Be sure to show your work.

A 11 feet 7 inches

B 1 feet 7 inches

C 18 inches

D 1 foot 1 inch

Name ______________________

PRACTICE

Common Core Standard 4.MD.2 – Measurement & Data

☐ Michael watches his favorite movie on Saturday evenings. It lasts 3 hours. How many minutes does it take for him to watch his movie? Be sure to show your work.

A 120 mins

B 180 mins

C 60 mins

D 90 mins

Common Core Standard 4.MD.2 – Measurement & Data

☐ LaShonda went shopping with her friends at the mall. She spent $132.6 to buy 6 t-shirts. What was the cost of each t-shirt that LaShonda bought, if she spent equal amount on each shirt? Be sure to show your work.

A $22.1

B $28.00

C $138.6

D $66.21

Common Core Standard 4.MD.2 – Measurement & Data

☐ Jonathan competes in the long jump for his school. Last weekend, Jonathan jumped 2 meters, how many decimeters did Jonathan jump last weekend? Be sure to show your work.

A 2 dm.

B 20 dm.

C 200 dm.

D 2,000 dm.

Name ____________________________

PRACTICE

Common Core Standard 4.MD.2 – Measurement & Data

☐ Christano helps his father on their peach farm. If Christano's father paid him $765 in Novemeber, how much does Christano's father pay him per day in Novemeber? Be sure to show your work.

A $24.67

B $27.32

C $25.50

D $36.50

Common Core Standard 4.MD.2 – Measurement & Data

☐ A fast moving cold front came through Farmington yesterday morning. At 9:00AM the temperature was 75° F. By noon it was 19° cooler. At 6:00PM the temperature had dropped another 6°. What was the temperature at 6:00PM? Be sure to show your work.

A 100° F

B 60° F

C 50° F

D 58° F

Common Core Standard 4.MD.2 – Measurement & Data

☐ Theo did his chores in 1 hour and 52 minutes. His sister did her chores in 125 minutes. How much less time did Theo spend on his chores than his sister? Be sure to show your work.

A 237 mins

B 15 mins

C 13 mins

D 65 mins

Name ____________________

PRACTICE

Common Core Standard 4.MD.2 – Measurement & Data

☐ Brandon came home at 7:15PM. He had been riding his bicycle for 35 minutes. What time did he begin riding his bicycle? Be sure to show your work.

A 7:40PM

B 6:40PM

C 7:00PM

D 6:45PM

Common Core Standard 4.MD.2 – Measurement & Data

☐ A science class conducted an experiment to see how long it takes an ice cube to melt. The temperature of the ice cube at the beginning of the experiment was 21°F. After 10 minutes, the ice cube's temperature had risen 7°F. At the end of the experiment, the melting ice cube's temperature had risen an additional 9°F. What was the temperature of the ice cube at the end of the experiment? Be sure to show your work.

A 5°F

B 37°F

C 25°F

D 15°F

Common Core Standard 4.MD.2 – Measurement & Data

☐ Marissa and her friend walked to the park on Saturday. The park was 600 meters away from Marissa's house. How far did the girls walk in kilometers? Be sure to show your work.

A 0.6 km

B 60 km

C 6 km

D .06 km

Name ___________________________

ASSESSMENT

Common Core Standard 4.MD.2 – Measurement & Data

☐ Joe's basketball game lasted 2 hours. How many minutes did Joe's game last? Be sure to show your work.

A 60 minutes

B 125 minutes

C 90 minutes

D 120 minutes

Common Core Standard 4.MD.2 – Measurement & Data

☐ Nora receives $60 from her mother and father for her birthday. If she receives 2/4 of the money from her mother, how much did her father give Nora? Be sure to show your work.

A $20.00

B $40.00

C $30.00

D $50.00

Common Core Standard 4.MD.2 – Measurement & Data

☐ Look at the clocks. Beth's mother jogs every morning before she goes to work. She leaves home at 5:45 and returns at 7:00. How long does it take her to complete her jog? Be sure to show your work.

A 45 minutes

B 1 hour 15 minutes

C 15 minutes

D 2 hours 15 minutes

Start

Return

Name ___________________________

ASSESSMENT

Common Core Standard 4.MD.2 – Measurement & Data

☐ Angela walks to a library every afternoon after school. It takes her 25 minutes to get from school to the library. If she leaves school at 2:15, what time will she get to the library? Be sure to show your work.

A 2:40

B 1:50

C 2:30

D 3:40

Common Core Standard 4.MD.2 – Measurement & Data

☐ Arthur needs $11.00 to buy a ticket for a concert. He raked 3 yards to earn money for his ticket to the concert. He earned $2.65, $3.15, and $1.75. How much more money does Arthur need before he can buy a ticket? Be sure to show your work.

A $5.45

B $3.55

C $4.55

D $3.45

Common Core Standard 4.MD.2 – Measurement & Data

☐ Brooks and his family went to visit his grandparents last weekend. They arrived at his grandparent's house at 9:25PM. It took them 3 hours and 45 minutes to make the trip. What time did Brooks and his family leave their home? Be sure to show your work.

A 12:30PM

B 6:25PM

C 6:40PM

D 5:40PM

Name ______________________

DIAGNOSTIC

Common Core Standard 4.MD.3 – Measurement & Data

☐ Amanda's mom wanted Amanda to measure her room to make sure that her new furniture will fit. Amanda measured 12ft as the length of her room and 8ft as the width of it. What would be the area of Amanda's room? Be sure to show your work.

A 120 square ft.

B 96 square ft.

C 86 square ft.

D 112 square ft.

Common Core Standard 4.MD.3 – Measurement & Data

☐ A farmer wanted to plant corn on his square shaped field. He measured the perimeter of his field to be 400 yards. What would be the length of one side of the farmer's field? Be sure to show your work.

A 400 yards

B 200 yards

C 800 yards

D 100 yards

Common Core Standard 4.MD.3 – Measurement & Data

☐ Paul decided to frame a picture he drew for his mother as a present for Mother's Day. He measured the length of his picture at 8in and the width at 3 inches more than the length. What would be the area of the frame that Paul needs? Be sure to show your work.

A 24 square inches

B 88 square inches

C 11 square inches

D 18 square inches

Name ___________________________

DIAGNOSTIC

Common Core Standard 4.MD.3 – Measurement & Data

☐ **The city is planning to build a new playground for kids at Woodrow Park. The city cleaned up an area of 120sq m. for the playground. If the length of the playground is 12m, what would be the width of the cleaned area? Be sure to show your work.**

A 10 m

B 12 m

C 11 m

D 120 m

Common Core Standard 4.MD.3 – Measurement & Data

☐ **What is the area of the shaded part of the rectangle below? Be sure to show your work.**

A 26sq. cm

B 13sq. cm

C 20 sq. cm

D 24 sq. cm

Common Core Standard 4.MD.3 – Measurement & Data

☐ **What is the perimeter of the given figure below? Be sure to show your work.**

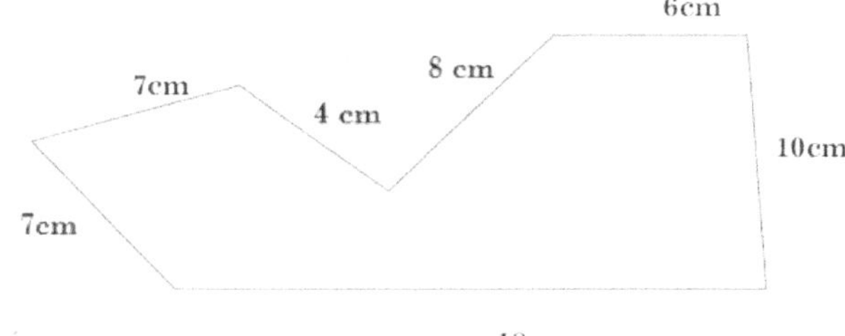

A 58 cm

B 60 cm

C 56 cm

D 62 cm

Name ____________________________ **PRACTICE**

Common Core Standard 4.MD.3 – Measurement & Data

☐ **Shiva is making a square desk for his room. To build the top of his desk, it will cost him $0.42 per square inch. He knows that the top of the desk will have a perimeter of 120 inches. Calculate the cost of the top of his desk. Be sure to show your work.**

A **$50.40**

B **$25.20**

C **$378.00**

D **$9.42**

Common Core Standard 4.MD.3 – Measurement & Data

☐ **What is the area of the right triangle below? Be sure to show your work.**

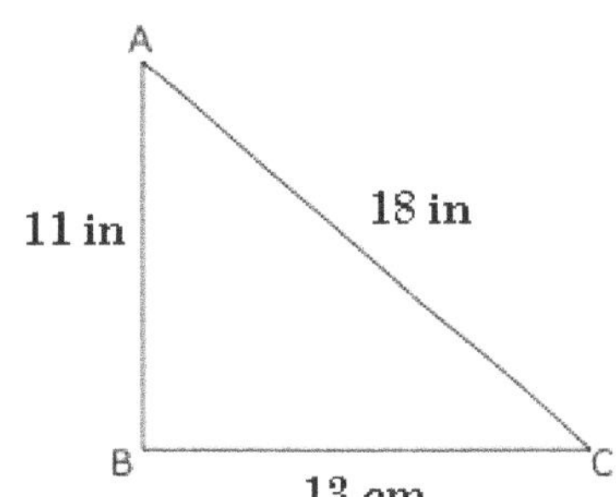

A **71.5 in**

B **198 in**

C **234 in**

D **42 in**

Common Core Standard 4.MD.3 – Measurement & Data

☐ **What is the perimeter of the parallelogram below? Be sure to show your work.**

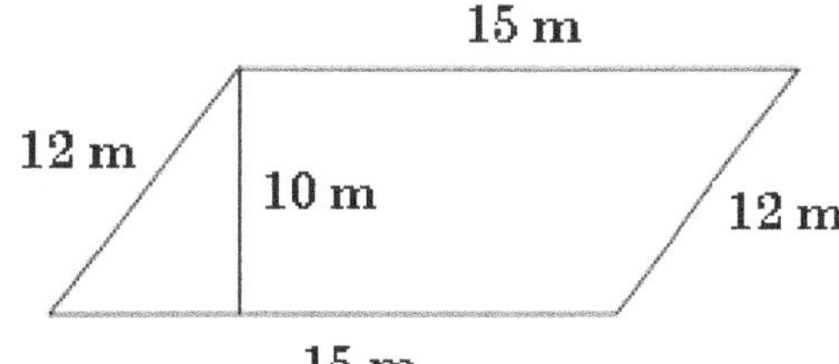

A **58 m**

B **54 m**

C **56 m**

D **62 m**

Name ___________________________

Common Core Standard 4.MD.3 – Measurement & Data

☐ What is the perimeter of the trapezoid below? Be sure to show your work.

A 78 ft

B 37 ft

C 31 ft

D 32 ft

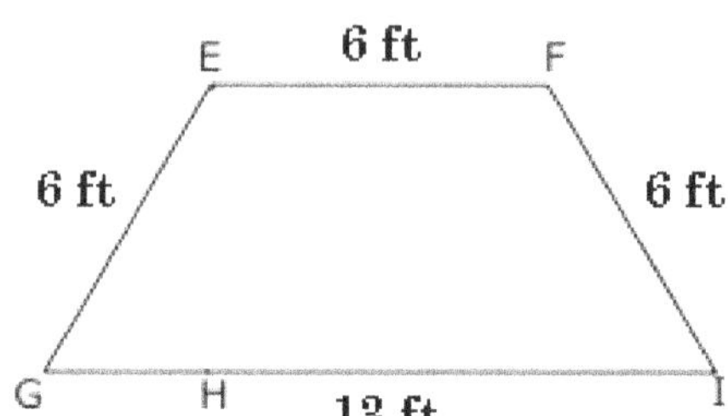

Common Core Standard 4.MD.3 – Measurement & Data

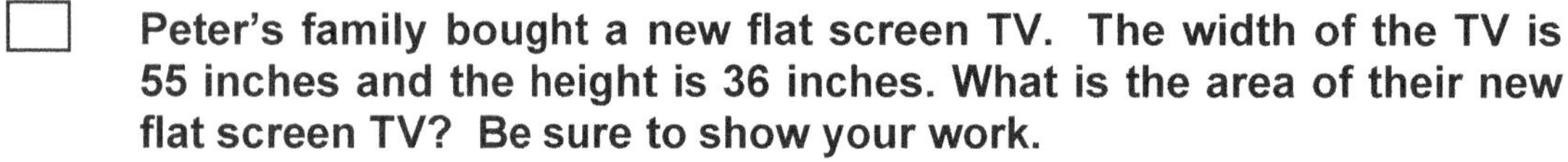

☐ Peter's family bought a new flat screen TV. The width of the TV is 55 inches and the height is 36 inches. What is the area of their new flat screen TV? Be sure to show your work.

A 182 inches

B 91 inches

C 220 inches

D 1,980 inches

Common Core Standard 4.MD.3 – Measurement & Data

☐ What is the area of the triangle below? Be sure to show your work.

A 10 km

B 8 km

C 16 km

D 13 km

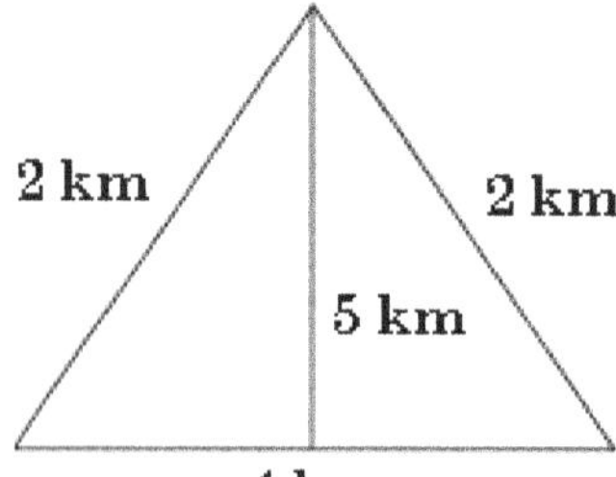

Name ________________________

PRACTICE

Common Core Standard 4.MD.3 – Measurement & Data

☐ **Nathan's family owns farm land that is in the shape of a square. The perimeter of the farm land is measured at 400 acres. What is the area of the farm? Be sure to show your work.**

A 400 sq. acres

B 10,000 sq. acres

C 200 sq. acres

D 1000 sq. acres

Common Core Standard 4.MD.3 – Measurement & Data

☐ **What is the perimeter of the figure below? Be sure to show your work.**

A 96 cm

B 42 cm

C 43 cm

D 21 cm

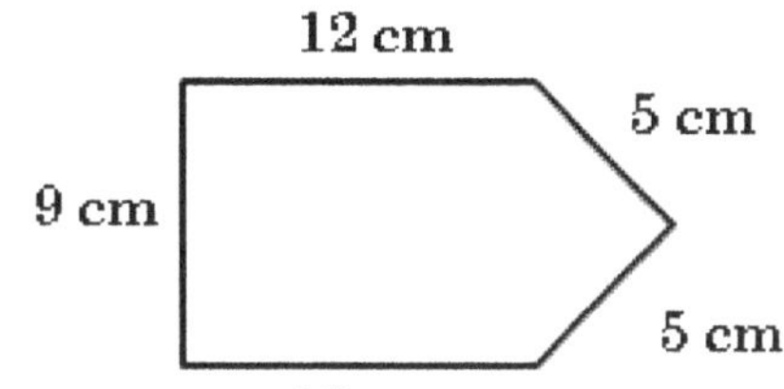

Common Core Standard 4.MD.3 – Measurement & Data

☐ **Adrian is going to help his father paint a mural on the side of a building. If the height of the wall is 14 feet and the base is 9 feet, what is the area of the wall Adrian and his father will paint?**

A 46 sq. ft.

B 23 sq. ft.

C 81 sq. ft.

D 126 sq. ft.

Name ___________________________

PRACTICE

Common Core Standard 4.MD.3 – Measurement & Data

☐ **Phillip helps his uncle build fences. His uncle charges $30 per square foot to build a fence. He built a 43 foot long by 8 feet high fence for Mrs. Smith. What will be the total cost of the fence when it is complete? Be sure to show your work.**

A $1,860

B $1,530

C $8,345

D $10,320

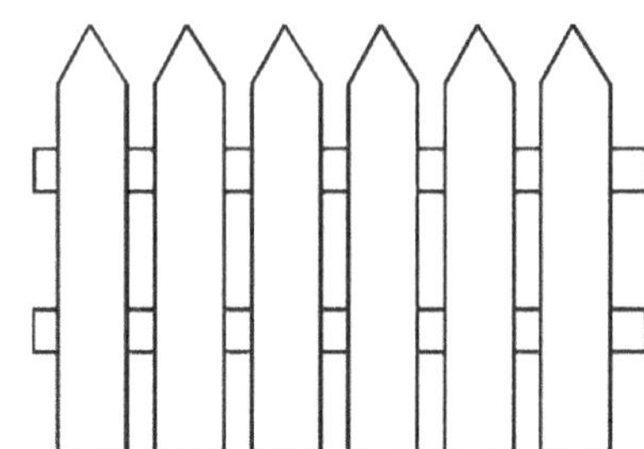

Common Core Standard 4.MD.3 – Measurement & Data

☐ **What is the area of the figure below? Be sure to show your work.**

A 60 mm

B 32 mm

C 45 mm

D 52 mm

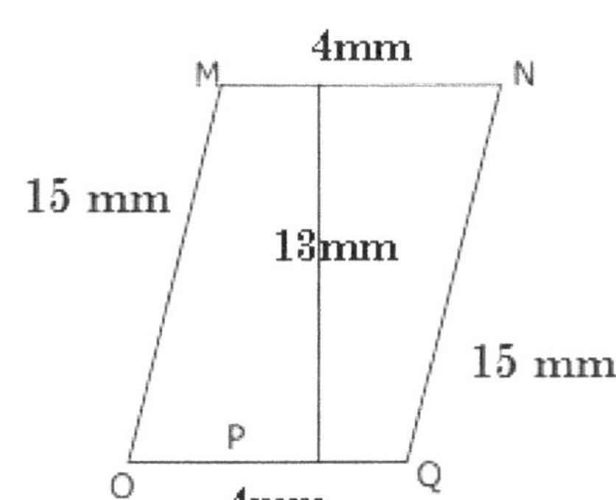

Common Core Standard 4.MD.3 – Measurement & Data

☐ **What is the perimeter of the pentagon below? Be sure to show your work.**

A 41 cm

B 32 cm

C 42 cm

D 54 cm

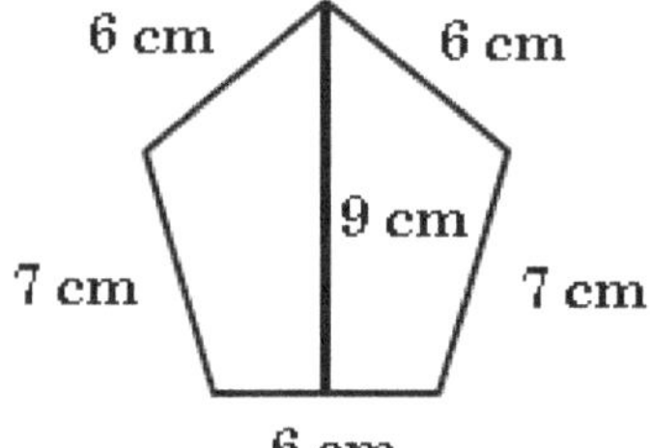

Name ___________________________

ASSESSMENT

Common Core Standard 4.MD.3 – Measurement & Data

☐ Mrs. Nguyen is making a square cookie cake for her class for a class celebration. The perimeter of the cookie cake measures 24 inches. What is the area of the cookie cake? Be sure to show your work.

A 36 square inches

B 12 square inches

C 16 square inches

D 24 square inches

Common Core Standard 4.MD.3 – Measurement & Data

☐ Jayson is getting a new comforter for his bed. He wants a race car theme. Jayson's mother measured his existing comforter and it was 7 feet wide and 10 feet long. If the cost per square foot for a comforter is $2, how much would it cost to make a new comforter for Jayson? Be sure to show your work.

A $34.00

B $68.00

C $54.00

D $140.00

Common Core Standard 4.MD.3 – Measurement & Data

☐ Stephen wanted to know the perimeter of his toy box. His toy box is in the shape of a parallelogram. The length of the toy box is 3 feet and the width is 2 feet. What is the perimeter of the toy box in inches? Be sure to show your work.

A 864 inches

B 10 inches

C 120 inches

D 6 inches

Name ______________________

ASSESSMENT

Common Core Standard 4.MD.3 – Measurement & Data

☐ **The rectangle blackboard in Mr. McShane's classroom measures 48 inches long and its perimeter is 168 inches. What is the width of the blackboard in Mr. McShane's classroom? Be sure to show your work.**

A 36 inches

B 3.5 inches

C 120 inches

D 48 inches

Common Core Standard 4.MD.3 – Measurement & Data

☐ **What is the perimeter of the triangle below? Be sure to show your work.**

A 629 cm

B 79 cm

C 100 cm

D 777 cm

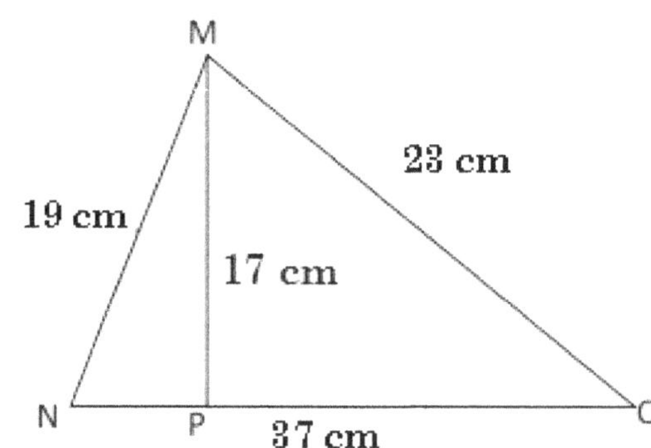

Common Core Standard 4.MD.3 – Measurement & Data

☐ **What is the area of the rectangle below? Be sure to show your work.**

A 136 sq. m

B 1,107 sq. m

C 1,681 sq. m

D 729 sq. m

41 m

27 m

27 m

41 m

Name ____________________________

DIAGNOSTIC

Common Core Standard 4.MD.4 – Measurement & Data

☐ **Henry's mom kept track of Henry's height since he was born. Look at the line plot below and find the correct answer to the questions below.**

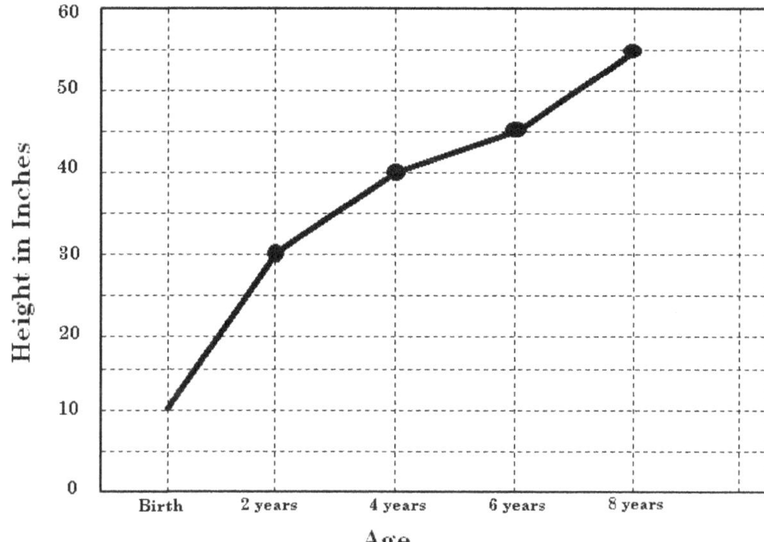

☐ How tall was Henry when he was four years old?

A 30 inches
B 40 inches
C 45 inches
D 35 inches

☐ How tall might Henry be at 10 years old?

A 65 inches
B 55 inches
C 50 inches
D 85 inches

☐ How old was Henry when he was 30 inches tall?

A 3 years old
B 5 years old
C 4 years old
D 2 years old

Name ______________________________

Common Core Standard 4.MD.4 – Measurement & Data

☐ Which object on the number line is at a position greater than $\frac{6}{8}$?

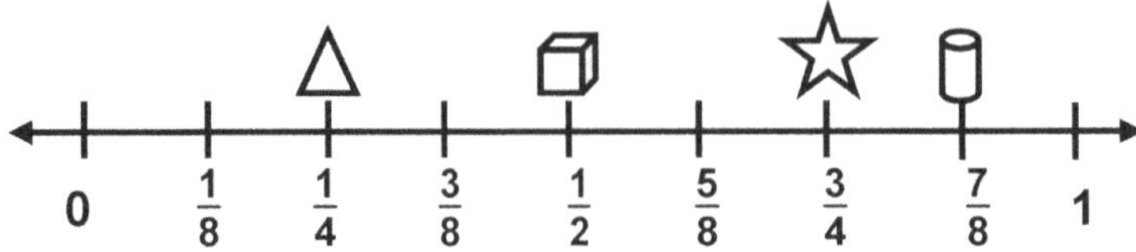

A Triangle

B Cylinder

C Star

D Cube

Common Core Standard 4.MD.4 – Measurement & Data

☐ Which point on the number line best represents $8\frac{3}{4}$?

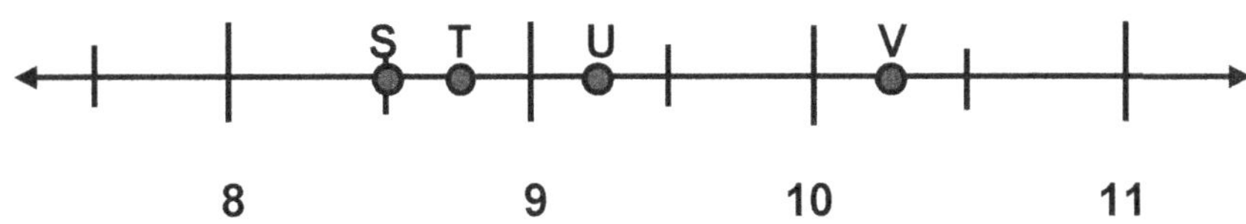

A V

B T

C S

D U

Common Core Standard 4.MD.4 – Measurement & Data

☐ Point P best represents which number?

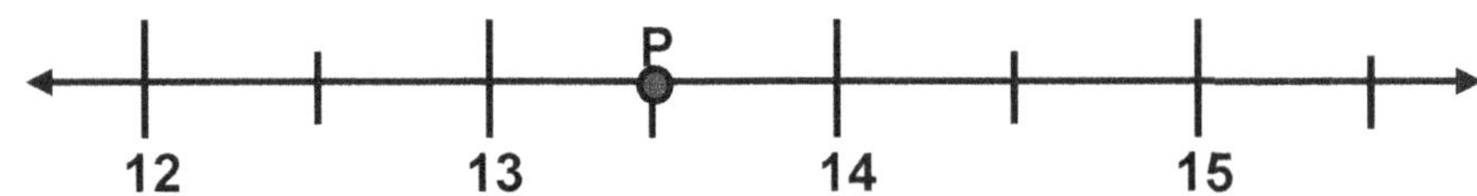

A $14\frac{3}{4}$

B $13\frac{3}{4}$

C $13\frac{1}{4}$

D $13\frac{1}{2}$

Name ____________________

PRACTICE

Common Core Standard 4.MD.4 – Measurement & Data

☐ Point X best represents which number?

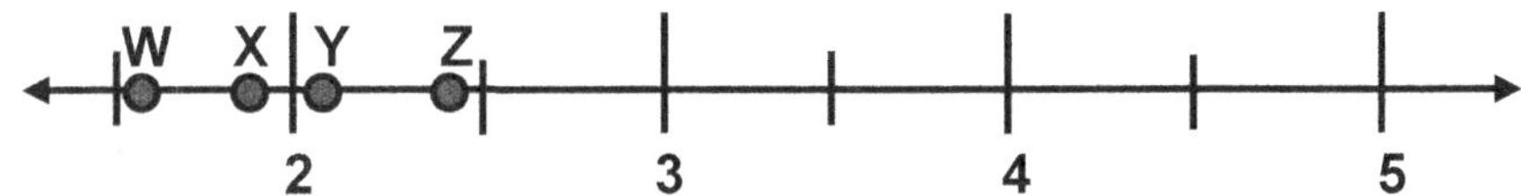

A $2\frac{7}{8}$

B $1\frac{5}{8}$

C $2\frac{1}{8}$

D $1\frac{7}{8}$

Common Core Standard 4.MD.4 – Measurement & Data

☐ Which object on the number line is at a position greater than $2\frac{3}{4}$?

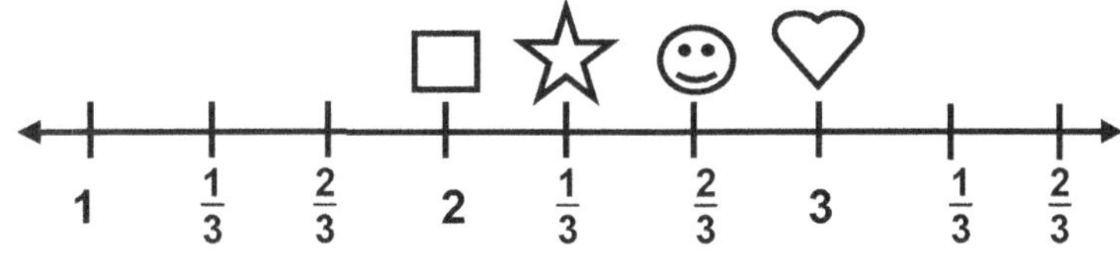

A Face

B Star

C Heart

D Cube

Common Core Standard 4.MD.4 – Measurement & Data

☐ An inchworm is racing along a number line. Which number tells how far the inchworm has gone?

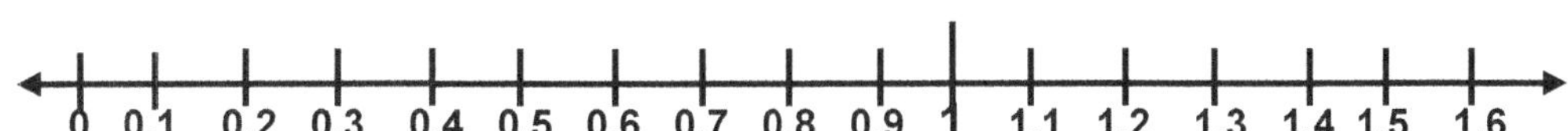

A 1

B 1.2

C 0.8

D 2

Name ____________________________

PRACTICE

Common Core Standard 4.MD.4 – Measurement & Data

☐ **The daily temperatures were tracked for Dallas last week and recorded on the line graph below. Use the graph to find the correct answer to the questions below.**

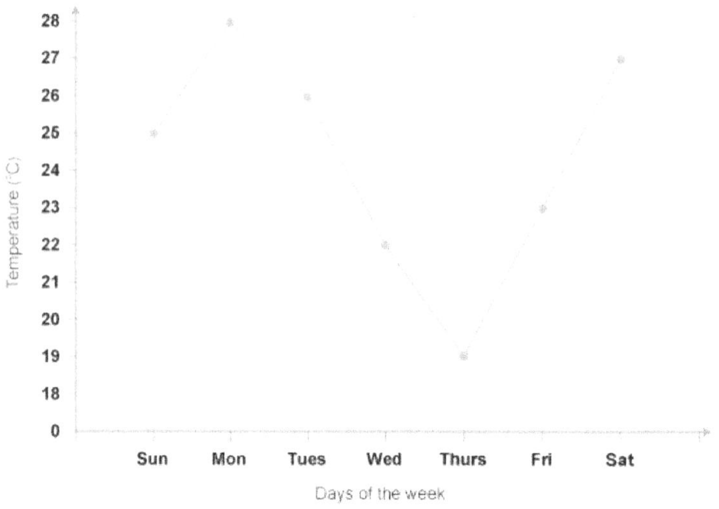

Temperature (°C)

28 27 26 25 24 23 22 21 20 19 18 0

Sun Mon Tues Wed Thurs Fri Sat

Days of the week

☐ **Which day experienced the highest temperature for the week?**

A	Thursday	C	Monday
B	Saturday	D	Sunday

☐ **What was the difference in temperature from Tuesday to Friday?**

A	5 degrees difference	C	4 degrees difference
B	3 degrees difference	D	2 degrees difference

☐ **What was the temperature for Wednesday?**

A	20°	C	19°
B	22°	D	18°

Name ____________________________ **PRACTICE**

Common Core Standard 4.MD.4 – Measurement & Data

☐ **Which point on the number line best represents $23\frac{2}{3}$?**

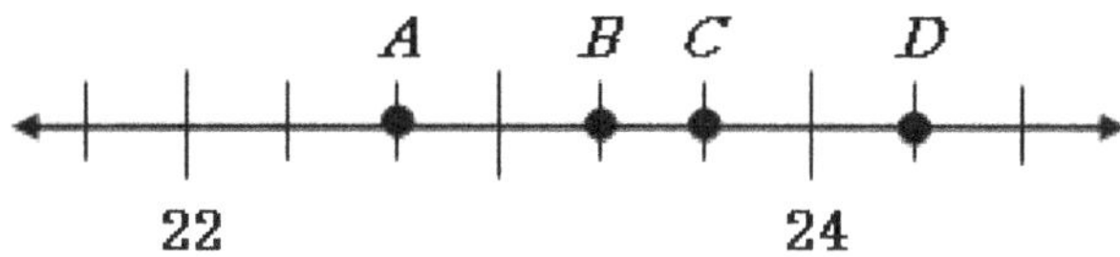

A Point *D* C Point *A*

B Point *B* D Point *C*

Common Core Standard 4.MD.4 – Measurement & Data

☐ **Which object on the number line is at a position less than $\frac{4}{8}$ and greater than $\frac{1}{8}$?**

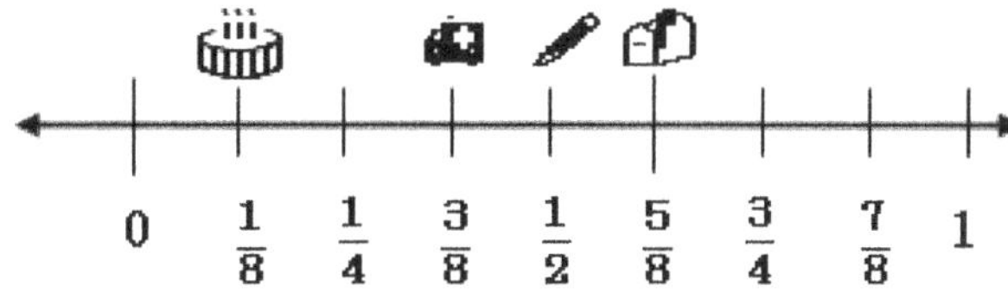

A Pencil C Birthday cake

B Ambulance D Mailbox

Common Core Standard 4.MD.4 – Measurement & Data

☐ **If ⬭ = $\frac{1}{4}$, △ = $\frac{1}{2}$, □ = $\frac{1}{8}$, and ☆ = $\frac{1}{3}$, which of the following would be in the correct order from greatest to least?**

A ☆ ⬭ □ △

B ⬭ △ □ ☆

C △ ☆ ⬭ □

D △ ⬭ ☆ □

Name ____________________

PRACTICE

Common Core Standard 4.MD.4 – Measurement & Data

☐ **Becky loves the World Cup and decided to track the number of goals scored in each game of her favority team. Use the plot below to find the correct answer to the questions.**

Game Number	1	2	3	4	5	6	7
Goals (x)	x x x x x x x	x	x x x x x x	x x x x x x x x	x x x x x	x x x x	x x x x x x

Each x = 1 goal scored

☐ **How many goals did Becky's team score in Game 3 and Game 6?**

A	Ten	C	Nine
B	Eleven	D	Eight

☐ **Which game did Becky's team score exactly one goal?**

A	Game 6	C	Game 4
B	Game 2	D	Game 1

☐ **What is the difference in the amount of goals scored in Game 1 versus Game 6?**

A	2 goals	C	4 goals
B	1 goal	D	3 goals

Name ________________________

ASSESSMENT

Common Core Standard 4.MD.4 – Measurement & Data

☐ **Point N best represents which number?**

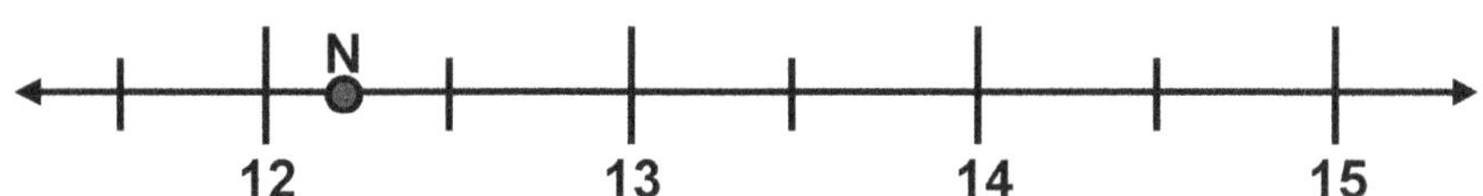

A $12\frac{1}{2}$

B $12\frac{3}{4}$

C $13\frac{1}{4}$

D $12\frac{1}{4}$

Common Core Standard 4.MD.4 – Measurement & Data

☐ **Which object on the number line is at a position greater than $4\frac{1}{4}$?**

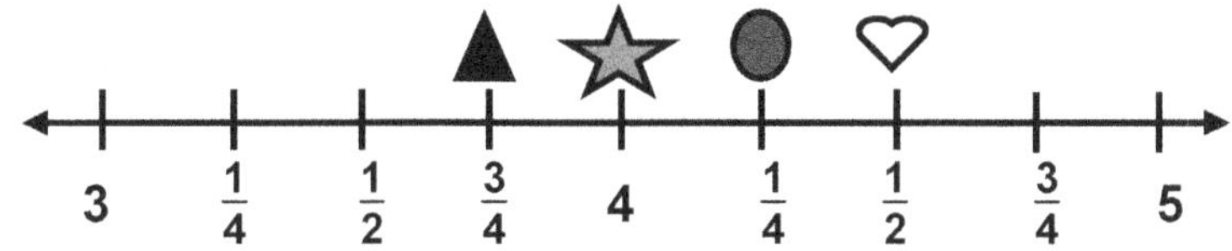

A Triangle

B Heart

C Oval

D Star

Common Core Standard 4.MD.4 – Measurement & Data

☐ **Tara's mother made cocoa for Tara, Julie, and Sydney. Tara's cup is $\frac{1}{8}$ full. Julie's cup is $\frac{3}{4}$ full, and Sydney's cup is $\frac{4}{8}$ full. Which answer shows the order of the cups from the greatest to the least amount of cocoa?**

A Sydney, Tara, Julie

B Julie, Tara, Sydney

C Tara, Sydney, Julie

D Julie, Sydney, Tara

Name ____________________________

ASSESSMENT

Common Core Standard 4.MD.4 – Measurement & Data

☐ **Mr. Reddy gave his classroom a math test on Friday. He was very happy to see that his class did well on the test. Use the plot below to find the correct answer to the questions.**

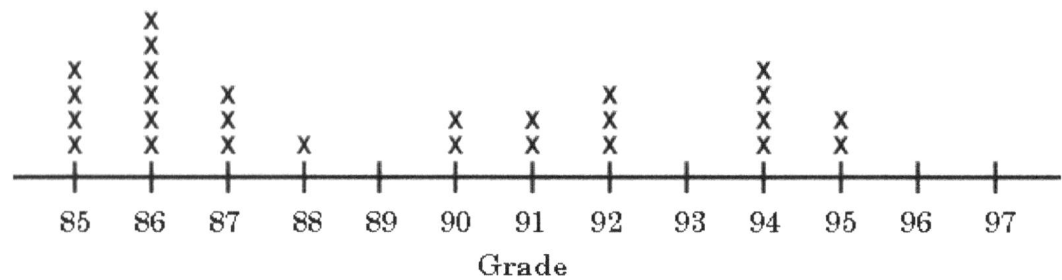

☐ **How many received a grade of 91 on their math test?**

A Three

B Four

C Two

D Five

☐ **What was the highest grade received by the students on the test?**

A 97

B 95

C 96

D 85

☐ **How many students scored less than a 90 on the math test?**

A 15 students

B 13 students

C 14 students

D 12 students

Name ___________________________

DIAGNOSTIC

Common Core Standard 4.MD.5 – Measurement & Data

☐ **Find the most likely measurement of the angle below.**

A 100°

B 45°

C 30°

D 80°

Common Core Standard 4.MD.5 – Measurement & Data

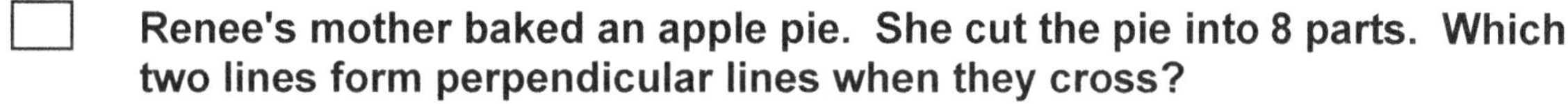

☐ **Renee's mother baked an apple pie. She cut the pie into 8 parts. Which two lines form perpendicular lines when they cross?**

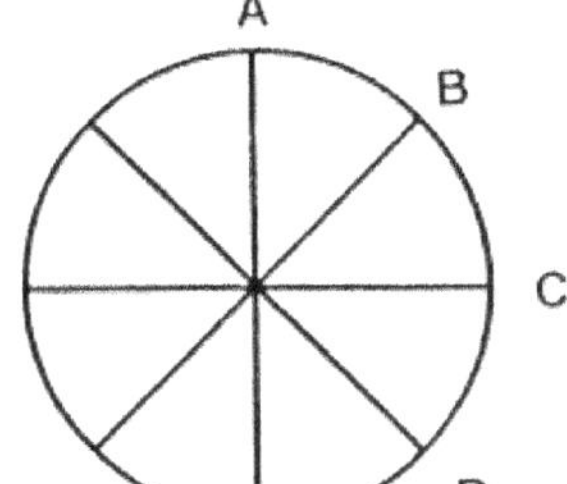

A (A and B)

B (A and D)

C (A and C)

D (B and C)

Common Core Standard 4.MD.5 – Measurement & Data

☐ **Find the most likely measurement of the angle below.**

A 180°

B 110°

C 100°

D 140°

Name ____________________

DIAGNOSTIC

Common Core Standard 4.MD.5 – Measurement & Data

☐ **Look at the sets of lines. Which answer shows a set of parallel lines?**

A D

B B

C C

D A

A

C 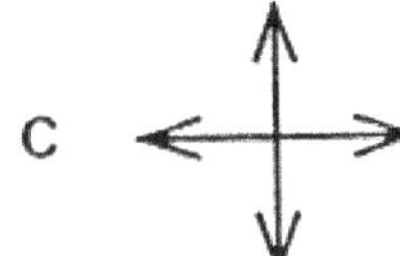

B

D 

Common Core Standard 4.MD.5 – Measurement & Data

☐ **Find the most likely measurement of the angle below.**

A 140°

B 70°

C 90°

D 115°

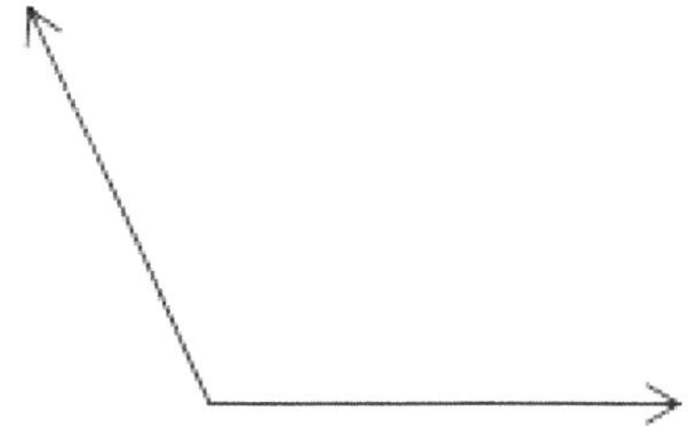

Common Core Standard 4.MD.5 – Measurement & Data

☐ **Look at the compass rose. Identify the type of lines the primary direction lines form.**

A Perpendicular

B Parallel

C Acute

D Curved

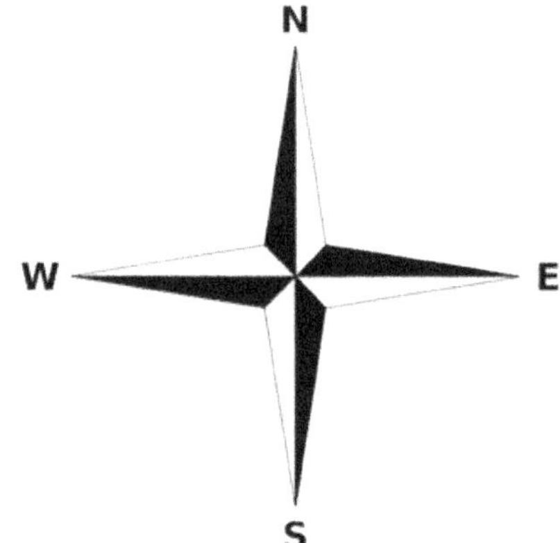

Name ____________________

PRACTICE

Common Core Standard 4.MD.5 – Measurement & Data

☐ Look at the map. Which streets are perpendicular?

A Jones Street and Avenue A

B Jones Street and Adams Avenue

C None of the streets

D Curved Road and Jones Street

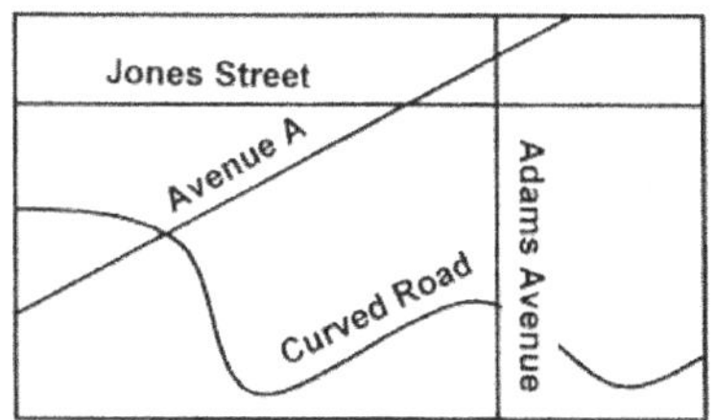

Common Core Standard 4.MD.5 – Measurement & Data

☐ Find the most likely measurement of the angle below.

A 300°

B 220°

C 350°

D 270°

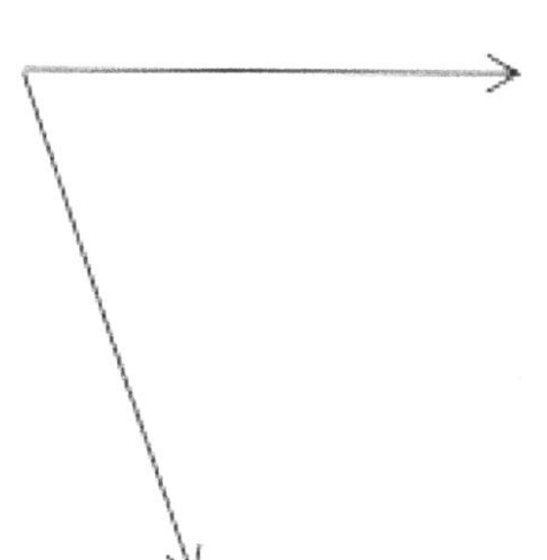

Common Core Standard 4.MD.5 – Measurement & Data

☐ Look at the calendar. Which kinds of lines are found on the calendar?

A Wavy

B Curved

C Parallel

D Diagonal

CALENDAR

Name ___________________________

PRACTICE

Common Core Standard 4.MD.5 – Measurement & Data

☐ **Find the most likely measurement of the angle below.**

A 150°

B 180°

C 90°

D 120°

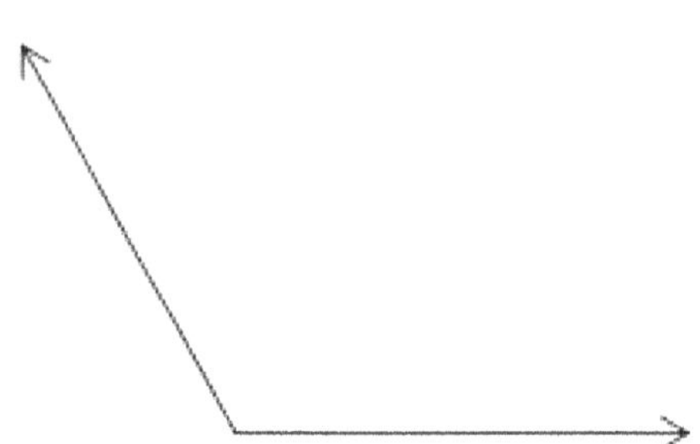

Common Core Standard 4.MD.5 – Measurement & Data

☐ **Look at the figure below. Which kinds of lines are found in the figure?**

A Point

B Ray

C Wavy

D Line

Common Core Standard 4.MD.5 – Measurement & Data

☐ **Find the most likely measurement of the angle below if the top line is at 180°.**

A 270°

B 345°

C 30°

D 250°

Name ____________________________

PRACTICE

Common Core Standard 4.MD.5 – Measurement & Data

☐ Find the most likely measurement of the angle below.

A 110°

B 160°

C 350°

D 180°

Common Core Standard 4.MD.5 – Measurement & Data

☐ Look at the figure below. Which kinds of lines are found in the figure?

A Point

B Ray

C Wavy Lines

D Intersecting Lines

Common Core Standard 4.MD.5 – Measurement & Data

☐ Find the most likely measurement of the angle below.

A 270°

B 60°

C 45°

D 90°

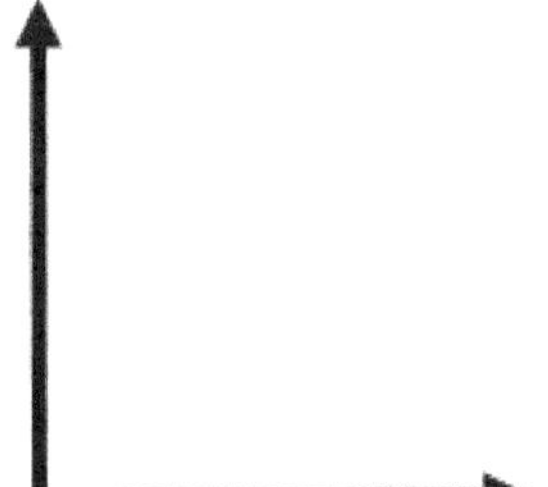

Name ______________________

PRACTICE

Common Core Standard 4.MD.5 – Measurement & Data

☐ Highway 28 and Highway 3 meet to form which kind of an angle?

A Straight

B Obtuse

C Acute

D Right

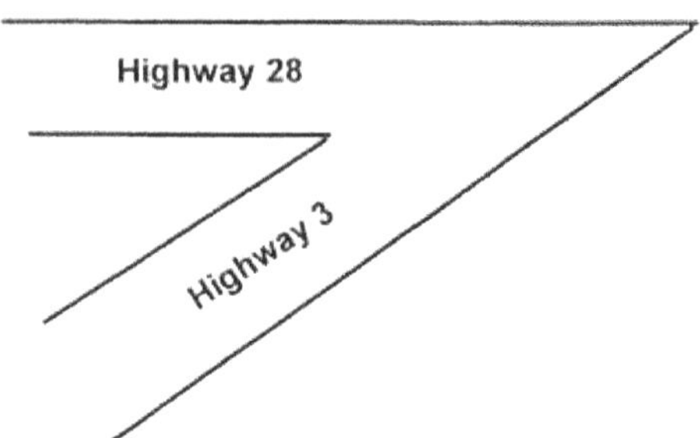

Common Core Standard 4.MD.5 – Measurement & Data

☐ Find the most likely measurement of the angle below.

A 340°

B 20°

C 60°

D 160°

Common Core Standard 4.MD.5 – Measurement & Data

☐ Which kind of angles form a square?

A Obtuse

B Right

C Straight

D Acute

Name ________________________

ASSESSEMENT

Common Core Standard 4.MD.5 – Measurement & Data

☐ **Find the most likely measurement of the angle below.**

A 190°

B 270°

C 150°

D 360°

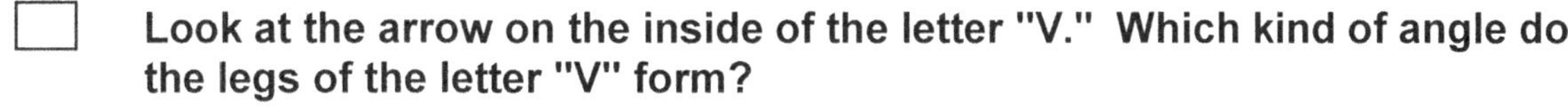

Common Core Standard 4.MD.5 – Measurement & Data

☐ **Look at the arrow on the inside of the letter "V." Which kind of angle do the legs of the letter "V" form?**

A Obtuse

B Right

C Straight

D Acute

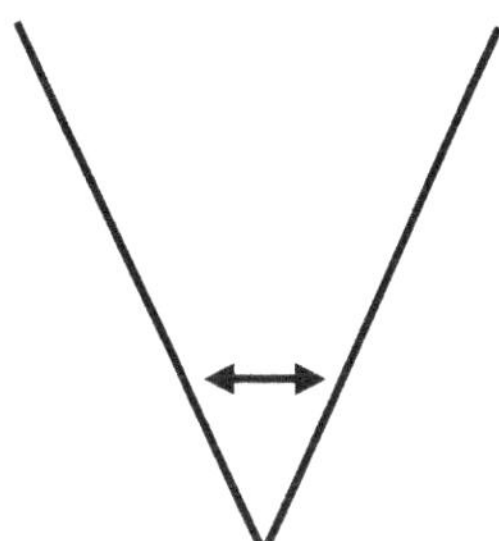

Common Core Standard 4.MD.5 – Measurement & Data

☐ **Find the most likely measurement of the angle below.**

A 70°

B 280°

C 90°

D 120°

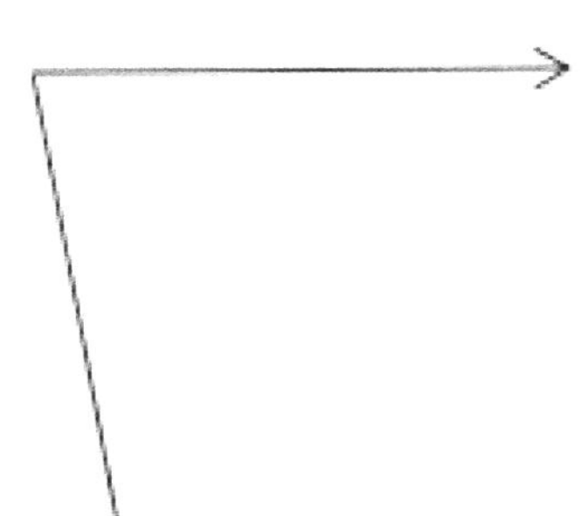

Name ___________________________

ASSESSMENT

Common Core Standard 4.MD.5 – Measurement & Data

☐ Look at the figure below. Which kind of line is found in the figure?

A Ray

B Segment

C Point

D Angle

Common Core Standard 4.MD.5 – Measurement & Data

☐ Find the most likely measurement of the angle below.

A 240°

B 20°

C 60°

D 70°

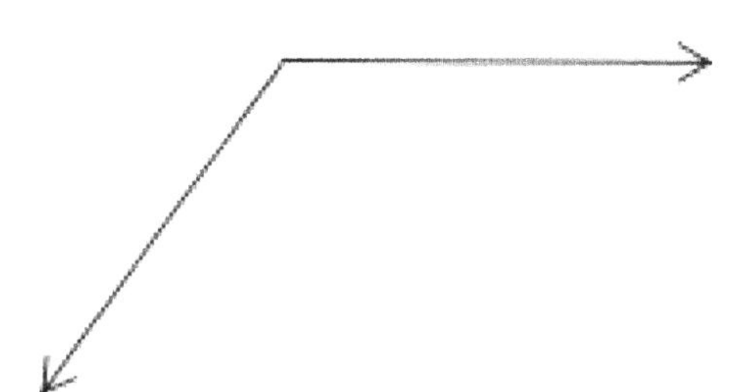

Common Core Standard 4.MD.5 – Measurement & Data

☐ In the closed figure below, which angle is a right angle?

A 5

B 1

C 3

D 2

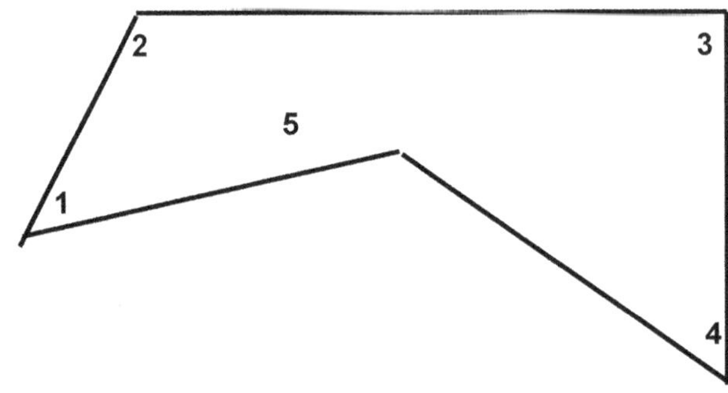

Name ____________________________

DIAGNOSTIC

Common Core Standard 4.MD.6 – Measurement & Data

☐ **Look at the protractor below. What is the angle measurement for lines *DAF*?**

A 105°

B 180°

C 75°

D 90°

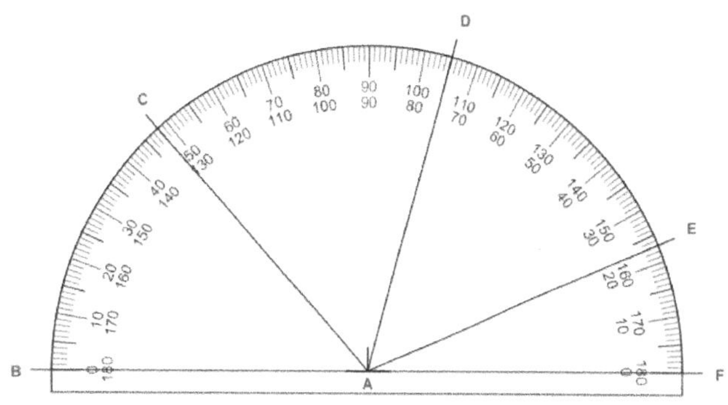

Common Core Standard 4.MD.6 – Measurement & Data

☐ **Look at the protractor below. What is the angle measurement for lines *CAB?***

A 48°

B 130°

C 180°

D 105°

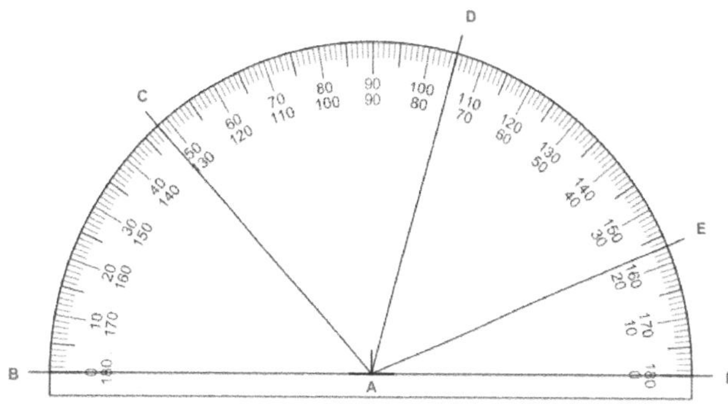

Common Core Standard 4.MD.6 – Measurement & Data

☐ **Look at the protractor below. What is the angle measurement for lines *EAF?***

A 157°

B 180°

C 35°

D 23°

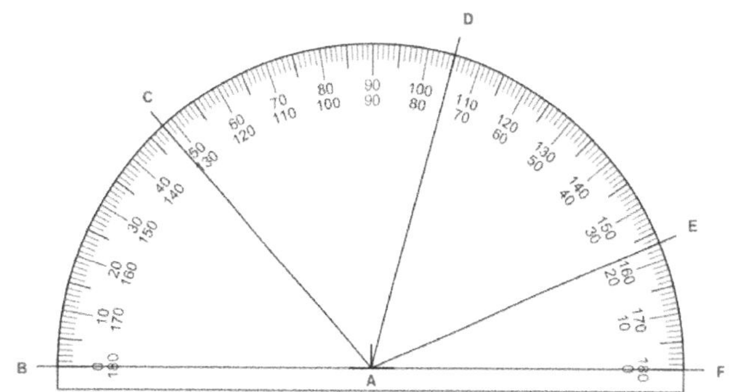

Name ____________________

DIAGNOSTIC

Common Core Standard 4.MD.6 – Measurement & Data

☐ Look at the protractor below. What is the angle measurement for lines *DAB*?

A 70º

B 109º

C 169º

D 180º

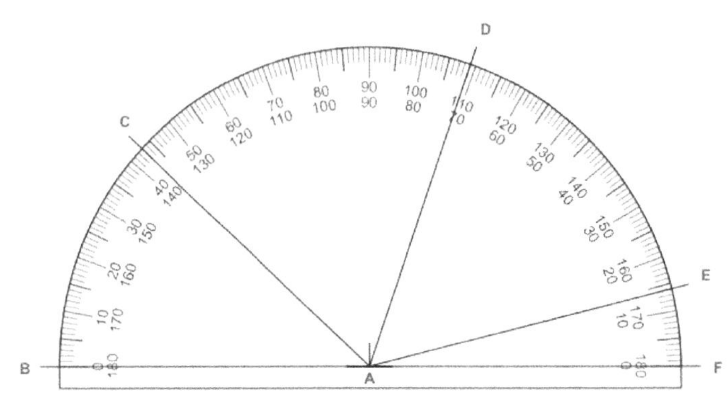

Common Core Standard 4.MD.6 – Measurement & Data

☐ Look at the protractor below. What is the angle measurement for lines *DAF?*

A 43º

B 109º

C 80º

D 71º

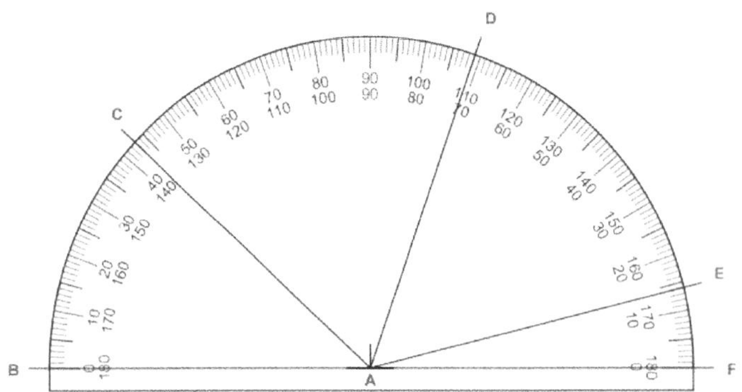

Common Core Standard 4.MD.6 – Measurement & Data

☐ Look at the protractor below. What is the angle measurement for lines *EAB?*

A 14º

B 170º

C 166º

D 180º

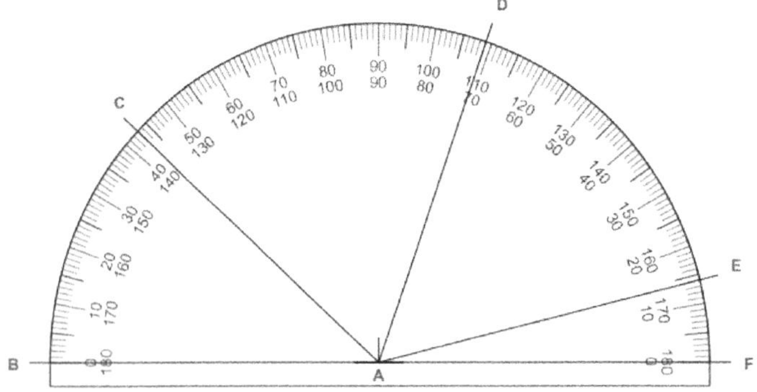

Name ____________________________

PRACTICE

Common Core Standard 4.MD.6 – Measurement & Data

☐ **Look at the protractor below. What is the angle measurement for lines *EAB*?**

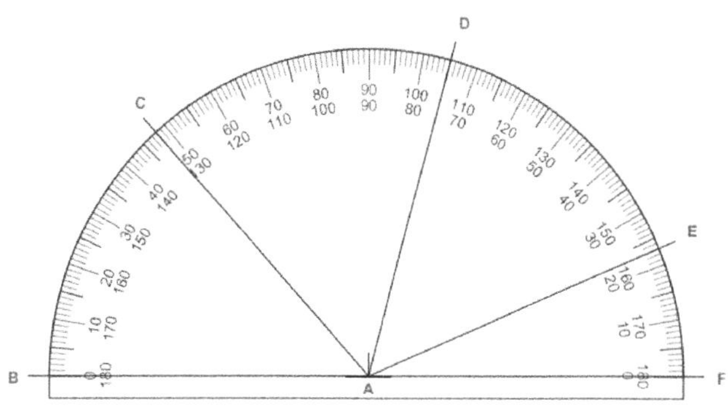

A **157°**

B **165°**

C **23°**

D **180°**

Common Core Standard 4.MD.6 – Measurement & Data

☐ **Look at the protractor below. What is the angle measurement for lines *CAF?***

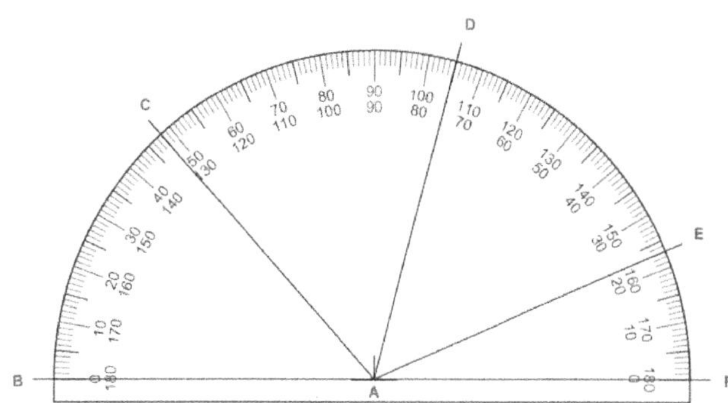

A **48°**

B **132°**

C **140°**

D **180°**

Common Core Standard 4.MD.6 – Measurement & Data

☐ **Look at the protractor below. What is the angle measurement for lines *DAB?***

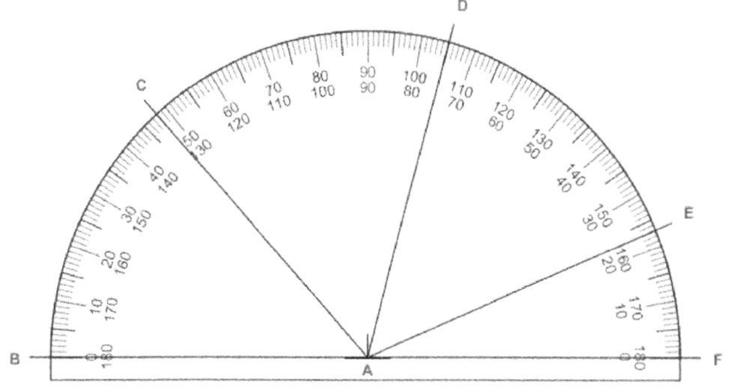

A **75°**

B **110°**

C **105°**

D **90°**

Name ____________________________

PRACTICE

Common Core Standard 4.MD.6 – Measurement & Data

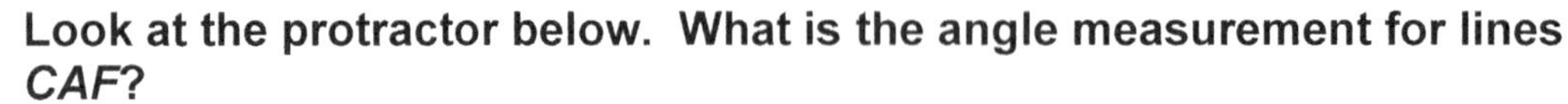

☐ **Look at the protractor below. What is the angle measurement for lines *CAF*?**

A 137°

B 43°

C 183°

D 166°

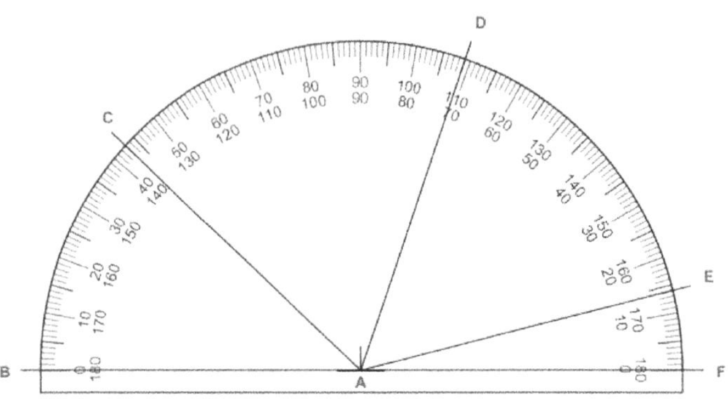

Common Core Standard 4.MD.6 – Measurement & Data

☐ **Look at the protractor below. What is the angle measurement for lines *DAF?***

A 175°

B 90°

C 81°

D 99°

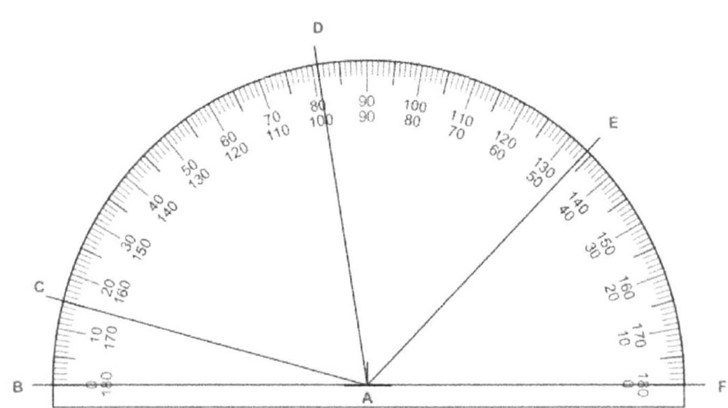

Common Core Standard 4.MD.6 – Measurement & Data

☐ **Look at the protractor below. What is the angle measurement for lines *EAB?***

A 180°

B 56°

C 134°

D 0°

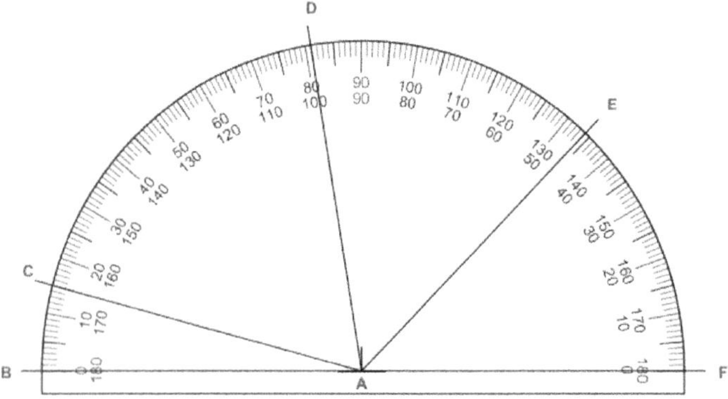

Name ______________________________

PRACTICE

Common Core Standard 4.MD.6 – Measurement & Data

☐ **Look at the protractor below. What is the angle measurement for lines *CAB*?**

A **151°**

B **160°**

C **29°**

D **88°**

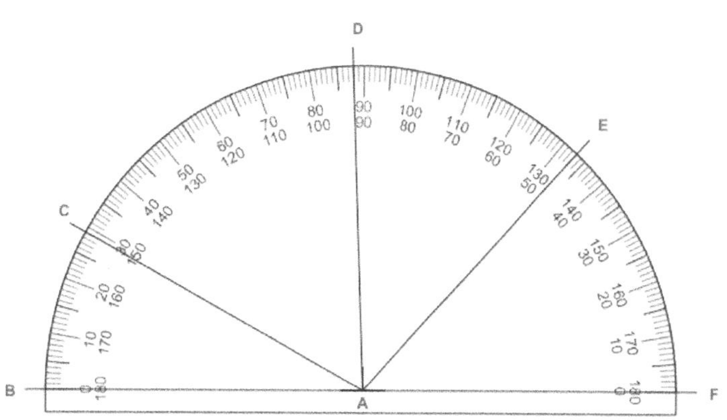

Common Core Standard 4.MD.6 – Measurement & Data

☐ **Look at the protractor below. What is the angle measurement for lines *DAF?***

A **92°**

B **90°**

C **80°**

D **180°**

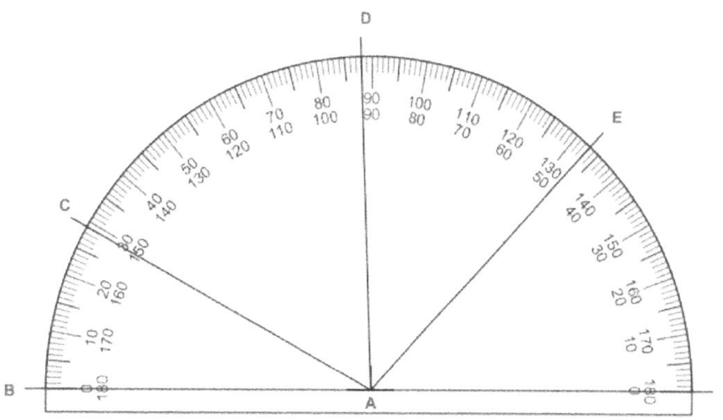

Common Core Standard 4.MD.6 – Measurement & Data

☐ **Look at the protractor below. What is the angle measurement for lines *EAB?***

A **55°**

B **133°**

C **135°**

D **53°**

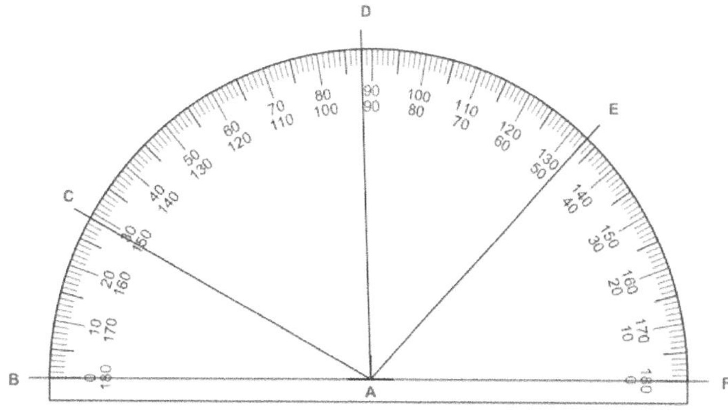

Name ____________________________

PRACTICE

Common Core Standard 4.MD.6 – Measurement & Data

☐ **Look at the protractor below. What is the angle measurement for lines *DAB*?**

A **78°**

B **80°**

C **103°**

D **100°**

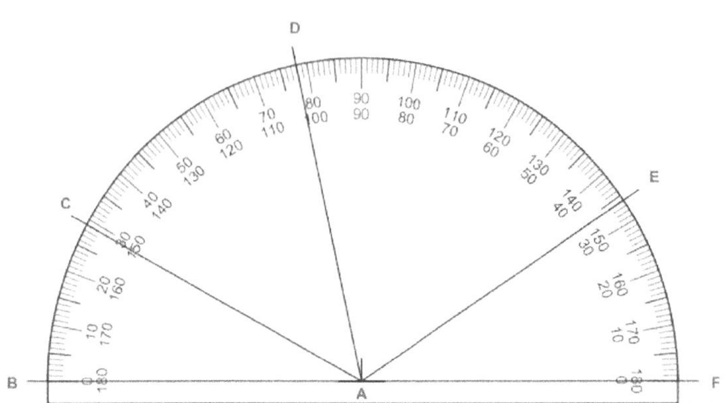

Common Core Standard 4.MD.6 – Measurement & Data

☐ **Look at the protractor below. What is the angle measurement for lines *CAF?***

A **150°**

B **30°**

C **151°**

D **180°**

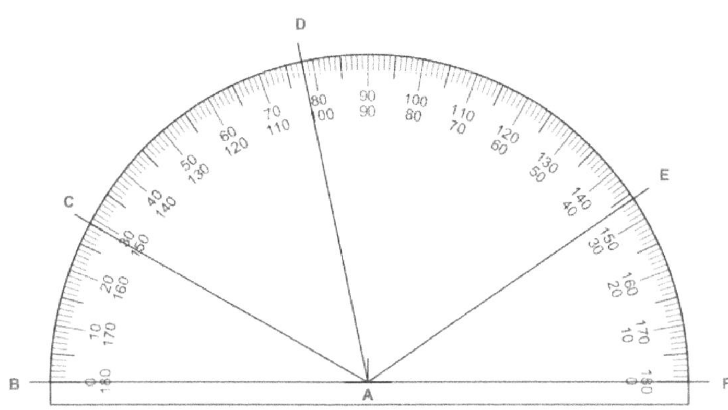

Common Core Standard 4.MD.6 – Measurement & Data

☐ **Look at the protractor below. What is the angle measurement for lines *EAF?***

A **147°**

B **34°**

C **33°**

D **150°**

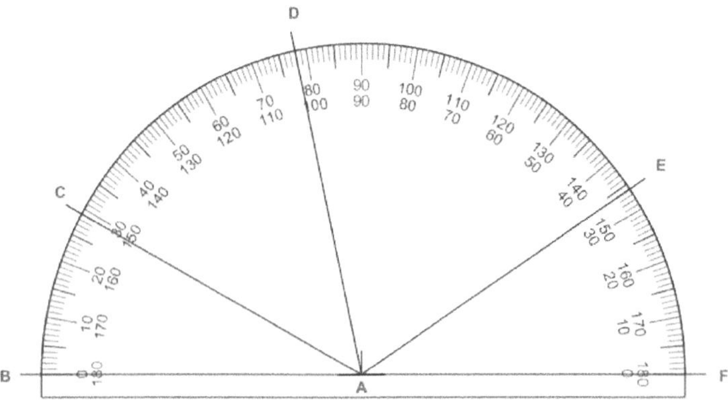

Name ____________________________

ASSESSMENT

Common Core Standard 4.MD.6 – Measurement & Data

☐ **Look at the protractor below. What is the angle measurement for lines *CAB*?**

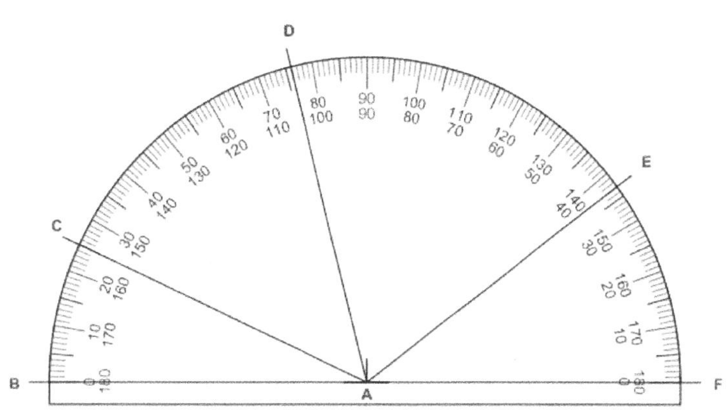

A **180º**

B **155º**

C **35º**

D **25º**

Common Core Standard 4.MD.6 – Measurement & Data

☐ **Look at the protractor below. What is the angle measurement for lines *CAF?***

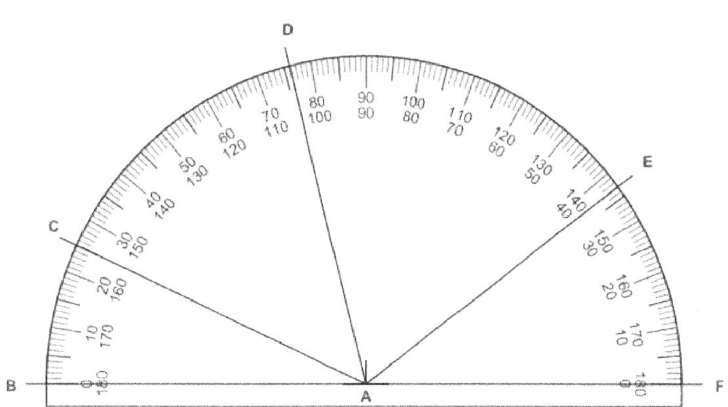

A **25º**

B **155º**

C **35º**

D **165º**

Common Core Standard 4.MD.6 – Measurement & Data

☐ **Look at the protractor below. What is the angle measurement for lines *DAF?***

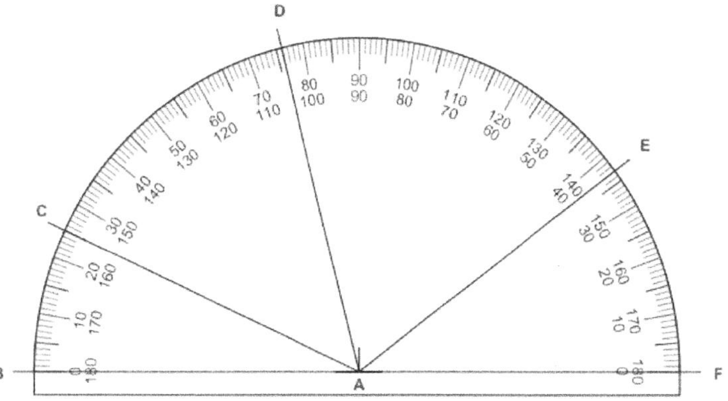

A **76º**

B **116º**

C **104º**

D **84º**

Name ___________________________

ASSESSMENT

Common Core Standard 4.MD.6 – Measurement & Data

☐ **Look at the protractor below. What is the angle measurement for lines *DAB*?**

A 113°

B 70°

C 115°

D 67°

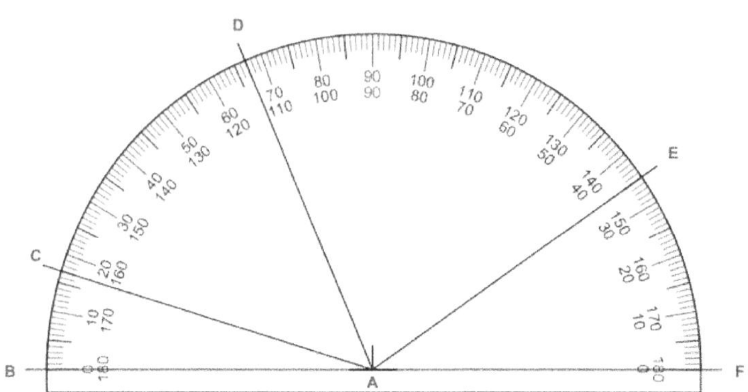

Common Core Standard 4.MD.6 – Measurement & Data

☐ **Look at the protractor below. What is the angle measurement for lines *CAF?***

A 17°

B 18°

C 163°

D 180°

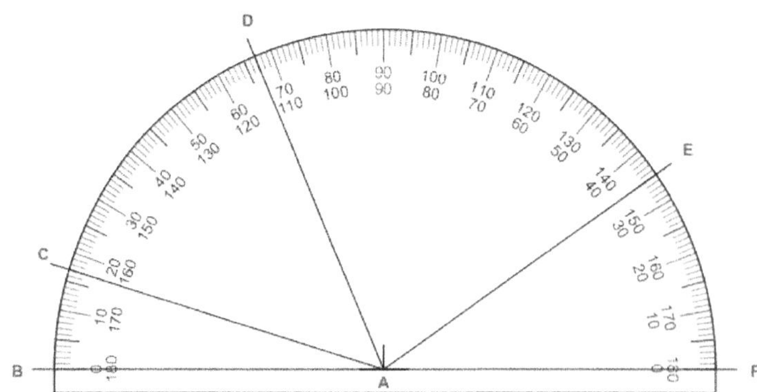

Common Core Standard 4.MD.6 – Measurement & Data

☐ **Look at the protractor below. What is the angle measurement for lines *DAF?***

A 113°

B 67°

C 72°

D 145°

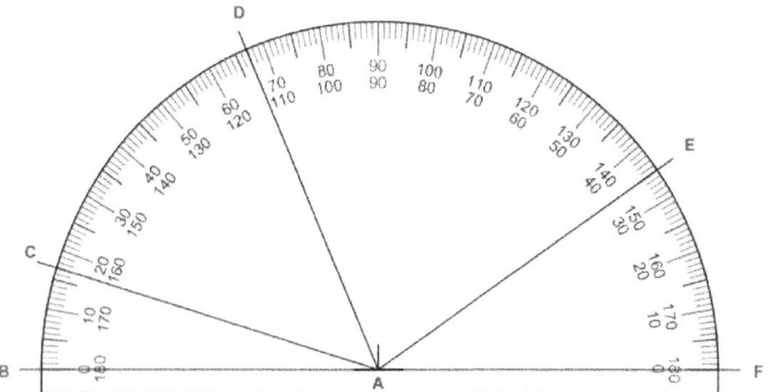

Name ____________________

DIAGNOSTIC

Common Core Standard 4.MD.7 – Measurement & Data

☐ **Find the measurement for ∠ABD if ∠ABC = 55° and ∠CBD= 25°.**

A 30°

B 80°

C 90°

D 55°

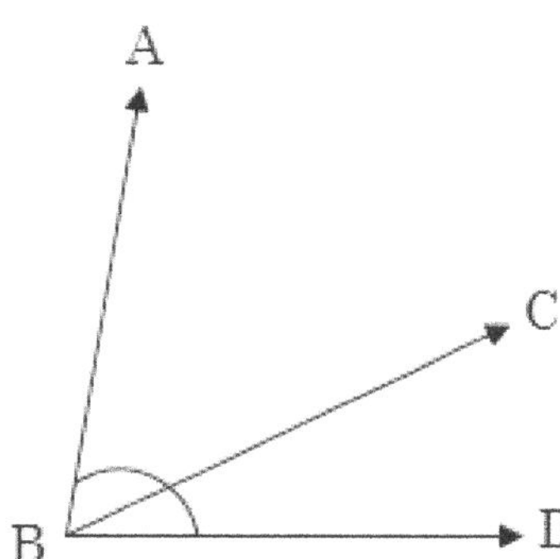

Common Core Standard 4.MD.7 – Measurement & Data

☐ **Find the measurement for ∠ GFH if ∠ EFH = 120° and ∠ EFG = 30°.**

A 80°

B 150°

C 90°

D 30°

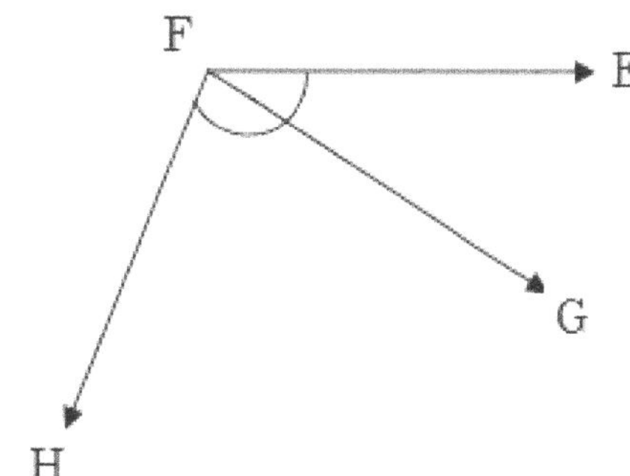

Common Core Standard 4.MD.7 – Measurement & Data

☐ **Find the measurement for ∠ IJL if ∠ IJK = 80° and ∠ KJL = 60°.**

A 130°

B 20°

C 80°

D 140°

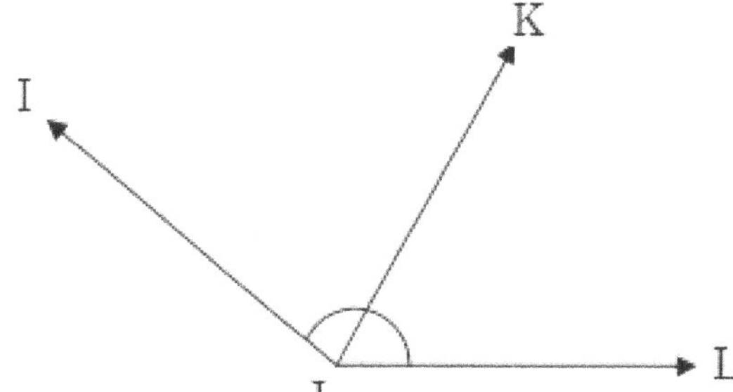

Name ____________________

DIAGNOSTIC

Common Core Standard 4.MD.7 – Measurement & Data

☐ **Find the measurement for ∠ CBD if ∠ ABD = 130° and ∠ ABC= 90°.**

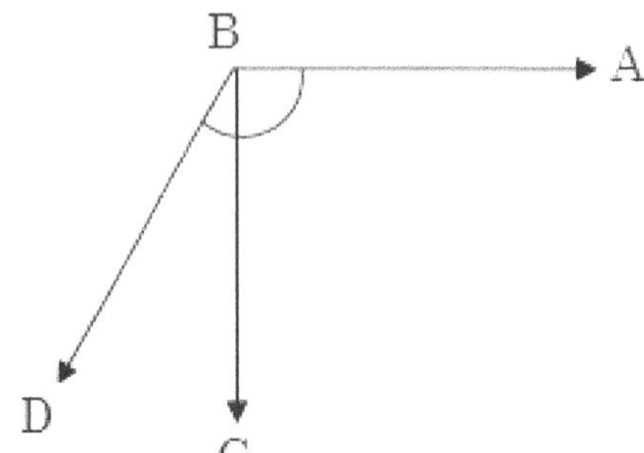

A 30°

B 240°

C 40°

D 90°

Common Core Standard 4.MD.7 – Measurement & Data

☐ **Find the measurement for ∠ EFH if ∠ GFH = 25° and ∠ EFG = 45°.**

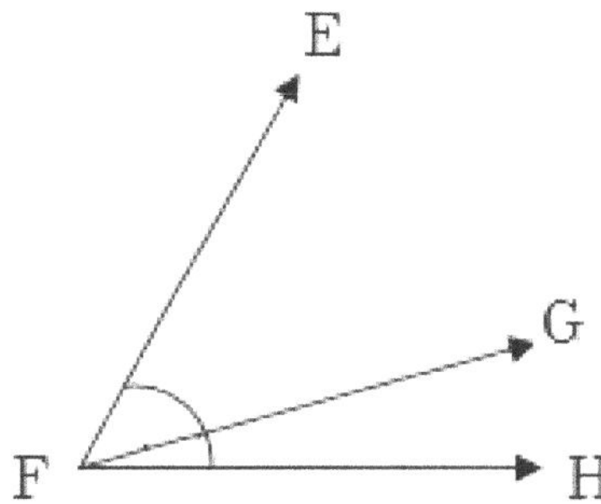

A 70°

B 20°

C 80°

D 45°

Common Core Standard 4.MD.7 – Measurement & Data

☐ **Find the measurement for ∠ KJL if ∠ IJL = 130° and ∠ IJK = 100°.**

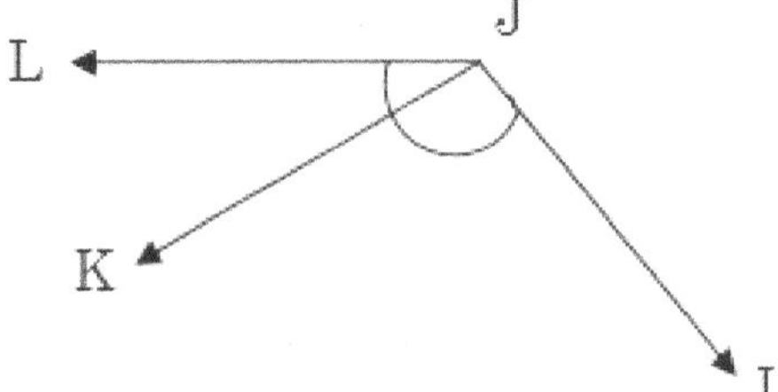

A 230°

B 40°

C 100°

D 30°

Name ____________________

PRACTICE

Common Core Standard 4.MD.7 – Measurement & Data

☐ **Find the measurement for ∠ ABD if ∠ ABC = 15° and ∠ CBD= 45°.**

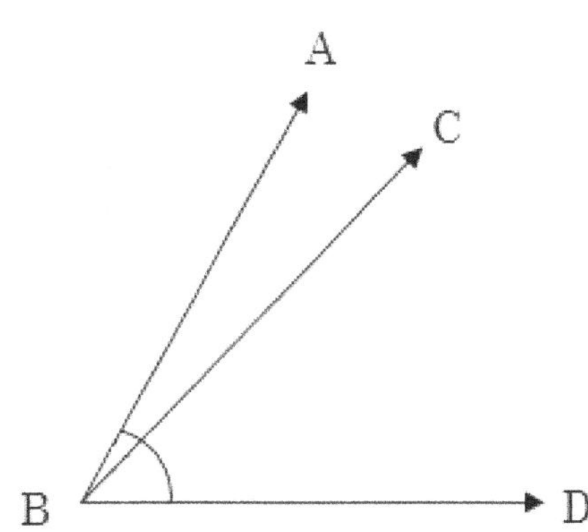

A 60°

B 80°

C 30°

D 45°

Common Core Standard 4.MD.7 – Measurement & Data

☐ **Find the measurement for ∠ GFH if ∠ EFH = 150° and ∠ EFG = 75°.**

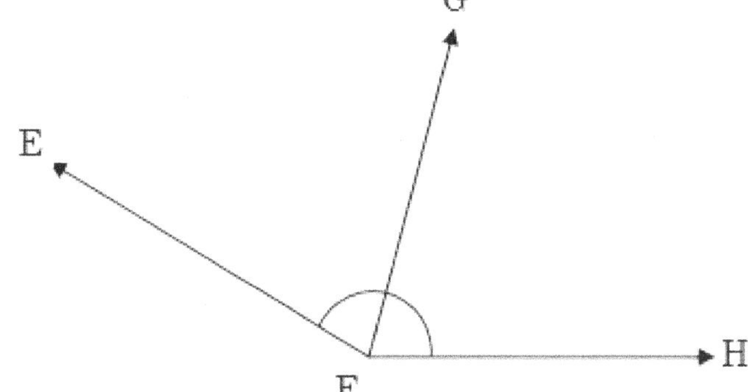

A 110°

B 150°

C 75°

D 80°

Common Core Standard 4.MD.7 – Measurement & Data

☐ **Find the measurement for ∠ IJL if ∠ IJK = 70° and ∠ KJL = 40°.**

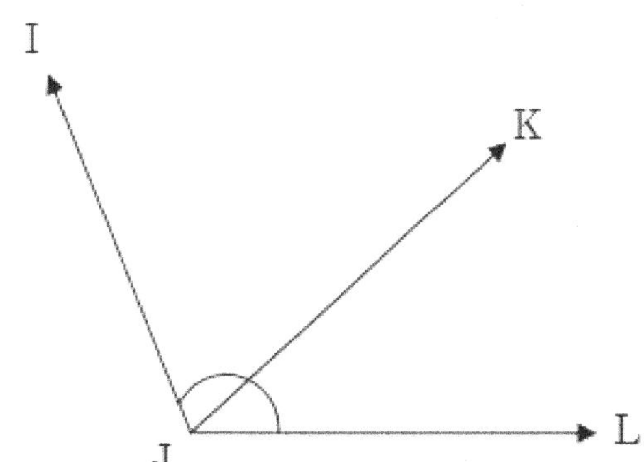

A 30°

B 112°

C 70°

D 110°

Name ____________________________

PRACTICE

Common Core Standard 4.MD.7 – Measurement & Data

☐ Find the measurement for ∠ ABC if ∠ ABD = 80° and ∠ CBD= 40°.

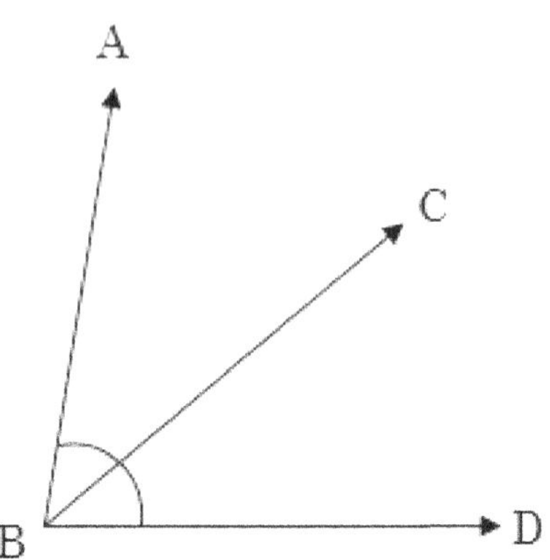

A 80°

B 120°

C 40°

D 45°

Common Core Standard 4.MD.7 – Measurement & Data

☐ Find the measurement for ∠ EFH if ∠ GFH = 55° and ∠ EFG = 55°.

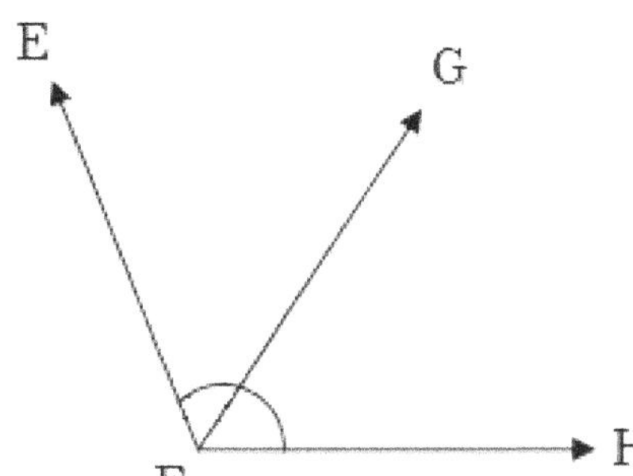

A 100°

B 120°

C 55°

D 110°

Common Core Standard 4.MD.7 – Measurement & Data

☐ Find the measurement for ∠ KJL if ∠ IJL = 80° and ∠ IJK = 30°.

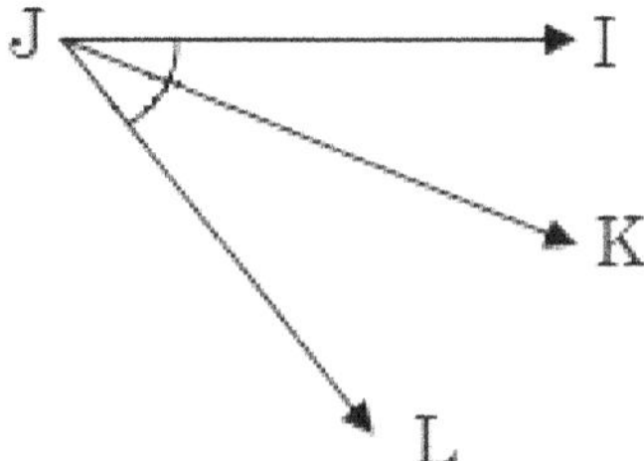

A 50°

B 60°

C 110°

D 30°

Name ____________________

PRACTICE

Common Core Standard 4.MD.7 – Measurement & Data

☐ 
Find the measurement for ∠ ABD if ∠ ABC = 50° and ∠ CBD= 100°.

A 50°

B 140°

C 100°

D 150°

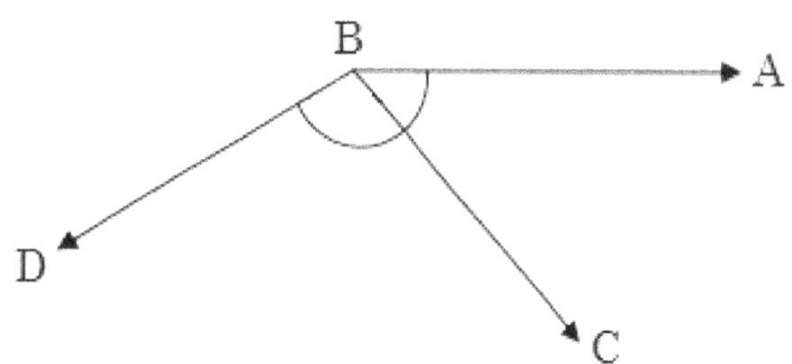

Common Core Standard 4.MD.7 – Measurement & Data

☐ 
Find the measurement for ∠ EFG if ∠ EFH = 160° and ∠ GFH = 70°.

A 160°

B 90°

C 230°

D 80°

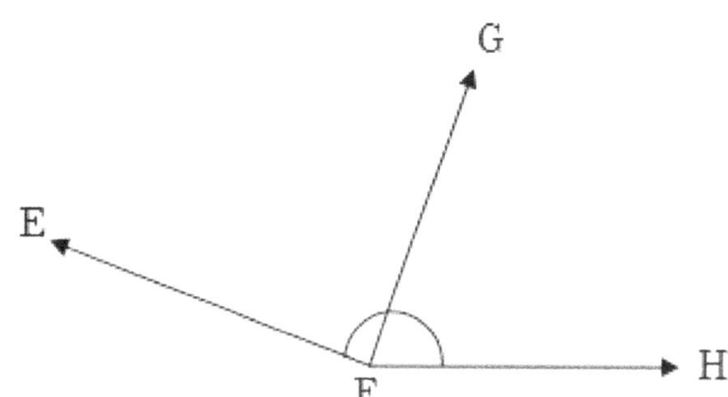

Common Core Standard 4.MD.7 – Measurement & Data

☐ Find the measurement for ∠ IJL if ∠ IJK = 95° and ∠ KJL = 55°.

A 40°

B 160°

C 95°

D 150°

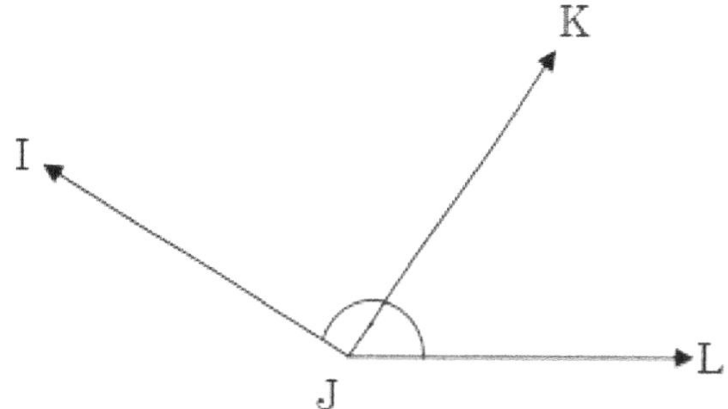

Name ____________________________

PRACTICE

Common Core Standard 4.MD.7 – Measurement & Data

☐ **Find the measurement for ∠ ABC if ∠ ABD = 120° and ∠ CBD= 60°.**

A 60°

B 70°

C 120°

D 180°

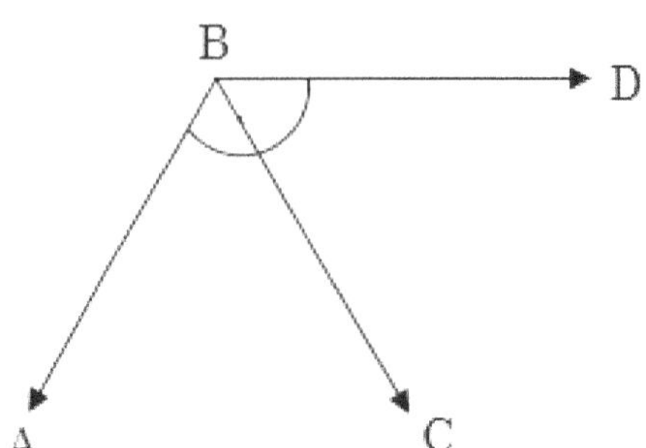

Common Core Standard 4.MD.7 – Measurement & Data

☐ **Find the measurement for ∠ EFH if ∠ GFH = 35° and ∠ EFG = 45°.**

A 10°

B 90°

C 80°

D 45°

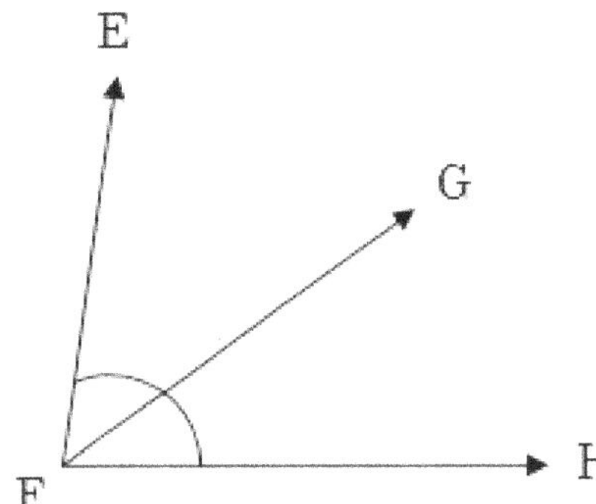

Common Core Standard 4.MD.7 – Measurement & Data

☐ **Find the measurement for ∠ KJL if ∠ IJL = 140° and ∠ IJK = 75°.**

A 215°

B 65°

C 70°

D 140°

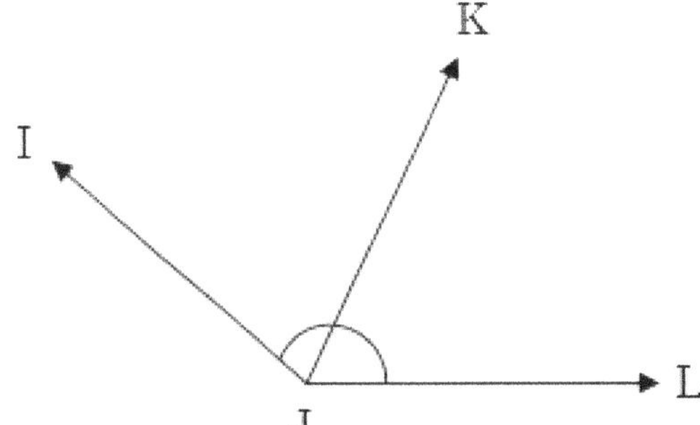

Name ___________________________

ASSESSMENT

Common Core Standard 4.MD.7 – Measurement & Data

☐ **Find the measurement for ∠ ABD if ∠ ABC = 81° and ∠ CBD = 34°.**

A **110°**

B **115°**

C **47°**

D **81°**

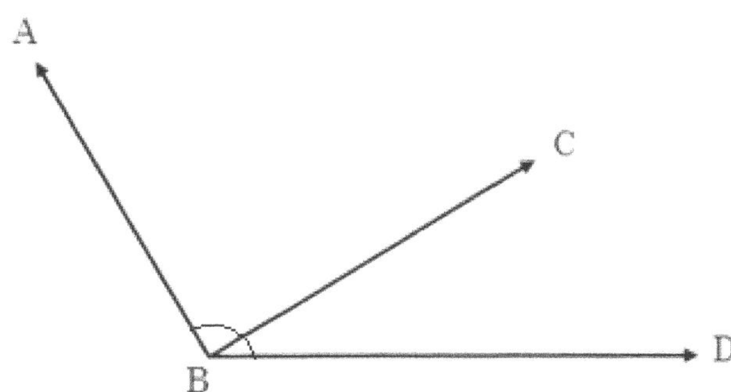

Common Core Standard 4.MD.7 – Measurement & Data

☐ **Find the measurement for ∠ GFH if ∠ EFG = 68° and ∠ EFH = 100°.**

A **100°**

B **40°**

C **168°**

D **32°**

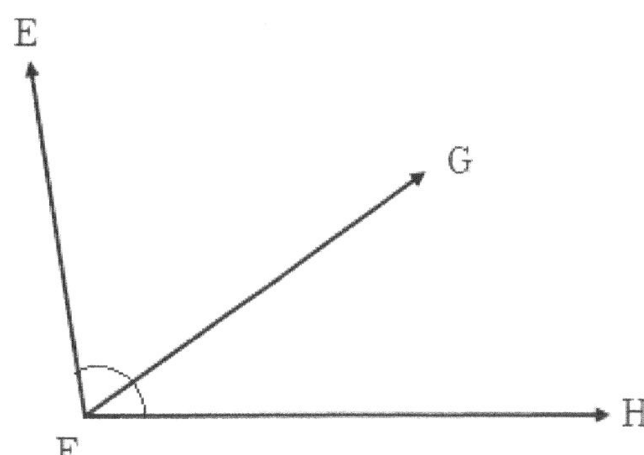

Common Core Standard 4.MD.7 – Measurement & Data

☐ **Find the measurement for ∠ IJL if ∠ IJK = 78° and ∠ KJL = 62°.**

A **140°**

B **16°**

C **62°**

D **150°**

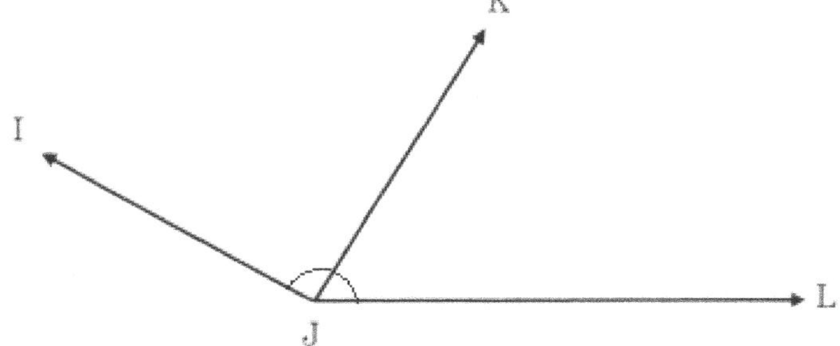

Name ______________________________

ASSESSMENT

Common Core Standard 4.MD.7 – Measurement & Data

☐ Find the measurement for ∠ ABC if ∠ ABD = 130° and ∠ CBD = 42°.

A 172°

B 90°

C 88°

D 130°

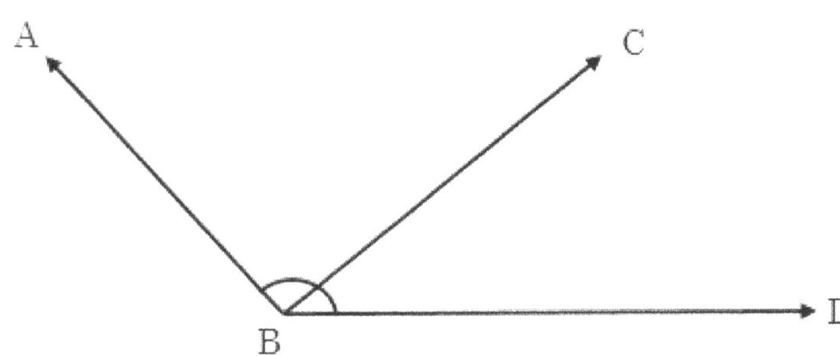

Common Core Standard 4.MD.7 – Measurement & Data

☐ Find the measurement for ∠ EFH if ∠ GFH = 37° and ∠ EFG = 113°.

A 140°

B 150°

C 113°

D 76°

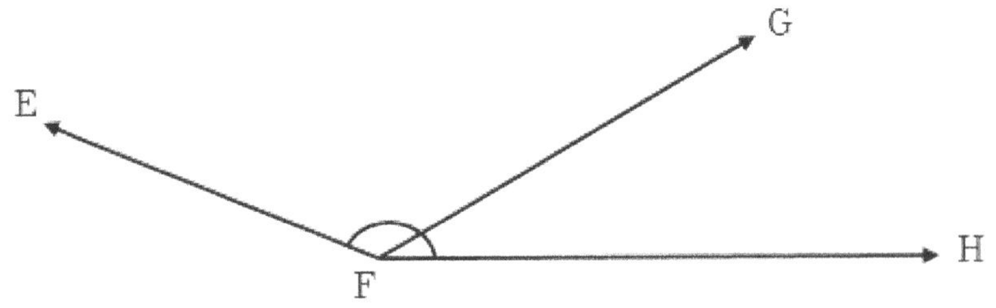

Common Core Standard 4.MD.7 – Measurement & Data

☐ Find the measurement for ∠ KJL if ∠ IJL = 135° and ∠ IJK = 95°.

A 230°

B 50°

C 95°

D 40°

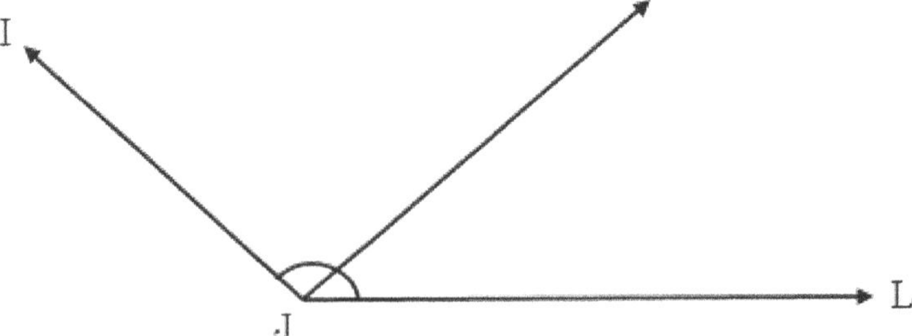

Name ___________________________

DIAGNOSTIC

Common Core Standard 4.G.1 – Geometry

☐ What kind of angle is angle "A" in the trapezoid?

A Acute

B Right

C Straight

D Obtuse

Common Core Standard 4.G.1 – Geometry

☐ Look at the hands on the clock. Which angle do they form?

A Right

B Acute

C Obtuse

D Straight

Common Core Standard 4.G.1 – Geometry

☐ What angle is formed when perpendicular lines meet?

A Right

B Straight

C Obtuse

D Acute

Name ____________________________

DIAGNOSTIC

Common Core Standard 4.G.1 – Geometry

☐ Which pair of angles could you put together to form a right angle?

A	B
B	D
C	C
D	A

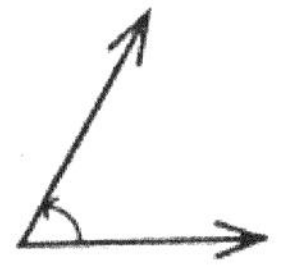

Common Core Standard 4.G.1 – Geometry

☐ Look at the drawing of the desk. Based on the drawing, the top of the desk *appears* to be made up of which of the following angles?

A Right angles only

B Right and obtuse angles

C Right and acute angles

D Acute and obtuse angles

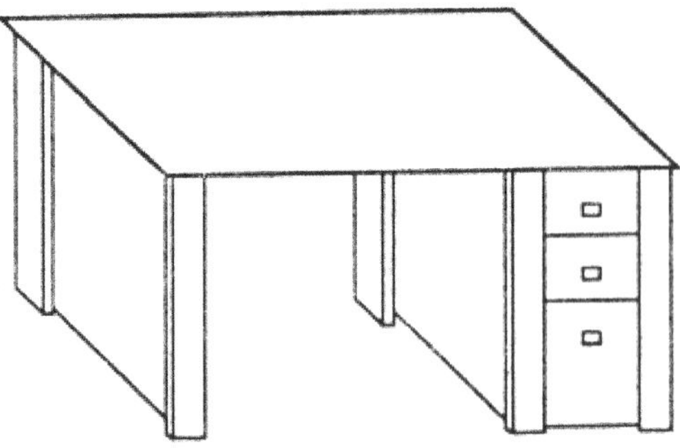

Common Core Standard 4.G.1 – Geometry

☐ Look at the angles. Which of the following is the *greatest* angle?

A	C
B	B
C	D
D	A

A

C

B

D

Name ___________________________

PRACTICE

Common Core Standard 4.G.1 – Geometry

☐ **Which triangle has an obtuse angle?**

A 

C 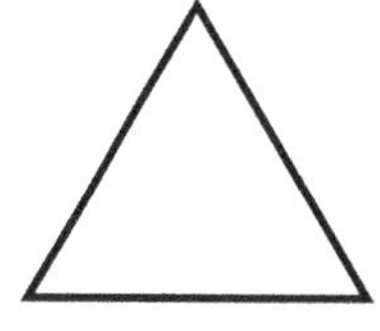

B 

D 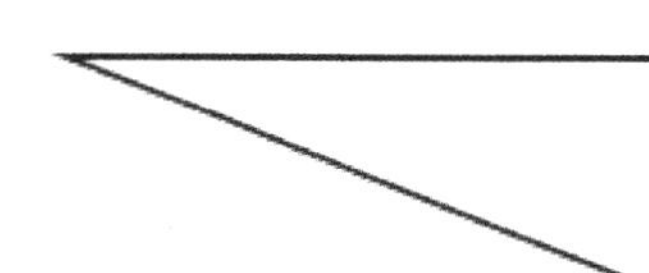

Common Core Standard 4.G.1 – Geometry

☐ **Look at the telescope and the angle it forms. What kind of angle is formed beneath the telescope?**

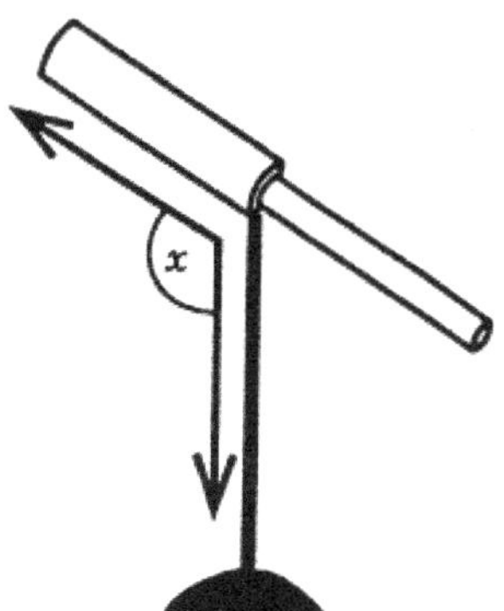

A Obtuse

B Right

C Acute

D Straight

Common Core Standard 4.G.1 – Geometry

☐ **What kind of angle is angle "B" in the trapezoid?**

A Acute

B Right

C Straight

D Obtuse

Name ____________________________

PRACTICE

Common Core Standard 4.G.1 – Geometry

☐ Look at the angles. Which of the following is the *least* angle?

A Angle B

B Angle A

C Angle D

D Angle C

A

C

B

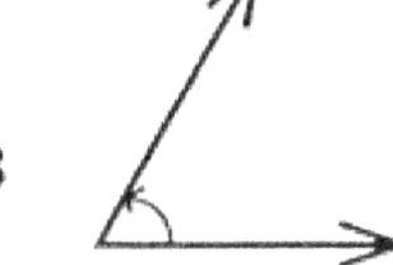

D

Common Core Standard 4.G.1 – Geometry

☐ Which of the angles represents an obtuse angle?

A Angle C

B Angle B

C Angle A

D Angle D

A

C

B

D

Common Core Standard 4.G.1 – Geometry

☐ The shelf is made up of 3 sections. Which of the following is an angle found in one of the sections of the shelf?

A Obtuse angle only

B Right angle only

C Right and obtuse angles

D Acute angle only

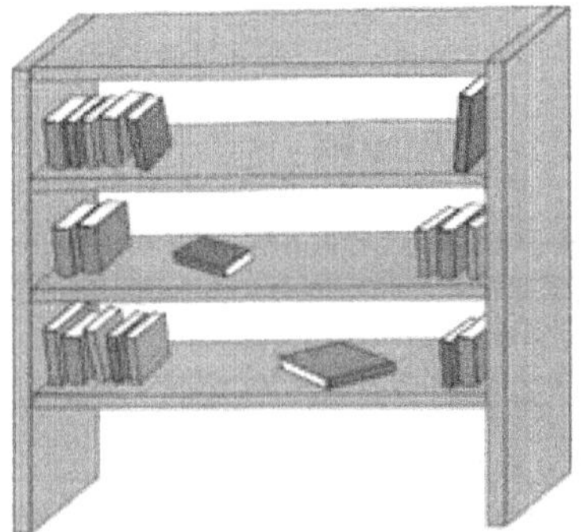

Name ______________________________

PRACTICE

Common Core Standard 4.G.1 – Geometry

☐ **In the closed figure below, which angles are obtuse angles?**

A 5,1

B 1,4

C 3,2

D 2,5

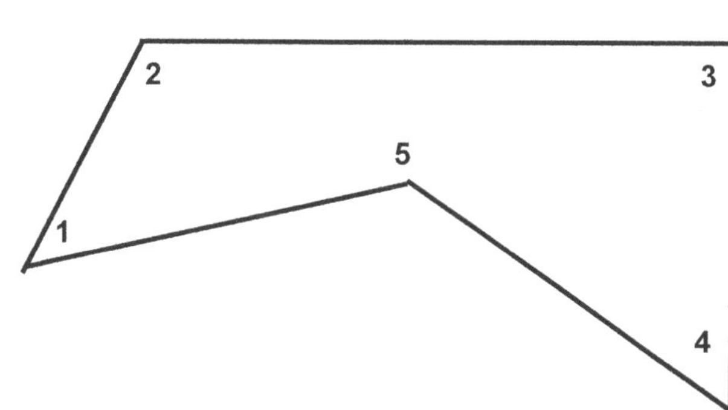

Common Core Standard 4.G.1 – Geometry

☐ **Look at the hands on each clock. Which clock's hands form an obtuse angle?**

A C

B B

C D

D A

A

B

C

D

Common Core Standard 4.G.1 – Geometry

☐ **Look at the arrow on the inside of the letter "V." Which kind of angle do the legs of the letter "V" form?**

A Obtuse

B Right

C Straight

D Acute

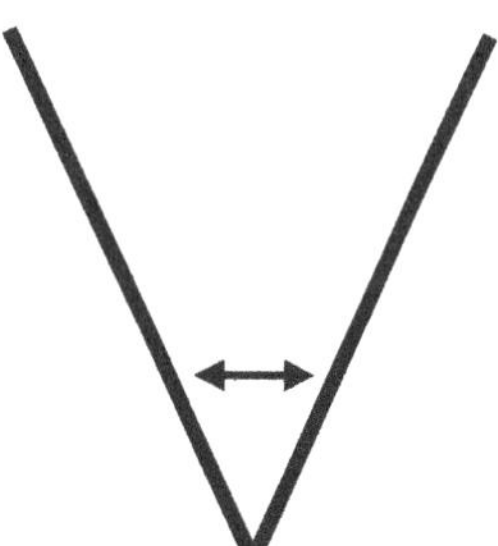

Name ____________________

PRACTICE

Common Core Standard 4.G.1 – Geometry

☐ **Which 2 angles could be put together to form an acute angle?**

A Angle C and D

B Angle B and C

C Angle A and C

D Angle B and D

A

B

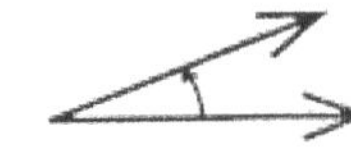

C

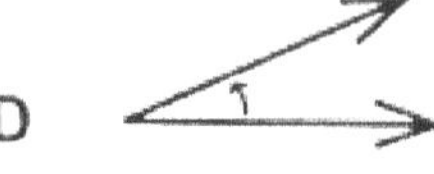

D

Common Core Standard 4.G.1 – Geometry

☐ **Which answer correctly describes the angle shown on the protractor?**

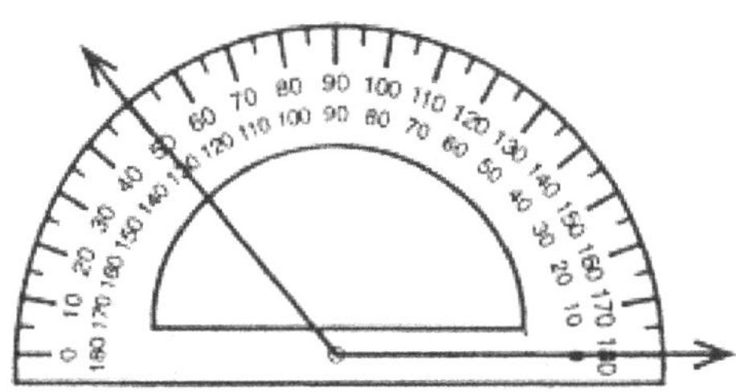

A Acute angle of 50°

B Obtuse angle of 50°

C Obtuse angle of 130°

D Acute angle of 130°

Common Core Standard 4.G.1 – Geometry

☐ **Which answer best describes the angle formed by the lawn chair?**

A Acute

B Right

C Obtuse

D Straight

Name ____________________

ASSESSMENT

Common Core Standard 4.G.1 – Geometry

☐ Angle *M* in the figure below appears to be which kind of angle?

A Right

B Straight

C Obtuse

D Acute

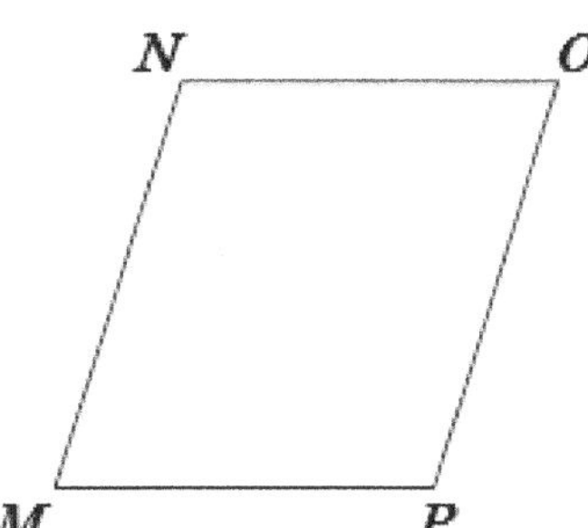

Common Core Standard 4.G.1 – Geometry

☐ What angle is formed when perpendicular lines meet?

A Obtuse

B Acute

C Right

D Straight

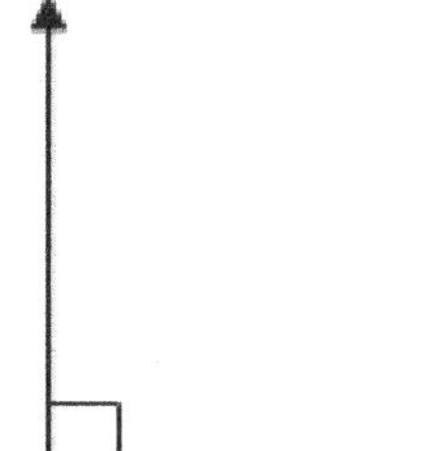

Common Core Standard 4.G.1 – Geometry

☐ What kind of angle does $\angle B$ appear to be in the hexagon?

A Acute

B Obtuse

C Straight

D Right

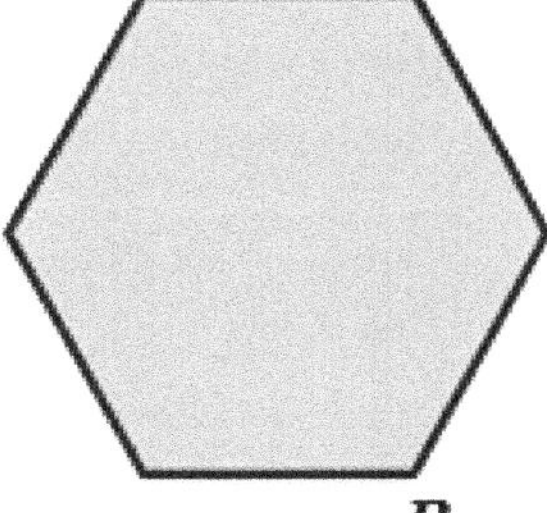

Name ____________________

ASSESSEMENT

Common Core Standard 4.G.1 – Geometry

☐ What kind of angle is formed on the inside of the football goal post?

A Obtuse

B Right

C Straight

D Acute

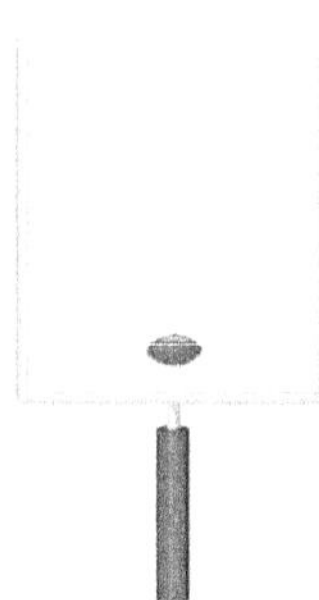

Common Core Standard 4.G.1 – Geometry

☐ Which clock's hands form an obtuse angle?

A 

C 

B 

D 

Common Core Standard 4.G.1 – Geometry

☐ Which answer best describes the angle formed by the slice of pizza?

A Acute

B Right

C Obtuse

D Straight

Name ___________________________

DIAGNOSTIC

Common Core Standard 4.G.2 – Geometry

☐ Which of the following figures has 4 right angles?

A Rhombus

B Rectangle

C Trapezoid

D Kite

Common Core Standard 4.G.2 – Geometry

☐ Which of the following figures has 1 pair of parallel sides?

A Rhombus

B Kite

C Square

D Trapezoid

Common Core Standard 4.G.2 – Geometry

☐ What kind of figure is shown below?

A Pentagon

B Octagon

C Triangle

D Hexagon

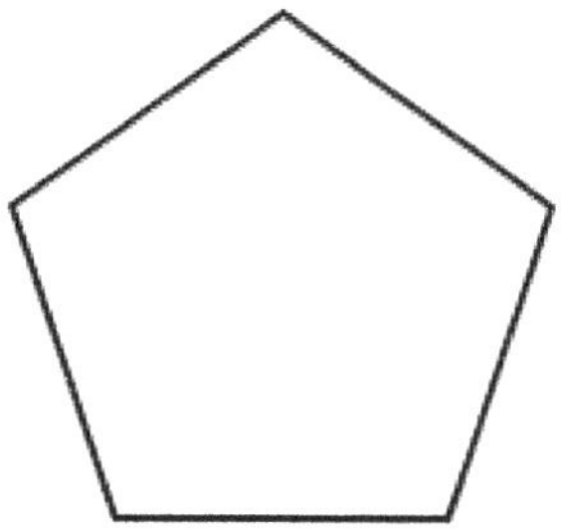

Name ____________________________

DIAGNOSTIC

Common Core Standard 4.G.2 – Geometry

☐ **Which of the following figures has 3 angles?**

A Square

B Triangle

C Hexagon

D Pentagon

Common Core Standard 4.G.2 – Geometry

☐ **Which of the following figures has no parallel sides?**

A Square

B Pentagon

C Hexagon

D Octagon

Common Core Standard 4.G.2 – Geometry

☐ **In which of the following figures the sum of the interior angles is less than 360°?**

A Hexagon

B Pentagon

C Square

D Triangle

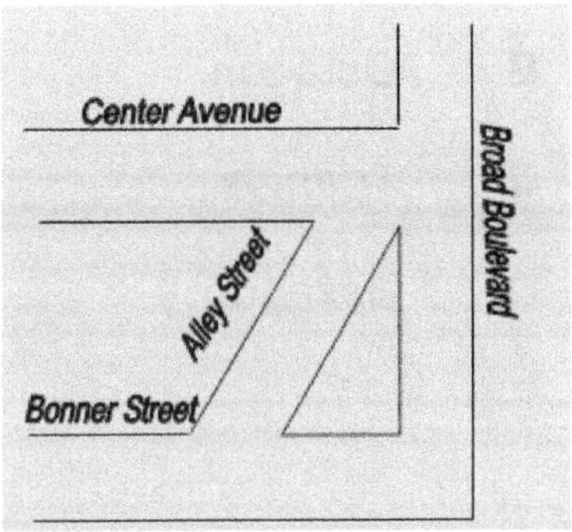

Name ___________________________

PRACTICE

Common Core Standard 4.G.2 – Geometry

☐ Which of the following figures doesn't belong to a group?

A Rhombus

B Hexagon

C Kite

D Rectangle

Common Core Standard 4.G.2 – Geometry

☐ Which drawing best represents a figure with only one pair of parallel lines?

A

C

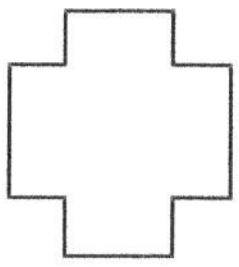

B

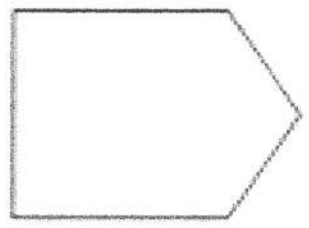

D

Common Core Standard 4.G.2 – Geometry

☐ Which of the following figures has 5 vertices?

A Octagon

B Heptagon

C Hexagon

D Pentagon

Name ______________________

PRACTICE

Common Core Standard 4.G.2 – Geometry

☐ Which of the following figures is a parallelogram?

A Triangle

B Rhombus

C Trapezoid

D Kite

Common Core Standard 4.G.2 – Geometry

☐ Which kinds of figures are found on the calendar?

A Triangles and squares

B Squares and rectangles

C Rectangles and kites

D Kites and pentagons

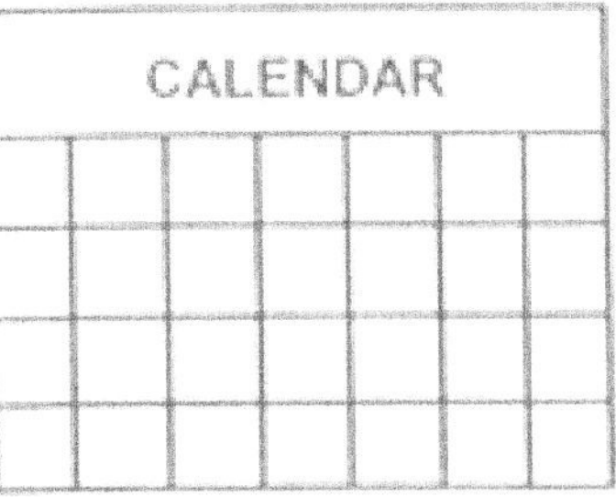

Common Core Standard 4.G.2 – Geometry

☐ What is the shape of the figure below?

A Square

B Polygon

C Diamond

D Hexagon

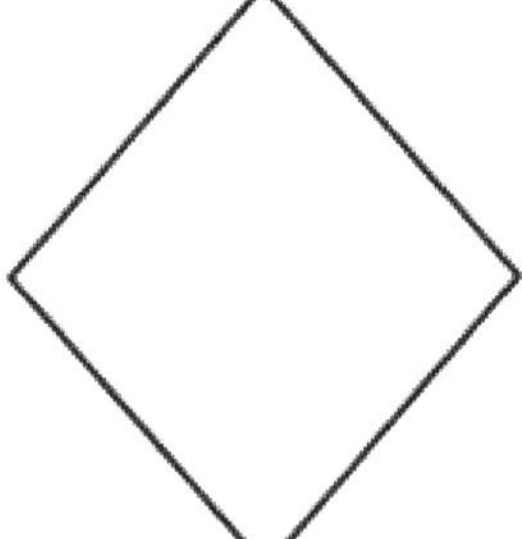

Name ___________________________

PRACTICE

Common Core Standard 4.G.2 – Geometry

☐ Which statement is true about the square below?

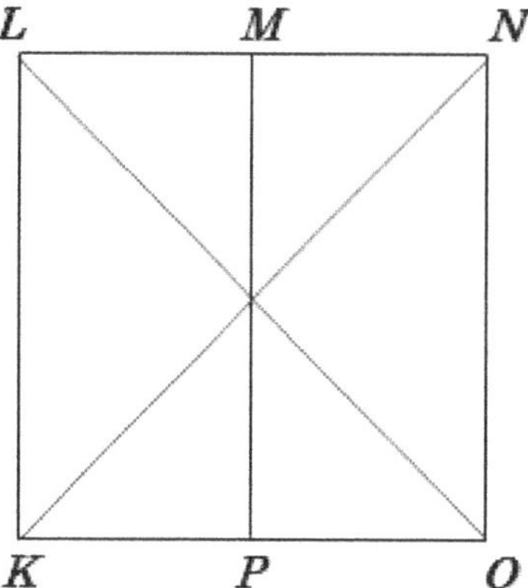

A Square KONL has 4 vertices and 7 sides.

B Square KONL has 5 vertices and 7 sides.

C Square KONL has 4 vertices and 4 sides.

D Square KONL has 5 vertices and 4 sides.

Common Core Standard 4.G.2 – Geometry

☐ Which drawing best represents a figure with two pairs of parallel lines?

A 

C 

B 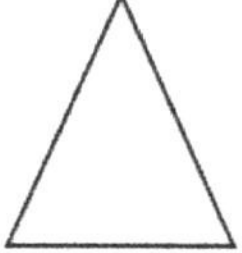

D 

Common Core Standard 4.G.2 – Geometry

☐ Which figures are shown on the US Flag?

A Pentagons

B Kites

C Rectangles

D Trapezoids

Name ___________________________

PRACTICE

Common Core Standard 4.G.2 – Geometry

☐ **Which statement about the following figure is true?**

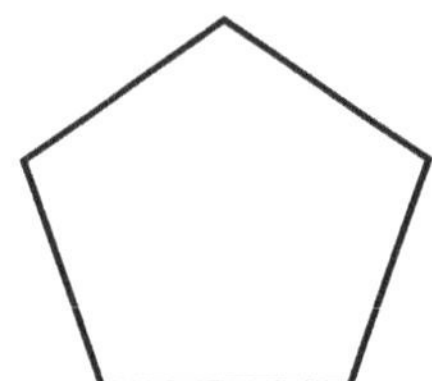

A It has more sides than vertices.

B It has more vertices than sides.

C It has an equal number of vertices and sides.

D It has 2 more vertices than sides.

Common Core Standard 4.G.2 – Geometry

☐ **Which of the following figures doesn't belong to a group?**

A Rhombus

B Trapezoid

C Rectangle

D Square

Common Core Standard 4.G.2 – Geometry

☐ **What is the shape of the figure below?**

A Octagon

B Rectangle

C Hexagon

D Diamond

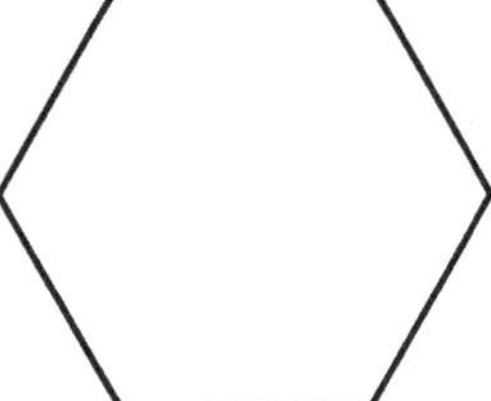

Name ____________________________

ASSESSMENT

Common Core Standard 4.G.2 – Geometry

☐ **Which of the following figures has 1 right angle?**

A Rhombus

B Trapezoid

C Obtuse triangle

D Right triangle

Common Core Standard 4.G.2 – Geometry

☐ **Which figure is MQR?**

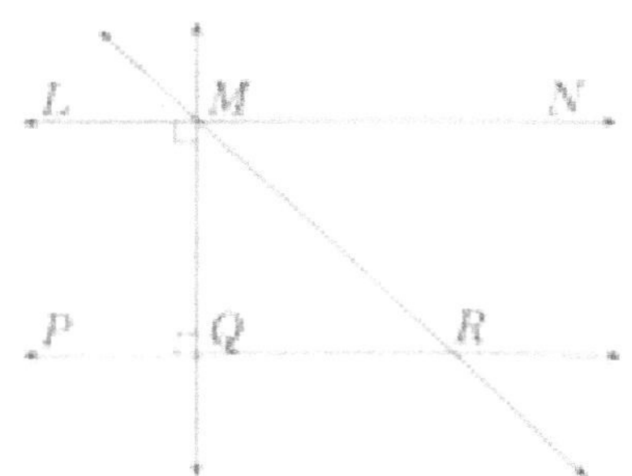

A Obtuse triangle

B Right triangle

C Quadrilateral

D None of the above

Common Core Standard 4.G.2 – Geometry

☐ **Which of the shapes below is a decagon?**

A

B

C

D

ASSESSMENT

Name 

Common Core Standard 4.G.2 – Geometry

☐ In the rectangle below, which statement is true?

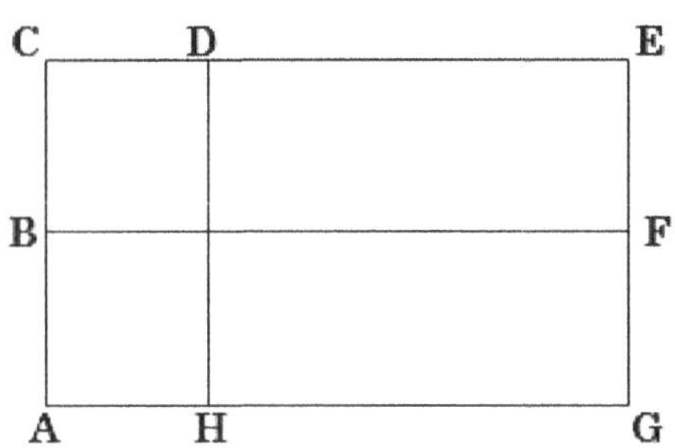

A Rectangle AGEC has 6 sides and 4 vertices.

B Rectangle AGEC has 6 sides and 5 vertices.

C Rectangle AGEC has 4 sides and 4 vertices.

D Rectangle AGEC has 4 sides and 5 vertices.

Common Core Standard 4.G.2 – Geometry

☐ In which of the following figures the sum of the interior angles is 360^0?

A Octagon

B Hexagon

C Pentagon

D Trapezoid

Common Core Standard 4.G.2 – Geometry

☐ Which of the following figures doesn't belong to a group?

A Rhombus

B Kite

C Triangle

D Trapezoid

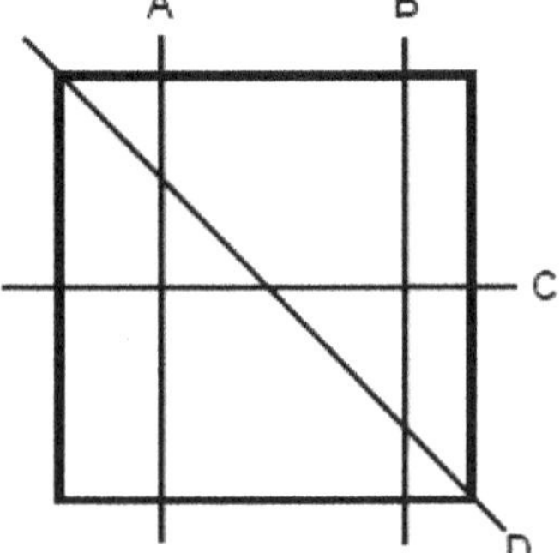

Name ____________________________

DIAGNOSTIC

Common Core Standard 4.G.3 – Geometry

☐ **Which does NOT show a figure with a line of symmetry?**

A

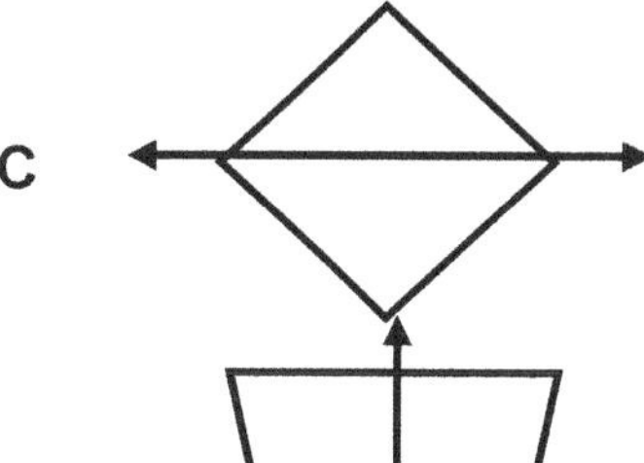

C

B

D

Common Core Standard 4.G.3 – Geometry

☐ **Which letter has 2 lines of symmetry?**

A **V**

B **T**

C **H**

D **C**

Common Core Standard 4.G.3 – Geometry

☐ **Which figure has more than 1 line of symmetry?**

A

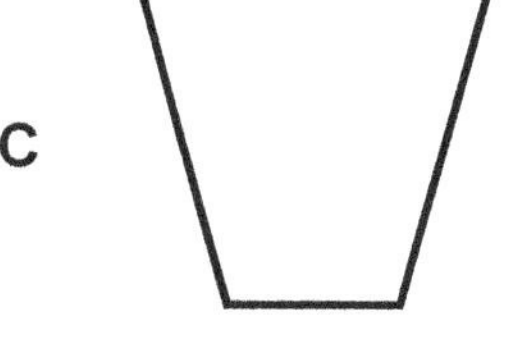

C

B

D

Name ______________________

DIAGNOSTIC

Common Core Standard 4.G.3 – Geometry

☐ **Which letter has a line of symmetry?**

A **J**

B **Q**

C **P**

D **B**

Common Core Standard 4.G.3 – Geometry

☐ **Which pair of figures shows a reflection?**

A 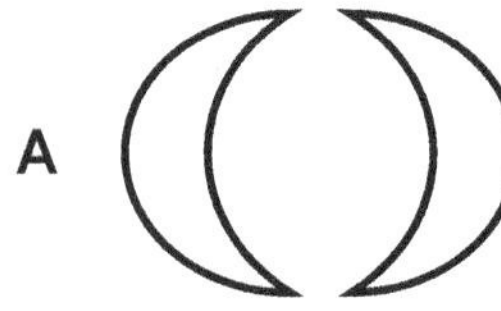

C 

B 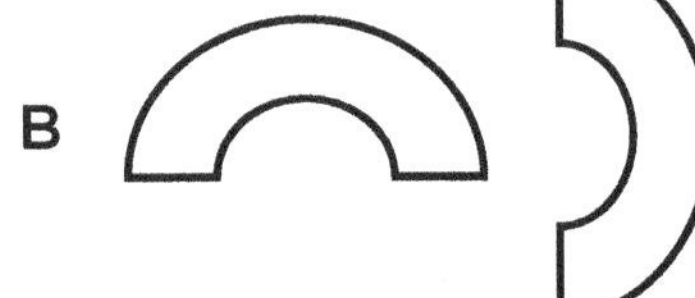

B 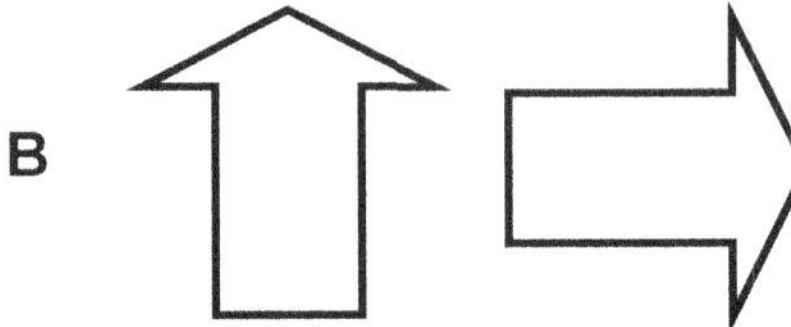

Common Core Standard 4.G.3 – Geometry

☐ **Which figure has a line of symmetry?**

A 

C 

B 

D 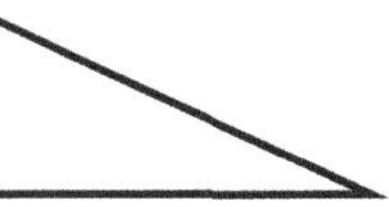

Name ____________________

PRACTICE

Common Core Standard 4.G.3 – Geometry

☐ **Which figure shows a line of symmetry?**

A 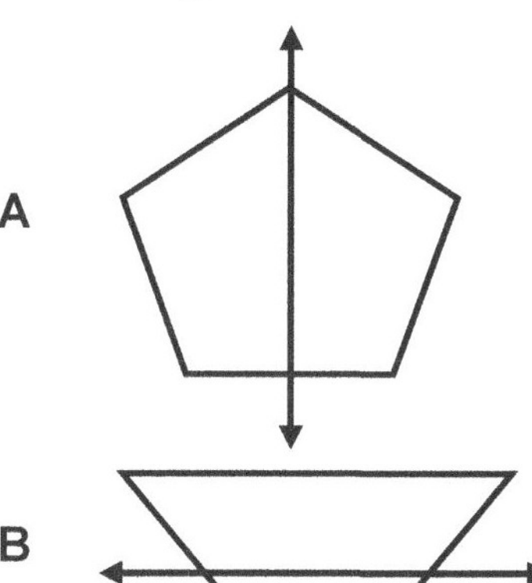

C

B

D 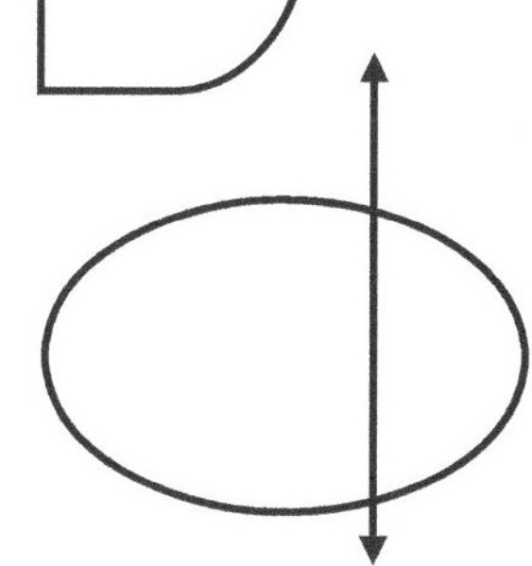

Common Core Standard 4.G.3 – Geometry

☐ **Which letter does NOT have a line of symmetry?**

A **Y**

B **D**

C **G**

D **E**

Common Core Standard 4.G.3 – Geometry

☐ **Which figure does NOT have a line of symmetry?**

A 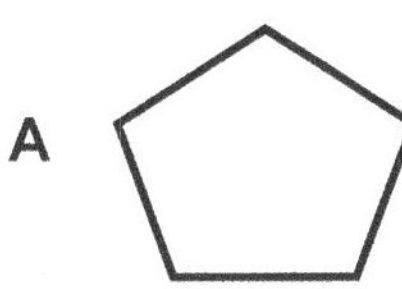

C

B

D

Name ____________________ PRACTICE

Common Core Standard 4.G.3 – Geometry

☐ **Which number has at least one line of symmetry?**

A **6**

B **5**

C **3**

D **4**

Common Core Standard 4.G.3 – Geometry

☐ **Which does NOT show a figure with a line of symmetry?**

A 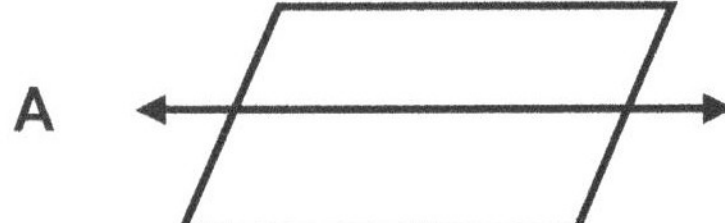

C 

B 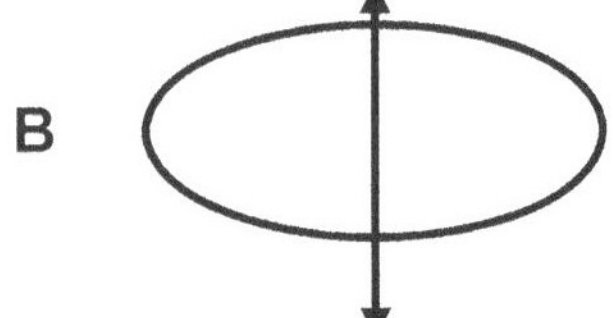

D 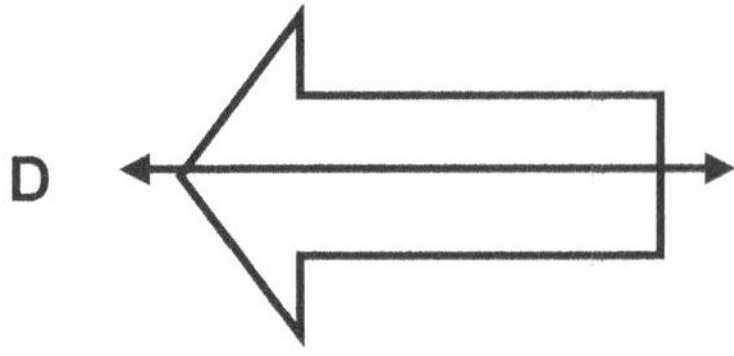

Common Core Standard 4.G.3 – Geometry

☐ **Which figure has a line of symmetry?**

A 

C 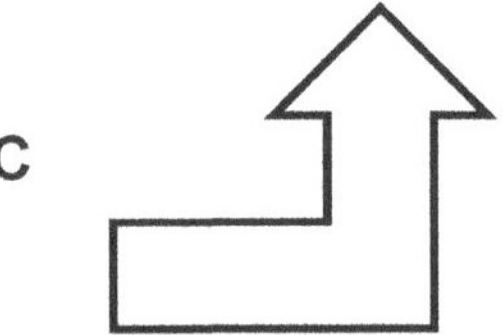

B

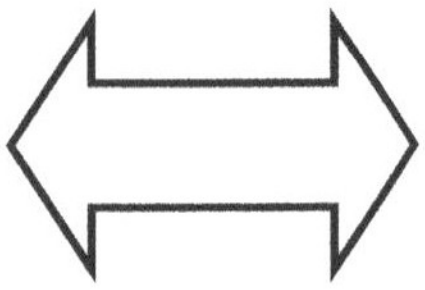

D 

Name ____________________________

PRACTICE

Common Core Standard 4.G.3 – Geometry

☐ **Which number does NOT have a line of symmetry?**

A **8**

B **7**

C **3**

D **0**

Common Core Standard 4.G.3 – Geometry

☐ **Which figure shows a line of symmetry?**

A 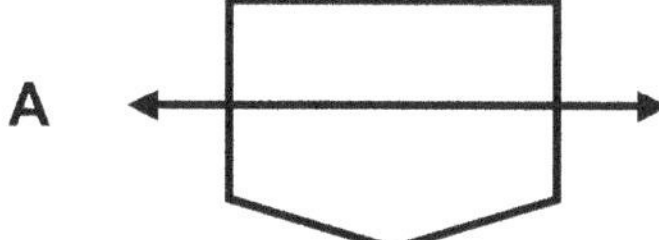

C

B 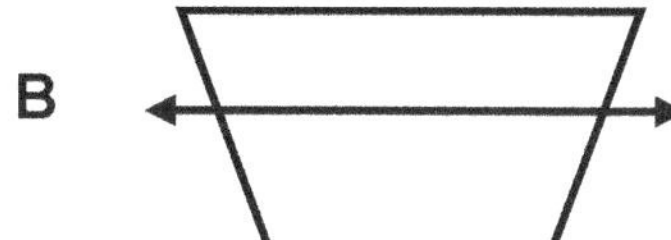

D

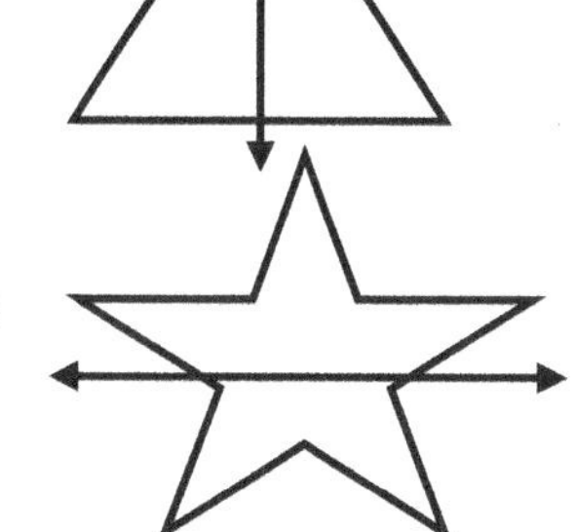

Common Core Standard 4.G.3 – Geometry

☐ **Which line divides figure into 2 congruent pairs?**

A a

B b

C c

D d

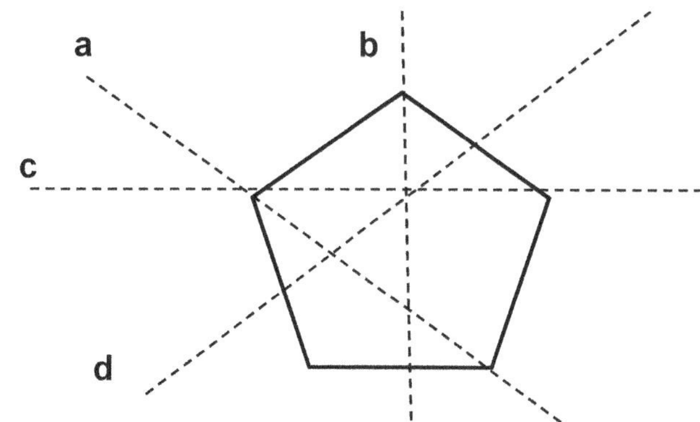

Name ____________________________

PRACTICE

Common Core Standard 4.G.3 – Geometry

☐ **Which word best describes the picture below?**

A Rotation

B Translation

C Reflection

D Not Here

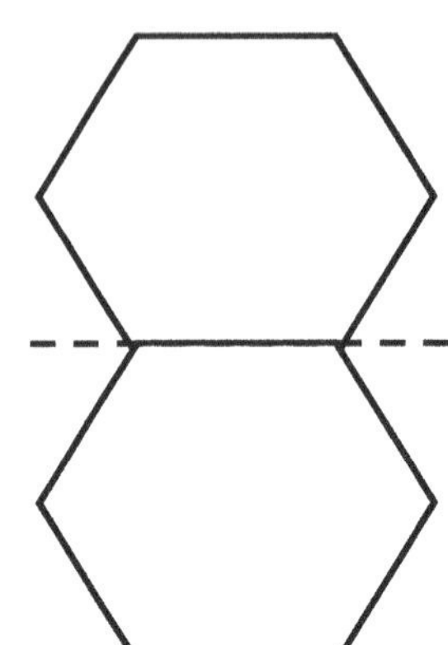

Common Core Standard 4.G.3 – Geometry

☐ **Which number has 1 line of symmetry?**

A **4**

B **7**

C **3**

D **9**

Common Core Standard 4.G.3 – Geometry

☐ **Which figure does NOT have a line of symmetry?**

A  

C  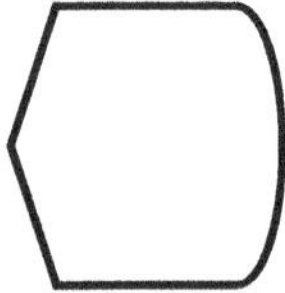

B 

D 

Name ______________________________

ASSESSMENT

Common Core Standard 4.G.3 – Geometry

☐ **Which does NOT show a figure with a line of symmetry?**

A

B

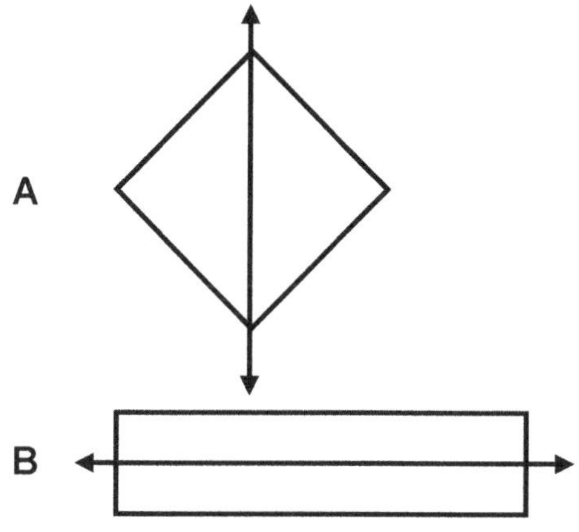

C

D

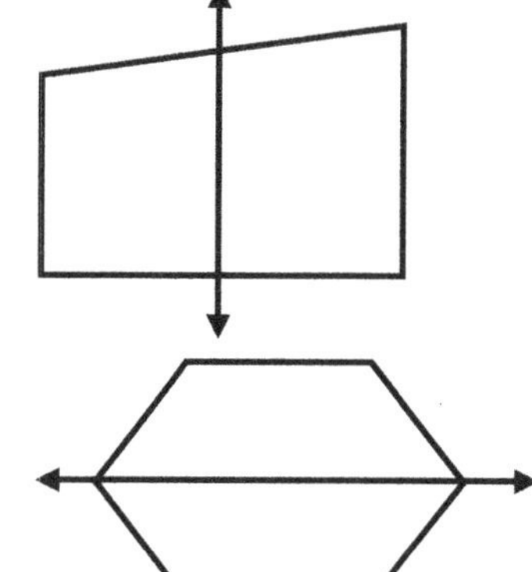

Common Core Standard 4.G.3 – Geometry

☐ **Which number has 2 lines of symmetry?**

A **8**

B **3**

C **9**

D **4**

Common Core Standard 4.G.3 – Geometry

☐ **Which figure does NOT have a line of symmetry?**

A 

B 

D 

Name ____________________

ASSESSMENT

Common Core Standard 4.G.3 – Geometry

☐ **Which letter does NOT have a line of symmetry?**

A **V**

B **T**

C **B**

D **J**

Common Core Standard 4.G.3 – Geometry

☐ **Which line divides figure into 2 congruent parts?**

A z

B y

C x

D w

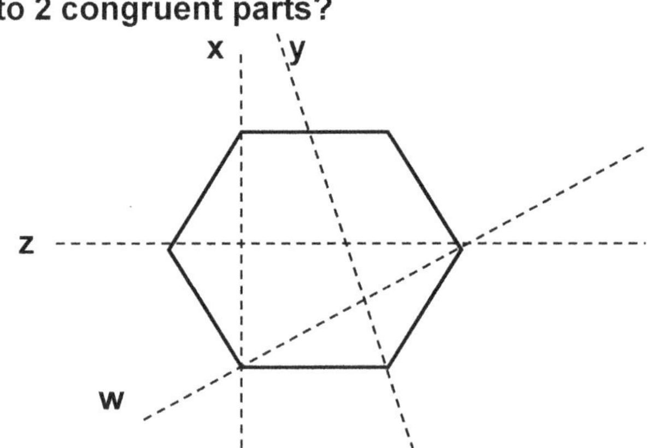

Common Core Standard 4.G.3 – Geometry

☐ **How many lines of symmetry does the square below have?**

A 2

B 3

C 4

D 5

ANSWER KEY

4.OA.1

Page 1 .... D, A, A
Page 2 .... D, C, C
Page 3 .... A, C, A
Page 4 .... D, A, D
Page 5 .... D, A, A
Page 6 .... D, A, A
Page 7 .... B, A, B
Page 8 .... B, A, B

4.OA.2

Page 9 .... B, C, B
Page 10 .... D, B, D
Page 11 .... B, C, B
Page 12 .... A, B, B
Page 13 .... A, C, B
Page 14 .... D, D, B
Page 15 .... A, A, D
Page 16 .... B, B, C

4.OA.3

Page 17 .... C, A, D
Page 18 .... C, B, C
Page 19 .... C, B, A
Page 20 .... D, D, B
Page 21 .... A, D, B
Page 22 .... A, D, B
Page 23 .... B, B, C
Page 24 .... B, B, D

4.OA.4

Page 25 .... 24; B; 4
Page 26 .... C; 13; B
Page 27 .... 16; D; 27
Page 28 .... D; 14; B
Page 29 .... 8; B; 7
Page 30 .... C; 11; B
Page 31 .... 12; B; 18
Page 32 .... C; 16; 7

4.OA.5

Page 33 .... C, B, B
Page 34 .... D, B, A
Page 35 .... B, A, C
Page 36 .... B, D, D
Page 37 .... C, A, C
Page 38 .... B, A, D
Page 39 .... B, A, B
Page 40 .... D, C, D

4.NBT.1

Page 41 .... D, B, A
Page 42 .... A, C, C
Page 43 .... D, D, B
Page 44 .... C, B, B
Page 45 .... C, B, A
Page 46 .... C, D, B
Page 47 .... D, B, D
Page 48 .... D, D, B

ANSWER KEY

4.NBT.2

Page 49 .... B, A, B
Page 50 .... D, C, C
Page 51 .... A, A, B
Page 52 .... B, A, C
Page 53 .... D, C, D
Page 54 .... C, B, A
Page 55 .... B, C, C
Page 56 .... A, C, D

4.NBT.3

Page 57 .... C, A, B
Page 58 .... C, D, C
Page 59 .... D, C, C
Page 60 .... B, A, C
Page 61 .... B, D, C
Page 62 .... B, B, D
Page 63 .... B, A, B
Page 64 .... A, D, B

4.NBT.4

Page 65 .... 1,255; 1,943; 2,674
Page 66 .... $2,181; 10,056; 1,601
Page 67 .... 284; 2,978; $159
Page 68 .... 2,867,822; 879; 1,581
Page 69 .... 3,101; 3,909; 5,380
Page 70 .... 7,064; 539; 9,205
Page 71 .... 2,104; $71; $2,396
Page 72 .... 527,831; $8,785; 1878

4.NBT.5

Page 73 .... 3,414; 624; 930
Page 74 .... 1,920; 1,071; 8
Page 75 .... 1,351; 551; 6
Page 76 .... 2,622; 1,384; 5,985
Page 77 .... 1,911; 1,344; 6
Page 78 .... 1,470; 42,232; 38
Page 79 .... 5,300; 5,184; 5,929
Page 80 .... 9; 9,207; 6

4.NBT.6

Page 81 .... 65; 315; 106
Page 82 .... 14; 1,930; 481
Page 83 .... 1,804; 182; 7
Page 84 .... 715; 1,056; 381
Page 85 .... 63; 817; 197
Page 86 .... 843; 722; 616
Page 87 .... 278; 2,307; 63
Page 88 .... 121; 511; 352

4.NF.1

Page 89 .... C, B, D
Page 90 .... A, D, C
Page 91 .... D, C, B
Page 92 .... A, B, B
Page 93 .... C, D, B
Page 94 .... C, D, A
Page 95 .... A, C, D
Page 96 .... B, D, C

ANSWER KEY

4.NF.2

Page 97 .... B, B, C

Page 98 .... C, B, C

Page 99 .... A, A, C

Page 100 .... B, A, D

Page 101 .... B, D, B

Page 102 .... C, A, D

Page 103 .... A, B, C

Page 104 .... C, B, D

4.NF.3

Page 105 .... B, B, A

Page 106 .... C, D, A

Page 107 .... B, D, A

Page 108 .... C, D, A

Page 109 .... A, B, A

Page 110 .... D, A, D

Page 111 .... C, B, D

Page 112 .... A, D, C

4.NF.4

Page 113 .... C, A, B

Page 114 .... D, B, B

Page 115 .... A, B, D

Page 116 .... C, D, B

Page 117 .... C, D, B

Page 118 .... C, C, D

Page 119 .... A, B, A

Page 120 .... D, A, D

4.NF.5

Page 121 .... A, B, C

Page 122 .... D, B, A

Page 123 .... D, D, A

Page 124 .... A, B, C

Page 125 .... C, D, A

Page 126 .... C, D, A

Page 127 .... C, A, B

Page 128 .... C, D, A

4.NF.6

Page 129 .... D, B, D

Page 130 .... A, A, C

Page 131 .... B, C, A

Page 132 .... D, D, B

Page 133 .... D, A, B

Page 134 .... A, B, D

Page 135 .... C, D, A

Page 136 .... C, A, D

4.NF.7

Page 137 .... B, D, C

Page 138 .... A, B, D

Page 139 .... C, A, A

Page 140 .... A, C, B

Page 141 .... B, D, B

Page 142 .... C, D, C

Page 143 .... C, C, B

Page 144 .... A, A, D

ANSWER KEY

4.MD.1

Page 145 .... D, B, B

Page 146 .... C, B, C

Page 147 .... D, A, A

Page 148 .... B, D, C

Page 149 .... C, C, B

Page 150 .... A, C, C

Page 151 .... C, B, A

Page 152 .... B, B, D

4.MD.2

Page 153 .... C, B, C

Page 154 .... B, C, D

Page 155 .... B, A, D

Page 156 .... B, A, B

Page 157 .... C, C, C

Page 158 .... B, B, A

Page 159 .... D, C, B

Page 160 .... A, D, D

4.MD.3

Page 161 .... B, D, B

Page 162 .... A, C, B

Page 163 .... C, A, B

Page 164 .... C, D, A

Page 165 .... B, C, D

Page 166 .... D, D, B

Page 167 .... A, D, C

Page 168 .... A, B, B

4.MD.4

Page 169 .... B, A, D

Page 170 .... B, B, D

Page 171 .... D, C, B

Page 172 .... C, B, B

Page 173 .... D, B, C

Page 174 .... A, B, D

Page 175 .... D, B, D

Page 176 .... C, B, C

4.MD.5

Page 177 .... B, C, D

Page 178 .... B, D, A

Page 179 .... B, A, C

Page 180 .... D, B, B

Page 181 .... B, D, D

Page 182 .... C, B, B

Page 183 .... A, D, B

Page 184 .... A, A, C

4.MD.6

Page 185 .... C, A, D

Page 186 .... B, D, C

Page 187 .... A, B, C

Page 188 .... A, D, C

Page 189 .... C, A, B

Page 190 .... A, C, B

Page 191 .... D, B, C

Page 192 .... D, C, A

ANSWER KEY

4.MD.7

Page 193 .... B, C, D

Page 194 .... C, A, D

Page 195 .... A, C, D

Page 196 .... C, D, A

Page 197 .... D, B, D

Page 198 .... A, C, B

Page 199 .... B, D, A

Page 200 .... C, B, D

4.G.1

Page 201 .... D, B, A

Page 202 .... C, D, B

Page 203 .... A, A, A

Page 204 .... D, B, B

Page 205 .... C, B, D

Page 206 .... A, C, C

Page 207 .... D, C, B

Page 208 .... B, B, A

4.G.2

Page 209 .... B, D, A

Page 210 .... B, B, D

Page 211 .... B, B, D

Page 212 .... B, B, C

Page 213 .... C, D, C

Page 214 .... C, B, C

Page 215 .... D, B, C

Page 216 .... C, D, C

4.G.3

Page 217 .... B, C, D

Page 218 .... D, A, A

Page 219 .... A, C, C

Page 220 .... C, A, B

Page 221 .... B, C, B

Page 222 .... C, C, B

Page 223 .... C, A, B

Page 224 .... D, A, C

Made in the USA
Middletown, DE
04 May 2023

30022307R00137